Praise for James Oliver and Lois E. Horton's
Slavery and the Making of America

"The Hortons demonstrate their wide mastery of the literature, telling the tragic and triumphant story of the 'peculiar institution' through the words and experiences of the people who lived it."
—Henry Louis Gates, Jr., Harvard University

"The oft-told tale is made fresh through up-to-date slavery scholarship, the extensive use of slave narratives and archival photos and, especially, a focus on individual experience. The well-known players (Attucks, Vesey, Tubman, Douglass) appear, but so do the more anonymous ones—the planter's wife and the slave driver share space with the abolitionist and the Confederate soldier, and all are skillfully etched. As the Hortons chronicle lives from freedom in Africa to slavery in America and beyond, they tell an integral American story, a tale not of juxtaposition but of edgy oneness."
—*Publishers Weekly*

"Shows how the history of American slavery and the history of the American nation are intertwined. Rare illustrations and scrupulous attention to the viewpoint of the slaves make this account especially interesting."
—*The Tampa Tribune*

"Ambitious. . . . Revises the historical record and overturns long-held beliefs about the institution of slavery and what it has meant to the country."
—*The Denver Post* (on PBS companion documentary *Slavery and the Making of America*)

"Dissects the incredible influences of the terrible moral fault in our history."
—*The Nashville City Paper*

"A terrific historical account of the roles and influence that the black slaves made on the United States. The Hortons provide an insightful look on how the slaves impacted all aspects of culture. . . . Anecdotal reciting and photographs augment this superb account. . . . Easy to read but difficult to put down because the book is so engrossing, this is a fabulous tome that history buffs will take immense delight in."
—*The Midwest Book Review*

"An excellent guide to an often difficult subject. Complete with dozens of images, a chronology of events, a list of recommended readings and website suggestions, *Slavery and the Making of America* is an up-to-date book, which offers not only a strong central storyline but also resources for further study."
—*North & South*

"Brings the appalling history of slavery into an especially clear focus by laying out of a fuller, more detailed historical/cultural timeline."
—*The Stamford Advocate*

SLAVERY
AND THE
MAKING of AMERICA

James Oliver Horton

Lois E. Horton

OXFORD
UNIVERSITY PRESS

OXFORD
UNIVERSITY PRESS

Oxford University Press, Inc., publishes works that
further Oxford University's objective of excellence
in research, scholarship, and education.

Oxford   New York
Auckland   Cape Town   Dar es Salaam   Hong Kong   Karachi
Kuala Lumpur   Madrid   Melbourne   Mexico City   Nairobi
New Delhi   Shanghai   Taipei   Toronto

With offices in
Argentina   Austria   Brazil   Chile   Czech Republic   France   Greece
Guatemala   Hungary   Italy   Japan   Poland   Portugal   Singapore
South Korea   Switzerland   Thailand   Turkey   Ukraine   Vietnam

First published by Oxford University Press, Inc., 2005
198 Madison Avenue, New York, NY 10016
www.oup.com

First issued as an Oxford University Press paperback, 2006
ISBN-13: 978-0-19-530451-0
ISBN-10: 0-19-530451-9

Oxford is a registered trademark of Oxford University Press

The Library of Congress has cataloged the cloth edition as follows:

Horton, James Oliver.
Slavery and the making of America / James Oliver Horton and Lois Horton.
p. cm. Includes bibliographical references (p.   ) and index.
ISBN-13: 978-0-19-517903-3   ISBN-10: 0-19-517903-X (acid-free paper)
1. Slavery—United States—History. 2. African Americans—History—To 1863.
I. Horton, Lois E. II. Title.

E441.H73 2004   973'.0496073—dc22   2004013617

Designed and Typeset by Alexis Siroc

1 3 5 7 9 8 6 4 2
Printed in the United States of America
on acid-free paper

Contents

Introduction • 7

1

The African Roots of Colonial America • 13

2

Slavery: From the Revolution to the Cotton Kingdom • 47

3

Westward Expansion, Antislavery, and Resistance • 85

4

Troublesome Property: The Many Forms of Slave Resistance • 119

5

A Hard-Won Freedom: From Civil War Contraband to Emancipation • 161

6

Creating Freedom During and After the War • 191

Notes • 232

Chronology • 243

Further Reading and Web Sites • 246

Index • 249

Introduction

Slavery played a profoundly important role in the making of the United States, as the institution grew from the handful of Africans landed in Virginia in 1619 to the four million African Americans held in bondage at the beginning of the Civil War in 1861. The bound labor of at least twelve generations of black people created great wealth for slaveholders, wealth that was translated into extraordinary political power. The slave trade and the products created by slaves' labor, particularly cotton, provided the basis for America's wealth as a nation, underwriting the country's industrial revolution and enabling it to project its power into the rest of the world. African slaves were not simply passive laborers. They brought many new cultures to America, and their religion, music, language, values, and skills helped shape America and its unique blended culture. Enduring a brutally oppressive system, African slaves also developed a deep commitment to liberty and became a living testament to the powerful appeal of freedom.

American slavery profoundly affected the concept and the actual development of American freedom. It provided a touchstone for patriots' demands for liberty and representative government. They believed, as John Dickinson of Pennsylvania claimed in the wake of the Stamp Act Crisis of the 1760s, that "Those who are taxed without their own consent, expressed by themselves or their representatives, are slaves." Because England had taxed the American colonies without their consent, Dickinson continued, "We are therefore–SLAVES." The argument that Britain sought to make Americans slaves in the mid-eighteenth century was a gross exaggeration, but Americans used the term metaphorically to impress Britain with the seriousness of their opposition to the loss of liberty. Dickinson's words carried a great irony when he wrote them in 1768, because he was the largest slaveholder in Philadelphia at the time, and his slaves were bound by chains much stronger than metaphors.[1]

This book is the story of American slavery and of the people whose loss of liberty under its yoke was much more than a deprivation of political representation. It is the story of African people becoming African Americans, for most under unimaginably oppressive and inhumane conditions, often told in their own words. It examines the great contradiction at the heart of American democracy—that a freedom-loving people tolerated human bondage that violated the values they professed to hold dearest. Generation after generation of Americans tried unsuccessfully to reconcile this contradiction, and America's history was shaped by this futile effort. This book is also about the determination of black Americans and their white allies to have the nation live up to the principles embodied in the Declaration of Independence, the Bill of Rights, and the other founding documents of American freedom.

By the time of the Revolution, Americans had wrestled with the meaning of slavery for more than 150 years. Slavery had created a hellish existence for the half million Africans caught in its grip and posed an ethical dilemma for liberal philosophers attempting to explain a slaveholders' revolution for freedom. It also created a struggle between the forces of slavery and the forces of freedom, which finally erupted in a bloody Civil War. Although slavery was at the heart of this conflict, most Americans have yet to understand its importance, the institution of slavery itself, or the lives of the slaves.

In the early twentieth century, popular interpretations of slavery were dominated by novelists, playwrights, and filmmakers whose works were largely based on the Old South view of slavery as a benevolent institution. In 1906 the Reverend Thomas Dixon, a North Carolinian who was pastor of the Twenty-third Street Baptist Church in New York City, published his best-selling novel, *The Clansman,* glorifying the political terrorism of the Ku Klux Klan during the volatile decades of the post–Civil-War Reconstruction era. Dixon's book depicted the Klan as a force for order and the restoration of southern honor. Film director D. W. Griffith brought Dixon's novel to the screen in 1915 in an innovative and powerful movie, *Birth of a Nation.* Screened at the White House and praised by President Woodrow Wilson as "history written with lightening," the film became a sensation, affirming racist assumptions underlying the system of racial segregation that was at its height in the early decades of the twentieth century.[2]

Interpretations of slavery by professional historians have changed over time as new historical sources became available and the times prompted new historical questions. One of the most influential academic historians of the early twentieth century was U. B. Phillips, who was born in Georgia, educated at Columbia University in New York City, and became professor of history and political science at the University of Wisconsin, Tulane University, the University of Michigan, and

Yale University. His portrayal of blacks as passive, inferior people, whose African origins made them uncivilized, seemed to provide historical evidence for the theories of racial inferiority that supported racial segregation. Drawing evidence exclusively from plantation records, letters, southern newspapers, and other sources reflecting the slaveholder's point of view, Phillips depicted slave masters who provided for the welfare of their slaves and contended that true affection existed between slave and master. This interpretation of slavery influenced most textbooks and popular media of the time and was reflected in the 1939 film classic *Gone with the Wind*, derived from Margaret Mitchell's best-selling 1936 historical novel set in the Civil War and Reconstruction periods.[3]

Some historical scholarship attempted to counter popular racist views and the defense of slavery during the 1930s and 1940s, but the benign view of slavery fit with the notion of white supremacy that was solidly entrenched in the society. Finally in 1956, in the wake of post–World War II civil rights protests and changing racial attitudes, historian Kenneth Stampp published a full-blown refutation of the idea of slavery as a benevolent institution. Stampp's book, *The Peculiar Institution: Slavery in the Ante-Bellum South*, was based on many of the same sources that Phillips had used, but it relied more heavily on diaries, journals, newspaper runaway-slave ads, and even a few slave narratives. Comparing slavery to the experience of the victims of World War II concentration camps, Stanley Elkins, in *Slavery*, posited slavery's damaging psychological impact on the personalities of the slaves. He painted a picture of the Sambo personality, child-like, dependent, and silly, as caricatured in minstrel shows. This personality distortion, he said, was created by the almost total helplessness of slaves and their reliance on the slave master.

By the late 1960s the impact of the modern civil rights movement had alerted scholars and many other Americans to the significance of African American history and its tradition of struggle. This raised new questions about the nature and impact of slavery and the response of black people to it. During the 1970s, scholars made greater use of the WPA slave interviews that historians sponsored by the federal government had conducted in the 1930s with the last living generation of former slaves,[4] and of hundreds of slave autobiographies published in the nineteenth century. Such scholars as John Blassingame, in the *Slave Community*, Eugene Genovese, in *Roll, Jordan, Roll*, Leslie Howard Owens, in *This Species of Property*, and Herbert Gutman, in *The Black Family in Slavery and Freedom*, found a much more complex story in which enslaved people played a more active role in shaping their own culture, calling Elkins's inter-pretation into question. Robert Fogel and Stanley Engerman brought computer analysis to bear on the issue of the quality of slave life in their influential and controversial *Time on the Cross*. Over the next decade there was a profusion of scholarship on slavery and the antislavery struggle. The field of African American history, for generations largely confined to segregated black public schools and colleges, burst onto the academic scene, bringing new insights to the study of American history, culture, and society. Finally, with Alex Haley's publication of his family history in *Roots* and the TV series that followed, the general public began to hear the voices of African Americans telling their own stories.[5]

In the decades since the 1970s, our understanding of slavery has changed dramatically, and a more complex and compelling picture of the slave experience has emerged. Thanks to groundbreaking work, we now see slavery as a more dynamic institution encompassing many different slave experiences in different times and places. We know that slavery originally existed in all original thirteen colonies, from New Hampshire to South Carolina. We know that before the American Revolution, New York City was second only to Charleston, South Carolina, in British North America as a major center of urban slavery. And we know that the shift in the chief slave crop from tobacco and rice in the eastern South before the Revolution to cotton in the deep South early in the nineteenth century profoundly changed slave life, the national economy, and politics. Debra Gray White showed us that slavery's impact on women was very different from that on men, and Jacqueline Jones gave us a sense of how varied the effects of work were on black women and their families during and after slavery. Peter Kolchin led us to compare the lives of American slaves and Russian serfs, while Phillip D. Morgan showed how the cultures and work of slaves in the Chesapeake region in the eighteenth century differed from those in South Carolina's Lowcountry. Brenda E. Stevenson pointed out the difficulties of maintaining families and the importance of extended kinship in the slave community, and Wilma King focused our attention on the lives of slave children. Ira Berlin's extensive research demonstrated how the Creoles of the Atlantic world became the Charter generation of American slaves, how Africans became African Americans, and how early slave communities were dislocated and disrupted in a second Middle Passage in the nineteenth century.[6]

In *Slavery and the Making of America*, we tell this complex story through the lives and words of the slaves themselves, looking at slavery from the vantage point of the enslaved. We follow individuals from African freedom to American slavery and beyond to freedom again. In the process, we seek to illustrate the inextricable link between American freedom and American slavery. This is a story of intense violence and determined resistance. People were not easily enslaved. Slavery was a coercive system sustained by the mobilization of the entire society, and its maintenance rested on the use of unimaginable violence and the constant threat of violence. It is also an inspiring story about those who would not allow their spirits to be broken by the violence of slavery, those who found ways to create families and communities, and those few who managed to escape to freedom. The story told here goes beyond the life of slavery as a legal institution, to the time after the Civil War when the nation struggled to determine the meaning of freedom for black Americans. It shows the ways that new systems of racial control came to replace the old rules of the slave system and how the system of legal segregation, called Jim Crow, came into existence in the South.

The history of slavery is central to the history of the United States, and so this is also a story about the values and events that shaped American society. White Americans committed to freedom and God-given rights found it necessary to justify their economic system based on slavery. Some could not, and they became part of an enduring campaign to abolish slavery from the country and the world. Others rationalized the contradiction with theories of racial inferiority, arguing that black people were particularly well-suited for enslavement, that they benefited from enslavement or that slavery was necessary for their control. Although slavery was abolished nearly a century and a half ago, the racism rooted in the nation's attempts to justify it remains with us today as the legacy of American slavery.

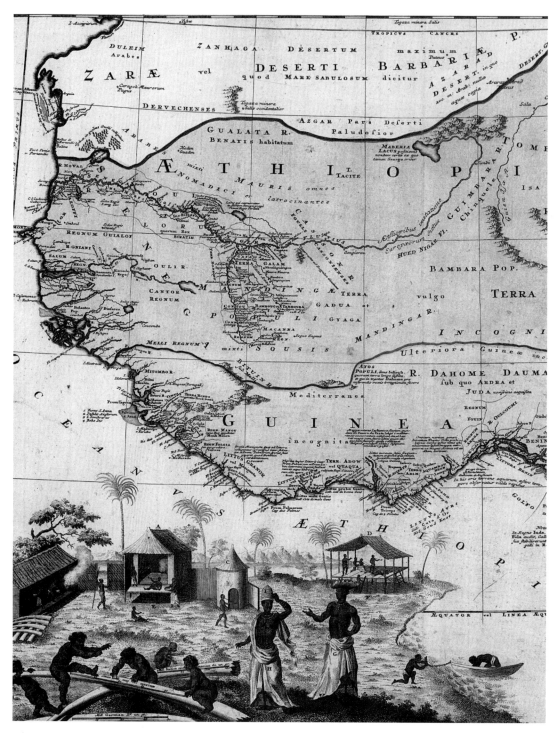

This mid-eighteenth-century map of the west coast of Africa shows the main ports of the slave trade, from present-day Senegal and Gambia in the northwest to Gabon in the southeast. The main commodity was of course Africans themselves, whose domestic and working lives are depicted in the illustration.

The African Roots of
Colonial America

Just before dawn on a spring morning in 1806, thirteen-year-old Anta Majigeen Njaay was asleep when men on horseback, their long, braided hair flying out behind them, charged into her prosperous West African village in Senegambia, just south of the Sahara Desert. Anta awoke to the terrifying sounds of battle, and by the end of the morning, these frightening men had killed her father, several of her uncles, and many of the village's other men. The invaders were warrior slaves, the special armed force of Amari Ngoone Ndella Kumba, king of Kajor, a coastal kingdom that had risen to power in Senegambia during the eighteenth century, carved out of the old Wolof empire of Jolof. Their job protecting Kajor and its ruler extended to raiding enemy villages and delivering valuable goods to the king. They also took prisoners to be traded to European slave dealers in return for fine fabrics, wines, and weapons. Occasionally, when too few enemies were available for slaves, they raided villages like Anta's, villages supposedly under the king's protection. By noon on the day of the raid, the soldiers had packed up looted goods and rounded up captives, including Anta, her mother, many of her other relatives, and the family servants. Slave traders cared little whether the captives were slaves, free artisans, or nobility like Anta, who was descended from the founder of the Jolof Empire and whose large Njaay family had provided generations of rulers.

Trade between Europe and Africa was centuries old. Ancient trade routes crossed the Sahara from West Africa to the Mediterranean, and Africa supplied most of Europe's gold from as early as the eighth century. Political and technological developments in the fifteenth century combined to change the nature of the trade and increased the importance of West African coastal nations. When the Turks captured Constantinople in 1453, they cut off Europeans' supply of slaves from the Slavic areas around the Black Sea. These slaves had provided the major workforce for the sugar plantations on the Mediterranean islands, so European

An ivory spoon made by the Edo people of the Benin Kingdom in the sixteenth or seventeenth century. The bird with outstretched wings on the spoon's handle is a feature of traditional Benin art. Edo artists also made such artifacts for export to Europe.

sugar producers increasingly looked to Africa for slave labor. Advances in navigation in the fifteenth century enabled the Portuguese to sail to the coast of West Africa, bypassing the Africans controlling the Sahara trade. There, in 1472, the Portuguese negotiated their first slave-trading agreement directly with a king's court, an agreement that included trade for gold and ivory as well. The African–European trade during the next two hundred years was complex: In addition to the trade in slaves and gold, African manufactured goods were exchanged for European manufactured goods. By the eighteenth century, European consumers coveted African textiles; ivory spoons, horns, and saltcellars; and woven mats from Senegambia, often used as bedcovers. Likewise, European textiles and beads were highly valued by fashion-conscious African consumers.[1]

The great empires of Ghana, lasting from the fourth century to the twelfth, and Mali, from the thirteenth century to the late fifteenth, controlled the African–European trade routes. As European nations claimed trade routes in the Atlantic Ocean, and as coastal areas provided new gateways for trade, competition for control of the trade intensified among both European and African nations, and trading dominance was more difficult to maintain. Songhay, the last of the great trading empires in West Africa, which arose in the late fifteenth century, collapsed by the early seventeenth century. The march of sugar cultivation, with its voracious appetite for slave labor, across the Atlantic Ocean to Brazil and the West Indies made the African trade even more lucrative for European nations, and they vied with each other and with African nations in attempts to control the markets. To this end, European nations organized such state-sponsored trading corporations as the Dutch West India Company and Britain's Royal Africa Company and established a string of fortresses along the African coast. One of the first of these fortresses was Elmina, a castle established by the Portuguese in 1481 and held by them until it was taken over by the Dutch in 1637. As the slave trade developed, European nations established more than fifty forts along the three-hundred-mile coastline from the Senegal River to Angola.[2]

Although contending European nations did establish control of the sea trade, they never managed to control the sources of goods and slaves. African nations continued to control the interior of the continent, and a class of private entrepreneurs cooperated with them to dominate the trade along the coast by the late seventeenth century. Many of these middlemen were mixed-race people originally from Cape Verde, an island located off the African coast where the Portuguese had established sugar plantations in the fifteenth century. As European trading activity expanded to the coastal areas of the continent, these people—Africans with intercultural skills and often with an interracial heritage, whom historian Ira Berlin has called Atlantic Creoles—played significant roles in the intercontinental trade. Many worked as agents for the Portuguese or for West African nations and European trading companies. Sometimes they went into business for themselves. By the middle of the eighteenth century the Dutch employed hundreds of mixed-race people as soldiers and trading officials in the trading forts along the Guinea coast. Multilingual and cosmopolitan, with ties to both African and European cultures, these people were invaluable to the commercial enterprises that negotiated vast cultural differences. Generally outcasts in the European societies and denied the right to inherit property, hold land, or marry in African societies, these brown-skinned people developed their own

In the fifteenth and sixteenth centuries Timbuktu was an intellectual and commercial center of the empire of Songhay. A visitor in the sixteenth century said it was "a wonder to see what plentie of Merchandize is daily brought hither and how costly and sumptious all things be. . . . Here are many shops of. . . merchants and especially of such as weave linnen."

This seventeenth-century bronze head represented a departed king of the powerful Benin Empire, a society in present-day southern Nigeria rich in artistic expression. It was the centerpiece of an altar for the king's ancestors, which commemorated the power and spiritual presence of past rulers.

subculture, including a synthetic language that became invaluable to trade throughout the Atlantic region. As the African–European trade grew, so did the enclaves of these Atlantic Creoles, expanding beyond the African coast to seaports in Europe and coastal areas of the Americas in the sixteenth and seventeenth centuries.[3]

Some of the best-known Atlantic Creoles were the canoemen who plied their trade carrying goods and people between European ships and coastal trading forts or who organized companies of African canoemen to do the work. By all reports, these men were usually independent merchants for hire to the highest bidder. Canoemen claimed the right to regulate their own work, refusing to venture out when they deemed the surf too rough for safety, when abused by their employer, or when they disputed the conditions of their labor. Because the African coast lacked harbors that could accommodate European ships, the canoemen were indispensable to the African trade.[4]

By the late eighteenth century, trade in weapons and human beings had created more changes in the power structure of West Africa. With guns and gunpowder, the kingdom of Kajor, for example, where Anta lived, developed a military force feared in the region, thereby extending its rule. Indeed, guns were the first European goods introduced into the African trade that Africans did not already produce, although iron had been used in Africa as early as 600 BCE. Long before Europeans arrived in the area south of the Sahara, African iron working produced steel that rivaled in quality the steel produced in Europe many centuries later.[5] The knives, swords, and other weapons made by Senegambian methods were of fine quality, but they could not compete with European guns. Guns were much more deadly, but at first some Africans were reluctant to use them, considering them weapons for cowards, since they didn't require the close-in fighting of earlier weapons. Coastal nations' direct access to European-supplied guns gave them an advantage over inland groups, increased their power, and encouraged efforts to maintain their control of the coastal trade by war if necessary. The nations of Europe and West Africa all maneuvered for maximum trade advantage, playing one competitor off against the others in commercial combat. During the early 1760s, for example, France and Britain competed over the trade with Senegambian rulers and allied themselves with rival warring Senegambian forces. From the African point of view, this was a war to deny Europeans access to inland areas and to determine which Africans would maintain control.

Although Europeans held a great advantage along the coast and along the banks of major rivers, where the heavy guns of their ships protected their positions, they were vulnerable inland beyond the reach of their artillery. European slavers could not remain inland for long, as exposure to such tropical diseases as malaria and yellow fever placed them at great risk. A study of European mortality in seventeenth-century West Africa found that 60 percent died within their first eight months on the continent.[6] The climate of sub-Saharan Africa and the power of African coastal nations combined to keep Europeans largely confined to the coastal trade. Thus, Anta Majigeen Njaay and the other captives from her village, like countless millions of Africans over the four centuries of the Atlantic slave trade, found themselves marched to the coast to be held for European traders. When they arrived at the town of Rufisque at the foot of the Cape Verde peninsula, French- and English-speaking merchants looked them

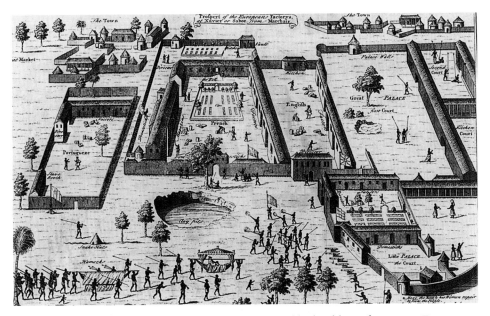

Slave factories on the West African coast were maintained by local kings for various European nations. There African captives from the interior were collected and sold into the Atlantic slave trade.

over and bid for each individually. Anta's group was unusual, with many more women than the normal preponderance of men wanted for heavy labor, but they were sold. Canoemen, with their long narrow canoes, then carried them to the trading fort on the small island of Goree. There, imprisoned in dark cells that opened to courtyards enclosed by high stone walls, they awaited the departure of a vessel bound for the Americas.[7]

Anta's reaction to her plight can only be imagined, since it was not recorded. She was a young girl on the threshold of womanhood, from a prestigious family who was captured and imprisoned along with surviving members of her family and village, including family servants and some of her uncles' slaves. She was familiar with African slavery, but she could not have been prepared for the next stage of her journey. A few other African captives did leave accounts of their experiences. Venture Smith was from Guinea, in the area bordering Africa's Gulf of Guinea. At the age of six, as he recalled, an "army supplied and incited by whites" captured him and marched him to the coast. They imprisoned him there in what he called a castle to await sale. Eventually, traders placed him and 250 others on board a Rhode Island–based ship bound for the British West Indian colony of Barbados. During his capture, the six-year-old had seen his father killed, a trauma that remained with him. As an adult he reported, "The shocking scene is to this day fresh in my memory."[8]

Uncertainty was one of the most distressing parts of another captive's initial enslavement. A small raiding party in Benin, in the eastern region of present-day Nigeria, captured Olaudah Equiano, the eleven-year-old son of an official of the Ibo nation. Although captured and at first enslaved in Africa with his sister, Olaudah later became part of the Atlantic trade, staying a few weeks in Barbados before being transported to Virginia. Once he left Africa, he spent most of his time alone or with Africans who spoke languages different from his own. His experience differed from people who were captured in large groups, and his inability to communicate with fellow captives intensified the shock of his situation.

Anta, Venture, and Olaudah were all children from West Africa, a vast area but only a small portion of an immense continent. Africa contains 11,700,000 square miles, is second only to Asia in size, and is almost six times the size of Europe. From the dry Sahara Desert in the north, an area the size of the United States, to the Kalahari Desert in the south, to the grasslands of the Sudan and tropical rain forests in the central regions, Africa has an extremely varied topography and climate. It is equally diverse in wildlife and human cultures. Africa's ancient civilizations changed partially in response to changes in geography and climate. Between 6000 BCE and 2500 BCE, the northern desert gradually encroached on the existing green belt, driving many societies southward and forcing those who remained to shift from farming to nomadic trading. Equiano's nation and its people were rooted in one of these scattered ancient civilizations. By the end of the fifteenth century, pepper grown in Benin and textiles manufactured there were in great demand in the European market, but by Olaudah's time, Benin's power had been eclipsed by other trading nations in the region. Venture's society in lower Guinea was also partly a product of this southward migration. By the seventeenth century, that region had become a thriving population center, more densely populated than most of Europe at the time.

The diversity of western Africa partly explains Olaudah Equiano's reaction to the things he saw as he reached the coast from his home a hundred miles inland. He was surprised by the ethnic and linguistic diversity of the Africans he met there and amazed by the ocean and the great ships anchored off the coast. His people had been traders, doing business with a number of other national and ethnic groups in the region, but he had never seen such a variety of Africans

European traders purchasing slaves who have been brought to the market yoked together. Often slaves were captured in warfare between competing West African nations and sold for guns and other goods.

as he encountered in the coastal slave-trading markets. He also saw Europeans there for the first time, adding to his confusion. "Their complexions... differing so much from ours, their long hair, and the language they spoke (which was very different from any I had ever heard)" all confirmed his fear that he would be killed by these "white men with horrible looks, red faces and long hair" whom he considered "bad spirits."[9]

Olaudah Equiano's fear and confusion were typical of the reaction of Africans brought from inland areas. His greatest relief came from finding an African with whom he could communicate, someone who helped him understand his situation. The white men would take him far away to their country in one of the huge ships, he was told. This was much better than he had feared. Having heard stories of cannibals, he was initially convinced that these strange men were going to eat him, apparently a common fear among those who had never before seen Europeans. According to contemporary observers, "slaves near the coast... know what to expect, but those from the interior are terrified by not knowing the purpose [of the trade]." As one eighteenth-century English trader noted, many captives from the more remote areas of the Senegambia region "imagined that all who were sold for slaves were generally eaten or murdered, since none ever returned."

Even well into the nineteenth century, white cannibalism remained a part of West African folklore. Apparently some assumed that the European style of kissing was a part of this cannibalistic tendency.[10] According to Equiano, the captives' fear of white cannibalism persisted during the entire voyage and remained so great even after their arrival in the West Indies that "at last the white people got some old slaves from the land to pacify us. They told us we were not to be eaten but to work, and were soon to go on land where we should see many of our country people. This report eased us much."[11] As a slave of white men, Equiano hoped, life might be no worse for him than for slaves in his homeland. Still, he was worried because "the white people looked and acted... in so savage a manner, for I had never seen among any people such instances of brutal cruelty."[12]

Most Africans understood slavery, since slavery was an ancient institution that had been established in North and West Africa before European involvement in the trade. In West Africa, land was not held as private property, and slavery, the ownership of other human beings and their labor, was a major basis of wealth. Slaves thus had measurable value, and trading in slaves was a part of commerce.

Those held in bondage were commonly captured in war, both fighters and their family members. Africans generally sold such captives to Europeans. Pacheco Pereira, a sixteenth-century Portuguese slave trader, commented on taking slaves in Benin, Equiano's homeland. Apparently, at the time, Benin was "usually at war with its neighbors [sic] and taking many captives, whom we buy at 12 or 15 brass bracelets each or for copper bracelets which they prize more." Slaves' value generally increased as

Herman Moll's 1714 map of "Africa Ancient and Modern." The abundant detail is indicative of Europe's keen interest in the opportunities offered by trade and military adventure in Africa.

they were farther from home, the distance making rescue or escape more difficult and political ties in the society less likely. Once on the coast, Pereira reported, the slaves were traded for gold.[13]

Before the fifth century, Romans were willing to pay high prices for North African slaves, largely because of the remoteness of their homelands. Muslims in the Middle East or North Africa especially valued slaves from far away as "strangers" who might be provided with trusted positions because they were thought to have no local loyalties other than to their masters. Masters often used these slaves as special military guards for households or harems. Slaves might be seen as less suitable for slavery as they became more familiar with the social customs and the politics of a region. Thus, the slaveholders might see children raised in the local society as unfit for slavery and release them from bondage. In such ancient kingdoms as Egypt in the north and Ghana and its successor Mali just to the south, slavery was an integral part of society. Slaves provided labor for a wide variety of tasks, including farming, clearing land, skilled wood or metal work, and domestic service. Holding slaves was also a sign of individual and national wealth and power. In some areas—such as along

continues on page 24

The Middle Passage: An Eyewitness Account

Olaudah Equiano was kidnapped from his home in Essaka, an Ibo village in present-day Nigeria, at age eleven, transported to the Atlantic coast, and sold into slavery. He was the first American slave to write an autobiography telling of his experiences. Published in 1791, the book became a sensation and was printed in nine different editions before Equiano died in 1797. He and his book were valuable resources for the early abolition movement. The following is his account of the horrors of the Middle Passage.

At last, when the ship we were in had got in all her cargo, they made ready with many fearful noises, and we were all put under deck, so that we could not see how they managed the vessel. But this disappointment was the least of my sorrow. The stench of the hold while we were on the coast was so intolerably loathsome, that it was dangerous to remain there for any time, and some of us had been permitted to stay on the deck for the fresh air; but now that the whole ship's cargo were confined together, it became absolutely pestilential. The closeness of the place, and the heat of the climate, added to the number in the ship, which was so crowded that each had scarcely room to turn himself, almost suffocated us. This produced copious perspirations, so that the air soon became unfit for respiration, from a variety of loathsome smells, and brought on a sickness among the slaves, of which many died, thus falling victims to the improvident avarice, as I may call it, of their purchasers. This wretched situation was again aggravated by the galling of the chains, now become insupportable; and the filth of the necessary tubs, into which the children often fell, and were almost suffocated. The shrieks of the women, and the groans of the dying, rendered the whole a scene of horror almost inconceivable. Happily perhaps for myself I was soon reduced so low here that it was thought necessary to keep me almost always on deck; and from my extreme youth I was not put in fetters. In this situation I expected every hour to share the fate of my companions, some of whom were almost daily brought upon deck at the point of death, which I began to hope would soon put an end to my miseries. Often did I think many of the inhabitants of the deep much more happy than myself; I envied them the freedom they enjoyed, and as often wished I could change my condition for theirs. Every circumstance I met with served only to render my state more painful, and heighten my apprehensions, and my opinion of the cruelty of the whites. . . .

One day, when we had a smooth sea, and a moderate wind, two of my wearied countrymen, who were chained together (I was near them at the time), preferring death to such a life of misery, somehow made through the nettings, and jumped into the sea: immediately another quite dejected fellow, who, on account of his illness, was suffered to be out of irons, also followed their example; and I believe many more would soon have done the same, if they had not been prevented by the ship's crew, who were instantly alarmed. Those of us that were the most active were, in a moment, put down under the deck; and there was such a noise and confusion amongst the people of the ship as I never heard before, to stop her, and get the boat to go out after the slaves. However, two of the wretches were drowned, but they got the other, and afterwards flogged him unmercifully, for thus attempting to prefer death to slavery. In this manner we continued to undergo more hardships than I can now relate; hardships which are inseparable from this accursed trade.[1]

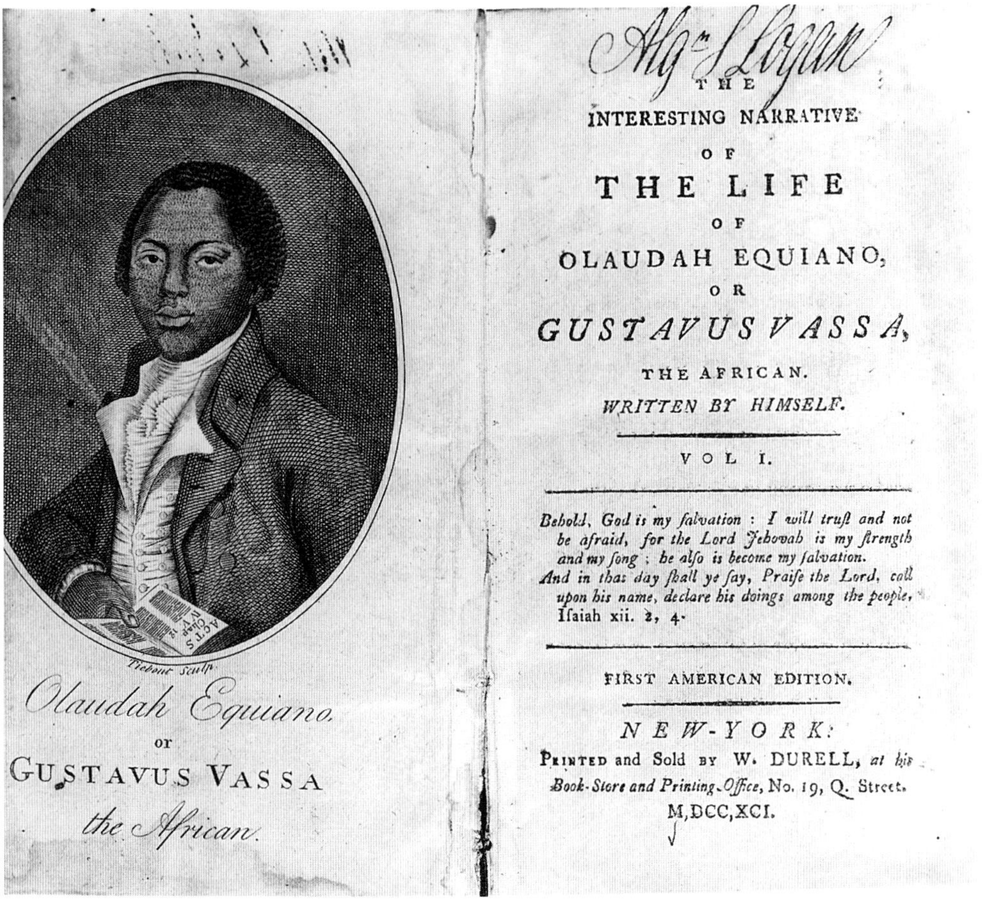

THE

INTERESTING NARRATIVE

OF

THE LIFE

OF

OLAUDAH EQUIANO,

OR

GUSTAVUS VASSA,

THE AFRICAN.

WRITTEN BY HIMSELF.

VOL I.

Behold, God is my salvation : I will trust and not
be afraid, for the Lord Jehovah is my strength
and my song ; he also is become my salvation.
And in that day shall ye say, Praise the Lord, call
upon his name, declare his doings among the people,
Isaiah xii. 2, 4.

FIRST AMERICAN EDITION.

NEW-YORK:

Printed and Sold by W. DURELL, at his
Book-Store and Printing Office, No. 19, Q. Street.
M,DCC,XCI.

Olaudah Equiano.

or

GUSTAVUS VASSA

the African.

continued from page 21

the Gold Coast, the region of West Africa along the Atlantic coast between the Komoe and Volta Rivers—only people of high social status could hold slaves.[14] Slaves, as property, could be a source of national, as well as personal, display. Between 1312 and 1332 Mali's great Muslim leader, Mansa Kango Musa, made regular pilgrimages to the holy city of Mecca. His camel caravans were weighed down with a thousand pounds of gold, were escorted by armies of servants and slaves wielding heavy golden staffs, and were calculated to impress rival states.[15] In terms of wealth, governmental organization, and military power, fourteenth-century Mali dominated its region and rivaled any nation in Europe.

African slavery could be brutal, but seldom did African masters hold life and death power over their slaves. Often slaves were people with acknowledged rights, and slavery frequently was paternalistic, in that masters had recognized responsibilities toward their slaves. In the Kongo empire of Central Africa the word "*nleke*" was used for both slave and child. Theoretically, slaves were treated as permanently subordinate family members with special responsibilities, the equivalent of perpetual children. In some societies slaves could own property, had the choice of marriage partners, and could even own their own slaves. One European observer of slavery in Anta Njaay's homeland, Senegambia, reported that agricultural slaves were allowed to work one day a week for themselves and their families. State officials often believed the undivided loyalty of slaves suited them for military and administrative service. Slaves could face harsh conditions and cruel punishment for disciplinary infractions, but African slavery contrasted greatly with the institution that developed in the Americas. Indeed, historian John Thornton has concluded that the life of an African slave was often comparable to the life of a European free tenant or hired worker.[16]

The slavery in the Americas that Anta Njaay, Venture Smith, and Olaudah Equiano faced was a different and ultimately a more devastating institution than that known in Africa. Equiano's reaction to being held by Europeans reflected his concerns about their plans. As he recalled, "Indeed such were the horrors of my view and fears at the moment, that if ten thousand worlds had been my own, I would have freely parted with them all to have exchanged my condition with that of the meanest slave in my own country."[17] Once taken to the coast, however, African captives were not likely ever to see their homes again. Their period of confinement in coastal forts varied, lasting until ships arrived to take them on to the Americas. Equiano explained the horrible conditions during this six- to eight-week journey known as the "Middle Passage." He reported that some of the children were allowed to remain on the ship's deck until the voyage got under way, but then all slaves were forced below decks, chained together in a tight space under conditions no human being should ever have to endure. "The heat of the climate, added to the number in the ship, which was so crowded that each had scarcely room to turn himself, almost suffocated us," he recalled.[18]

Under these harsh conditions some decided that death might be preferable. One enslaved African recalled being sick with dysentery and unable to eat for days. Many

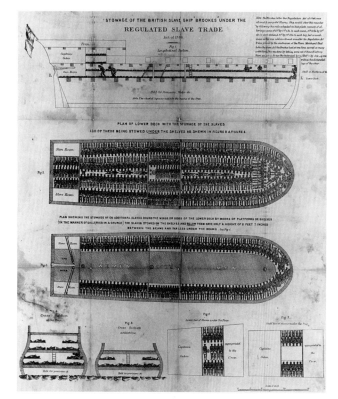

The deck plan of the British slave ship Brookes illustrates the inhuman method of transporting slaves, effectively making them human cargo. This broadside, published by the British Abolitionist Society in 1789, was a highly effective propaganda tool for the antislavery movement.

others decided not to eat at all, whereupon their captors often resorted to such tortures as thumbscrews, burning their lips with hot coals, or using force-feeding devices in attempts to prevent their suicide by starvation. Though some slaves did starve themselves to death, others found opportunities during brief respites on deck to jump overboard and drown, perhaps preferring to return home in spirit rather than endure enslavement.[19]

One British surgeon who traveled on a slave ship from West Africa to the West Indies a generation after Equiano's experience confirmed the deplorable conditions. Slaves were locked in irons that were attached to a long chain fixed to the lower deck, binding fifty or sixty men to the ship and to one another. At one point when the doctor ventured below decks to attend the sick, he was forced to step on chained bodies, as slaves covered the entire floor. He reported that slaves were fed "chiefly of horse beans, boiled to the consistency of a pulp;

of boiled yams and rice, and sometimes of a small quantity of beef and pork."[20] Depending on the weather, twice a day, at about eight in the morning and four in the afternoon, slaves were allowed above decks for food and exercise. This minimal privilege was permitted not as an entitlement but as a means of protecting the value of the slave cargo. Even so, records of this Atlantic slave trade reveal that mortality rates were generally about 15 percent and could range as high as one-third of the slaves during this Middle Passage.

Life aboard a slave ship was unbearable and often deadly for the slaves, but it was also dangerous for slave ship crews. They faced the hazardous job of all sailors and the threat of tropical diseases. Angry slaves posed additional dangers. "The Negroes [fight] like wild beasts," warned one veteran slave trader. "Slavery is a dangerous Business at sea as well as ashore."[21] Mortality among slave ship crews, some of whom were unpaid workers impressed into service or convicts serving on the crew in lieu of a prison term, was almost as high as among the slaves, although it did decline over the course of the eighteenth century. A number of captains lost their lives in slave revolts on their ships, a danger even if the revolt was unsuccessful. Heavily armed sailors generally managed to quell shipboard rebellions, but a notable few were successful. Several days out from the Guinea Coast of Africa en route to Rhode Island in 1730, slaves aboard the *Little George* managed to kill three crewmen and subdue and imprison the captain and the rest of the crew. The slaves sailed the ship back to Sierra Leone and negotiated with the captain, exchanging the freedom of the ninety-six slaves for the freedom of the captain and crew.[22] Investors were willing to chance the risks of this inhuman enterprise because profits

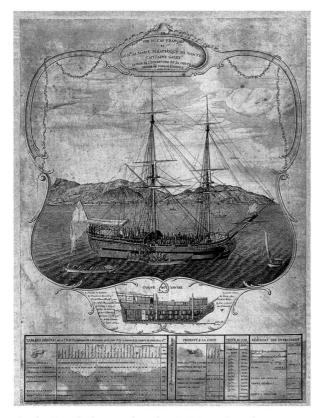

On the French slave-trading ship La Marie-Séraphique, *an iron fence was constructed to confine the enslaved Africans when they were on deck.*

could reach up to 100 percent or 150 percent of the investment for each voyage. Such profits overcame moral scruples, spurred the growth of the trade, and increased the numbers of enslaved Africans brought to the Americas. In fact, by the time of the American Revolution, despite the high rate of Middle Passage mortality, enslaved Africans composed the largest group of immigrants to the Western Hemisphere.

Olaudah Equiano was one of the slaves who survived the Middle Passage, and, like most, he came ashore in the West Indies. Only about 6 percent of slaves transported to the Americas came directly to British North America. About 40 percent were landed in Brazil, where Portuguese colonial slave masters used huge numbers of Angolan and Congolese slaves to cultivate sugarcane. Sugar was also the major crop in other parts of Latin America and in the Caribbean, where slaves working in the cane fields produced the sugar that sweetened European food and drink and generated great wealth for European merchants and American slaveholders. Equiano was too young for the cane fields, and no one bought him in Barbados. He spent only a short time there before traders took him to the English colony of Virginia on the North American mainland.

By the mid-eighteenth century when Equiano arrived, slavery had existed for nearly two generations in Virginia. The first Africans had come to the colony in 1619, little more than a decade after its founding in 1607. They arrived on a Dutch warship fresh from a military engagement in the Caribbean, where its crew had captured a number of African slaves. The ship made port in Jamestown greatly in need of supplies and willing to trade its human cargo for food. Jamestown colonist John Rolfe described the encounter in a letter to officers of the Virginia Company, the London-based sponsor of the colony, in early January 1620. He reported that "about the latter end of August, A Dutch man of War…brought not anything but 20 odd Negroes which the Governor and Capt. Merchant brought for victualle [food]." Although Africans had come with Europeans to other parts of the Americas, this was the beginning of the African presence in British colonial North America.

Jamestown settlement was a corporate venture financed by the sale of stock in the Virginia Company of London. English businessmen, following the Spanish example in Latin America, hoped to bring huge returns on stockholders' investments. The Spanish had found rich gold deposits in Mexico and other parts of Latin America that, for a time, had made Spain one of the richest nations in the world. But very soon it became clear that Virginia offered no gold, and the first decade of settlement was not encouraging. Many colonists died of malnutrition during the "starving times"; others succumbed to disease or were killed in warfare with the powerful Powhatan confederacy of Algonquian Indian tribes. English settlers soon recognized that the lack of gold in Virginia meant that the promise of the colony was in longer-term agricultural production. Negotiations with the Powhatan Confederacy provided a respite from hostilities long enough for colonists to plant crops for food to sustain themselves.

Local tribes taught the Virginia colonists to grow tobacco, which became an important cash crop for the Europeans. The introduction of this noxious and addictive drug to the general European population ensured a ready market. Tobacco

British North American colonial maritime trade, symbolized by the shells and anchor at center, depended heavily on tobacco production in the Chesapeake area of Virginia. By the eighteenth century tobacco industry was based almost entirely on slave labor.

was the Chesapeake region's most promising cash export, but the shortage of labor needed to cultivate it posed a problem. Colonists had tried impressing Native Americans into service, but deadly retaliation discouraged the practice. Young workers imported from England seemed promising for a time, but even the many Europeans who came to America as indentured servants bound for a term of service did not satisfy the labor needs of the Chesapeake colonies. Nor was the supply of indentured servants dependable, especially when prosperity in Europe improved workers' prospects there and siphoned off those who might otherwise have been willing to accept passage to America in return for years of labor. For British colonials in search of labor, the abundant supply of African slaves was irresistible.

The Africans brought to Jamestown in the early seventeenth century were bound laborers who worked long hard hours in the fields and in the homes of the white Virginians, who increasingly shunned field work. Not all Africans, however, were treated as slaves in the familiar nineteenth-century sense. There was no consistent regulation of African labor within the British American colonies in the first half of the seventeenth century. In some cases Africans served for specified periods, much as white indentured servants did, and their slave status did not necessarily pass on to their children. Angolan-born Antonio arrived in Jamestown during the early 1620s and served fourteen years before being released from bondage. He then married Mary, an African slave working in the same household. By the early 1640s Antonio had taken the name Anthony Johnson, and the couple, both free, had at least four children. They bred cattle and pigs on their substantial landholdings on Virginia's eastern shore.

Although the Johnsons had not had contracts of service as white servants did, their former owner apparently granted land to them as freedom dues, land customarily provided to those emerging from indentured servitude. During the next decade the Johnsons increased their landholdings by at least 250 acres, awarded under the headright system whereby many colonies granted land to a person for paying his own passage or the passage of a servant brought into the colony. Virginia awarded fifty-acre grants under this system, and the Johnsons had at least five servants working for them by the mid-seventeenth century. In Anthony's thirty years of freedom, before he died in 1670, he and his family had achieved something few blacks in succeeding generations could duplicate. Indeed, after Anthony's death a Virginia court allowed a white planter to seize a portion of the family's estate on the grounds that, as a black man, Anthony Johnson had never been a citizen of the colony. His children managed nevertheless to maintain much of their inheritance and their lives as free farmers.[23]

During this early colonial period, American concepts about race, slavery, and standards for race relations were still being formulated and were not yet as fixed as they would become in the eighteenth century. Still, by the mid-seventeenth century it was becoming clear that Africans and white servants received different treatment. In 1640 three servants, one of them a black man named John Punch, escaped from their duties in Virginia. When they were apprehended, the white servants were punished by having time added to their period of service. Punch, on the other hand, was sentenced to service for the rest of his life. In the same year in Virginia, an African servant named Emanuel and six white servants were recaptured after escaping. Emanuel was apparently already serving for life. The captors chained, branded, and whipped all of the fugitives, and the white servants had their time in service extended, but no extension was needed for Emanuel.

By the 1660s the Chesapeake colonies began establishing the legal foundation for racial distinctions that created the formal structure for eighteenth-century racial slavery. Colonial Virginia authorities formulated regulations to stabilize the emerging slave system in a way that worked to the advantage of slaveholders. Under traditional English common law, a child took the father's status. In 1662, Virginia changed the law to allow status to travel through the maternal line, so that children produced by unions between slave women and their free white masters would be slaves, not free. Thus, Englishmen could increase the supply of perpetual servants and more easily maintain the racial distinction between slave and free, enslaving their own children.

In attempts to attain more clarity in racial distinctions, colonies passed laws against interracial relationships and marriages, although the prohibition against interracial relationships was not applied to slave owners. In 1664, Maryland discouraged certain interracial relationships with a law stating that any white woman marrying an African slave could be forced to serve her husband's master for as long as her husband lived.[24] In defiance of the law, in 1681 Eleanor Butler, a white servant commonly known as Irish Nell, married a black slave called Negro Charles. The marriage caused great concern among local whites, who wondered why a white woman would enter such a marriage, since it would mean that she and her subsequent children would be enslaved. Nevertheless, Nell married Charles, and she and their children became the slaves of Charles's master. Eventually, in 1787, two of their grandchildren sued for their freedom and won on a legal technicality.[25]

The first racially based law in Virginia banned interracial marriages in the late seventeenth century. In 1705 Massachusetts prohibited interracial relationships, providing that black men and women involved in these relationships be whipped and sold into slavery outside the colony. White men were to be whipped, fined, and held responsible for any children resulting from the relationship, and white women were to be whipped and bound into a period of indenture. A 1726 Pennsylvania law declared that any free black person who married a white person could be sold into slavery.[26]

Colonial officials' attitudes toward interracial relationships reflected their concerns about how interracial sexual relationships might complicate racial definitions and affect the developing system of racial slavery. But they also had more immediate practical political concerns. Occasionally dramatic events illustrated the potential danger of alliances between unfree blacks and whites. Such an event took place in 1676, when white Virginia planter Nathaniel Bacon led a group of poor white farmers, white servants, and black slaves in a campaign to appropriate Native American lands in western Virginia. When Virginia authorities condemned his action and labeled him and his men criminals, Bacon turned his forces against the colony. In the fight that ensued, Bacon's army burned the colonial capital and drove the governor from his residence. Bacon's death from dysentery weakened his interracial forces, and Virginia's militia eventually overcame them. Bacon had attracted some of his followers by promising freedom to any slaves and indentured servants who joined him, and his rebellion illustrated the power of such a promise to create a dedicated interracial force. The last of his troops to be defeated were eighty blacks and twenty whites.[27]

This painting portrays two "luxuries" of white Virginians—the sexual exploitation of an enslaved woman, and the physical abuse of a male slave. The painting was found undated and unsigned on the back of a formal portrait—few would dare publicly attack the open secret of slaveowners' sexual relationships with their slaves.

Virginia's elites found this strike at colonial authority deeply disturbing. Most of all, they were disturbed by the dangers of insurrectionary interracial alliances among the lower classes. In the years after Bacon's Rebellion, they passed laws specifically designed to discourage interracial associations, attempting to combat such alarming threats to the public order and to their control of the developing racial order, of which slavery was a part. Bacon's Rebellion reflected the complex, shifting interracial alliances that emerged during the eighteenth century. Some American Indians were allies of British colonials in their conflicts with rival Europeans; others were their enemies. Blacks occasionally joined with Indians in actions against white colonists. Sometimes, however, even in areas of large slaveholdings, they helped defend the colonists against European or Indian enemies. Yet, potential black alliances with Indians became another area of concern for colonial legislative assemblies.

In 1691, South Carolina provided British North America with its first comprehensive slave code. Drawing on the code of the British island colony of Barbados, South Carolina defined "all Negroes, Mulattoes, and Indians" sold into or intended for sale into bondage as slaves. After 1700 other British North American colonies followed suit, although it was at least fifty years before the precise legal status of property in slaves was clearly defined. A 1696 South Carolina law treated slaves as property attached to specific land, as in European serfdom, and discussions continued in southern colonies as to whether slave ownership should be akin to land ownership, should involve chattel (moveable property, such as horses and cows), or should be a combination of the two.

By the time of the Revolution, slavery, formerly a legally inconsistent system, was set in the law of all the colonies: a slave inherited that status from the mother, served for a lifetime, was of African descent, and was chattel property able to be bought and sold independently of the land. Part of the necessity for the early formalization of slavery in South Carolina was the proportion of slaves in that colony's population. By 1680, slaves accounted for 17 percent of the population, and this percentage soared to 70 percent by 1720. The percentage of the population in slavery increased in other colonies as well during that period, rising from 7 percent to 30 percent in Virginia, for example. But the vast numbers of slaves in South Carolina, many newly arrived from Africa, gave the colony a distinctly West African quality. It seemed to one European "more like a negro country than like a country settled by white people."[28]

Many of the Africans in South Carolina were from the rice-growing regions of western and central Africa. Africans began growing rice in the colony for their own consumption, but their knowledge of rice cultivation soon enabled European settlers, largely unfamiliar with the process, to produce the cash crop that sustained the colony's economy. Rice became so critical to South Carolina that slaves from rice-growing regions of Africa were especially prized. Some traders, realizing the marketing advantage, claimed to be able to supply Africans from what was advertised as the "Rice Coast" in return for premium prices. Other African slaves, especially West African Fulani herdsmen, were sought after to tend the cattle shipped to the West Indies to feed British masters and their slaves on the large and profitable sugar plantations of Barbados.

TO BE SOLD on board the Ship *Bance-Island*, on tuesday the 6th of *May* next, at *Ashley-Ferry*; a choice cargo of about 250 fine healthy NEGROES, just arrived from the Windward & Rice Coast. —The utmost care has already been taken, and shall be continued, to keep them free from the least danger of being infected with the SMALL-POX, no boat having been on board, and all other communication with people from *Charles-Town* prevented.

Austin, Laurens, & Appleby.

N. B. Full one Half of the above Negroes have had the SMALL-POX in their own Country.

The announcement of a sale of 250 newly arrived Africans in Charleston, South Carolina, in the 1780s notes that more than half of them had immunity from smallpox, a fact that made them particularly valuable.

The major slave-produced crops in British North America were tobacco in the Chesapeake region and rice in South Carolina, but slavery also provided the labor needs of colonies farther north without large cash crops.[29] There, both the slaveholdings and the black populations were smaller. This was especially true in New England, where great profits were more often made in slave trading than in slaveholding. Even as the numbers of North American slaves grew, by 1750 the only New England colony with a slave population that exceeded 3 percent of the total population was Rhode Island, where slaves were 10 percent of the population. In New England slaves were likely to work as domestic servants, as field hands on small farms, or as laborers in the towns and port cities. Rhode Island needed a relatively large percentage of slaves because of the large number of extensive estates in the tobacco-growing areas of the Narragansett region of the colony. There, slaveholdings were more like the plantations of South Carolina than those in most other regions of the North.

Large tobacco estates were also located on Long Island and in the Hudson River Valley; these fell under British control in 1660 when Britain ousted the

Dutch from the colony. New Netherlands became New York, and the British replaced the Dutch system of slavery with their own. People of African descent had played key roles in the establishment of New Netherlands. As early as 1613 the Van Tweenhuysen Company, a Dutch trading enterprise, employed Jan (or Juan) Rodrigues, a free African sailor of mixed racial heritage from San Domingo, to organize a fur trade with Native Americans. Rodrigues settled on what is now Governor's Island, just off Manhattan in New York Bay, becoming the first non–Native American resident of the colony. The company hoped to build a trade monopoly on the relationships with the Indians that Rodrigues would establish. Rodrigues changed allegiance, however, taking with him his Native American connections, and commercial competition between Dutch traders broke out in violence. In the summer of 1614, crews from rival ships clashed when one trader "arrested" Rodrigues, claiming that he had broken his agreement to work exclusively for their enterprise. They injured him and confiscated his equipment before the other crew came to his rescue. Conversant with the cultures of Europe, West Africa and eastern Native Americans, Rodrigues was a valuable asset to Dutch traders, one worth fighting over.[30]

During the seventeenth century, the Dutch established New Netherland as their major American trading post, and the colony grew in population and economic importance. The first eleven African slaves arrived in 1626, and by 1640 African slavery was an increasingly important form of labor in the colony. Yet this was a different system from that developing in the British colonies. The Dutch West India Company held many of its slaves in New Amsterdam in a flexible system of bondage called half freedom. Under this system Africans could pay a yearly tax and live independently of their masters. As a part of the agreement, they were also required to labor for the company when called upon. They were not free, but they lived as free people much of the time. Those who were married lived with and supported their own families. Their children also owed their labor to the company for life under half freedom, but this system offered more independence than any other form of North American slavery. Free blacks were freer in Dutch North America than they were in the British colonies. If freed, blacks in New Netherland could own property, pursue trades, and even intermarry with whites[31]. When Great Britain took over New Amsterdam in 1664, it changed the system of slavery there to conform to the practices of other British colonies. By 1750, New York was the major slaveholding colony north of Maryland, with more than ten thousand slaves who constituted about 15 percent of the population.

In the middle colonies of New Jersey and Pennsylvania, slavery was controversial from the beginning, even though slaveholding was relatively widespread and very lucrative. In New Jersey slaves accounted for only 7 percent of the population, and most were in the northeastern region of the colony near the border of New York. There were fewer slaves in the western and southern parts of the colony, where Quaker influence was strongest. Initially, William Penn, the founder and first governor of the Quaker colony of Pennsylvania, had proposed a system of African indenture instead of slavery, with land given in return for fourteen years of service. Although not voluntary and with a longer term of service, this term labor was more like the indentured servitude of many whites. Before the end of the 1680s Pennsylvania's demand for labor was so great that Penn abandoned his plan in favor of slavery. Thereafter the black population grew steadily to approximately five thousand by 1721, leading some white laborers to complain of job competition from slave labor. Concerned about the growing black population, the colonial assembly attempted to limit their number by levying a tax on slave imports, but the tax had little effect, since slaves were smuggled into the colony from New Jersey. Pennsylvania's black population grew to eleven thousand by 1750. By this time, slavery had all but replaced white indentured servitude in all the colonies, and importing bound labor generally meant importing Africans.

Young Olaudah Equiano experienced slavery in both the South and the North, but his age and relative good fortune protected him from the worst of slave labor. In 1756, after the trader failed to find a buyer interested in purchasing him for labor in the sugarcane fields of Barbados, a Virginia tobacco planter bought him. Separated from his family and countrymen and working as a house slave in a strange culture, Equiano felt intensely lonely. Not yet able to speak English and not finding anyone who spoke his language,

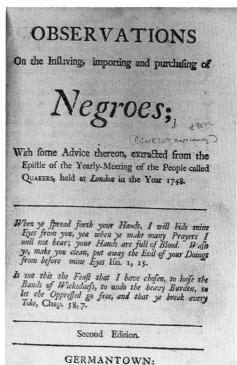

Abolitionist Anthony Benezet wrote this treatise urging fellow Quakers to stop enslaving, importing, and purchasing Africans. It was published in Germantown, Pennsylvania, in 1760 as part of a campaign against slavery begun early in the century that resulted in Quakers disowning slave-owning members and ended slavery among Quakers by the end of the eighteenth century.

he spent his time in dreadful isolation. Slavery seemed to have robbed him of all the things that marked his identity, even his name. His new owner called him Jacob, and he was expected to answer to this new name or be harshly punished. This was an important part of the process of enslavement. The free human being was stripped of the markers of freedom and humanness and never was openly to challenge this new status. Equiano, and other Africans undergoing this process, soon learned the importance of accepting, or at least appearing to accept, names provided by masters. It was an important symbol of a master's power to deprive captives of their former identities, an indication of the totality of the master's authority. Within a month, Equiano was sold again, this time to an English sea captain, and once again his name was changed. This time he was called Gustavus Vassa.

When the captain became a naval officer during the French and Indian War, Equiano went with him to work as a cabin boy. There he shared the dangers of the military life at sea, serving until the end of the war in 1763. While aboard ship, he mastered English and learned to read. Now that he was old enough for the cane fields, Equiano's owner sold him to the West Indian trade. He was resold on the island of Montserrat, but once again his luck held and a Quaker from Philadelphia bought his labor. His new owner allowed him to work for wages for part of his time, and after five years agreed to allow Equiano to purchase his own freedom with money he had saved from his wages. In 1766 Equiano embarked on a twenty-year career as a seaman, based in London and traveling to various ports in Europe and the Caribbean.[32]

Olaudah Equiano's African name meant fortunate one, and he was more fortunate than most captives. Few Africans were so lucky, but most yearned for freedom, and some sought to break slavery's hold in any way possible, violently if necessary. Deeply aware of the dangers of holding human beings in bondage, all colonies attempted to control the slave population by passing legislation and instituting sometimes horrific punishments. Slaveholders everywhere were acutely aware of the danger of slave rebellion. Rumors of savage uprisings and the slaughter of white people tormented whites, especially in areas with large numbers of enslaved people.

The presence of substantial numbers of captives in their midst also made the British colonies vulnerable to European rivals vying for power in North America. South of British Carolina lay Spanish Florida. The Spanish were quick to take advantage of the situation, encouraging British slaves to escape southward, convert to Catholicism, and join the effort to curb the southern expansion of the English colonies. In 1693 Spain promised freedom to British slaves who escaped to Florida, and many Carolina slaves made the attempt. Although not all Spanish officials made good on the promise, many runaways became part of the Spanish militia, defending Florida, raiding Carolina, and freeing slaves in the process. Throughout the early eighteenth century the Spanish recruited these African allies and even freed many of their own slaves to fill out

the military forces stationed at the Spanish garrison at Gracia Real de Santa Teresa de Mose near St. Augustine, a fort manned by free African troops. This black settlement, offering freedom to slaves escaping from British colonies, became legendary among Carolina slaves.[33]

In the fall of 1739 slaveholders' fears were realized. More than one hundred slaves staged a rebellion at the Stono River in South Carolina. Twenty of the rebels were former Kongolese soldiers who had been captured in battle in Central Africa, then brought to America as slaves in South Carolina near Charles Town (later called Charleston). Led by a man named Jemmy, the twenty recruited other South Carolina slaves, trained them in the military tactics and strategies of the Kongo, and staged a mass escape. Near the Stono River the party broke into a store and confiscated guns and ammunition, killing two shopkeepers in the process. Then, hoping to capitalize on the war between Britain and Spain, they marched south toward Spanish Florida in search of Fort Mose. The

This page from the South Carolina Assembly Journal shows some of the authorities' reactions to the Stono Rebellion of 1739. A committee considered "means to relieve the People about Stono from the dangers arising from domestic enemies." The assembly required all land- and slaveholders to provide white men for the state militia.

Africans and their recruits marched in military ranks, flying colors and accompanied by the beat of drums. Their banners were "like the unit flags that African armies flew in their campaigns." They freed slaves as they went, and their ranks had increased to more than fifty by midmorning.[34] Their forces continued to grow and numbered more than a hundred by that afternoon, but by then, South Carolina authorities had been alerted, and the royal governor had called out the colonial militia. In the fighting that ensued, most of the rebels were killed, but some escaped to the woods and swamps, where they were pursued by the militia for more than a year. The news of the Stono Rebellion profoundly affected colonists throughout British North America. South Carolina and Georgia mounted a land-and-sea military campaign against Fort Mose. The invading forces suffered fifty dead and twenty captured when a Spanish force that included many former slaves from South Carolina routed them. Blacks at the fort continued to menace the southernmost British colonies. South Carolina also reacted to the Stono Rebellion by tightening restrictions on blacks with a new slave code. This harsh law, for example, prohibited slaves from testifying, even under oath, made the murder of a slave by a white person only a misdemeanor, and provided that a slave be executed if convicted of planning a revolt, conspiring to run away, committing arson, making poisons, or teaching another slave about poisons. In 1740, in another effort to forestall rebellion, colonial authorities passed a law providing stiff fines for slaveholders who failed to give slaves sufficient food or clothing or to allow them the customary Sundays off from work.[35]

Gentlemen and ladies of the colonial elite class found rebellions and rumors of rebellion especially disturbing when uprisings involved lower class whites as well as blacks, people they called the "the herd," the "degraded rabble," or the "mean and vile" ranks. In these ranks were white indentured servants, other poor whites, black slaves, and black indentured servants. In highly class-conscious British colonial America, upper-class status, a matter of background, breeding, and social and political connections, was expressed by dress and manner. Race, always a factor, was only one of the distinctions dividing elite Americans from "the lower sort" at the bottom of colonial society. The comparable living conditions of blacks and whites at the bottom reinforced their association in the minds of the upper class. Although conditions for white indentured servants were never identical to those of slaves, on a day-to-day basis their situation might be very similar. As one white servant complained, he and his fellow servants were often "subject to the same laws as the Negroes and [had] the same coarse food and clothing." Other accounts made the point even more vividly. "They sell the [white] servants here as they do their horses, and advertise them as they do their beef and oatmeal," reported a British visitor to colonial Philadelphia.[36] The perception of many whites, blacks, and Indians that the oppressed, regardless of race, shared unjust and brutal treatment encouraged a sense of shared disadvantage among those at the bottom of society. It also opened possibilities for such interracial alliances as those formed between the servants and slaves who escaped bondage together or those who joined in Bacon's rebellion. Understanding the dangerous consequences, colonial authorities sought to prevent such alliances.

During the eighteenth century, one colony after another added new racial regulations to those already prohibiting interracial marriage. A 1708 Rhode Island law declared that a free person could not entertain a slave in his or her home if the slave's master was not present. In New York, complaints about social gatherings of blacks and whites in private homes or public drinking houses sparked calls for strict regulation. Authorities viewed such interracial contacts as dangerous to peace and "destructive to the morals of servants and slaves." One newspaper reported them to be "the principal bane and pest of the city." Colonial elites were right to fear these alliances, since the least powerful did join forces in violent strikes against authority. As early as 1712 slaves and Indians had united in New York City, where they set fires, killed nine whites, and wounded several others. When repelled by the militia, they escaped to the woods. Authorities eventually captured the rebels and exacted a price that reflected the level of popular fear. They tortured and hanged several slaves, burned others at the stake, starved some to death, and broke others on the wheel. They executed two Indians for their part in the conspiracy, and repressive laws were enacted against blacks and Indians.[37]

In 1741, testimony taken during a trial on charges of conspiracy involving a group of slaves, poor whites, and others engaged in criminal activity in New York City again raised fears in the colonies. Coming soon after the Stono Rebellion in South Carolina, it was another chilling reminder of the continuing danger of slave uprisings with the particularly ominous feature of interracial collusion. Witnesses told of a bold plan hatched in taverns and dance halls frequented by an interracial group of shady characters. One of these places, a saloon operated by a white proprietor, John Romme, was suspected of being a clearinghouse for goods stolen by several urban gangs. The Geneva Club, a black gang well known in New York's underworld, gathered there regularly with some of the city's interracial and white gangs.[38]

Romme's was only one of the New York establishments that concerned city authorities. John Hughson, a shoemaker, was another white underworld character who operated an interracial bar, and officials had strong evidence that his establishment was a front for a fencing operation that served the city's criminals, including free blacks, slaves, and poor whites. Patrons were entertained by Margaret (Peggy) Sorubiero, "the Newfoundland Irish beauty." On weekends, slaves who were customarily allowed Saturday nights and Sundays to themselves joined whites and free blacks to dance, enjoy the music, and eat good food, including goose and mutton and fresh baked bread, and drink strong rum and cider. On occasion, even off-duty British soldiers joined the lively urban social scene.[39] In Hughson's tavern, with the assistance of Romme and his associates, blacks and whites hatched a plot that seemed to confirm the worst fears of colonial elites and urban authorities. Courtroom testimony revealed their plan to consolidate New York's criminal activity and to divert attention from widespread thievery by setting fires in the city. The officials' response was swift and extreme. They burned thirteen blacks at the stake, hanged sixteen other blacks and four whites, and banished more than seventy blacks and seven whites from the British colonies.[40]

Sometimes interracial, class-based action took the form of economic protest. Boston's poor workers reacted strongly to the combination of inflation and rising unemployment they suffered during the 1730s. A Boston minister complained about "murmuring against the Government & the rich People" during the harsh winter of 1737. Eventually, full-scale rioting by "young People, Servants and Negroes" forced colonial officials to adopt measures that finally diminished the economic crisis.[41] African Americans, European Americans, and Native Americans also forged alliances to oppose the press gangs that entered communities to forcibly remove young able-bodied men and impress them into service in the British navy. Only those whose family or political connections protected them from what amounted to little more than legalized kidnapping were immune. Their only other protection was group resistance. In 1745 and again in 1747 Boston men, angered by the appearance of press gangs, mounted violent resistance, what one report called a "riotous, tumultuous assembly of foreign seamen, servants, Negroes and other persons of mean and vile condition." They then turned their rage on the colonial troops who attempted to subdue the mob, a mob that also apparently included several men from the middling classes.[42] Violent resistance was not unique to Boston. Impressment sparked interracial resistance in major port cities throughout the mid-eighteenth century. In Newport, Rhode Island, during the summer of 1765, five hundred "seamen, boys and Negroes" took direct action against press gangs that had operated in the city for more than a month. Protest exploded in New York City and Norfolk, Virginia, as well.[43]

In 1770, on the eve of the American Revolution, Africans and African Americans were a significant part of the population in the colonies of British North America. Their numbers had grown as slavery's importance to the economy had grown, and the overwhelming majority were slaves. By 1750 there were almost a quarter million slaves in the mainland colonies of British North America, all but 30,000 held in the southern colonies. Their numbers continued to grow in the last half of the century, so that the black proportion of the population in the colonies had grown from 4 percent in 1700 to nearly 40 percent by 1770, doubling between midcentury and the Revolution. Although the Africans had come from many different ethnic groups, spoke many different languages, and practiced different religions, there were cultural commonalities that, along with the shared experience of slavery, facilitated their creation of families and communities. Most came from traditional agricultural societies, where kinship was the basis of political and economic life. They had well-developed craft traditions and accomplished artists and artisans who worked with woods, metals, yarns, reeds, grasses, and clay. Music, musical instruments, including stringed and percussion instruments, singing, and dancing were integral to these African cultures, as was the storytelling common to oral traditions. Virtually all valued invention and improvisation, and many greatly prized the idea of maintaining their dignity both as individuals and as a people. Upon such commonalities, Africans and people of African descent built a syncretic African American culture that preserved

Late-eighteenth-century slaves in South Carolina perform the Juba, a dance of the Yoruba people of West Africa. The male dancer's cane and the women's scarves are typically African, as are the molo *(banjo) and drum.*

important parts of their African heritage while adapting to their environment and to their situation in America.[44]

The cultural traditions, skills, and sensibilities that Africans brought with them helped shape the lives of all Americans. This was particularly true in areas heavily dependent on slave labor. African laborers brought their own styles and beliefs to the northern colonies, but their influence there was less than in the southern colonies because they were only about 4 percent of the northern population. In the Chesapeake region, on the other hand, African influence was stronger. There were found the greatest number of slaves, more than three hundred thousand in 1770, making up about 37 percent of the total population. Although less densely settled in 1770, the Lower South surrounding Charleston contained more than ninety thousand slaves, and more than seven thousand slaves lived in the Deep South of the Lower Mississippi Valley. In both these areas, the African cultural influence was particularly strong, since Africans and their descendants were well over half of the total population.

The Africans who handled much of the work of the colonies, particularly in the southern colonies, brought with them concepts of how the work should be done and ideas about the design of tools to accomplish that work. The enslaved workers who planted, cultivated, and harvested rice in South Carolina drew on their agricultural experience in Africa. They created the large round shallow-sided reed winnowing baskets used in the South Carolina rice fields, following the coiled grass method of their homeland. The Virginia slave ironworkers who forged the hoes and axes used on local farms followed an ancient African skill. These eighteenth-century slave blacksmiths made more than tools. They expressed their culture in artistic productions and created spears as weapons for slave rebellion as well. Slave cooks introduced African cooking methods and tastes to the American diet, often emphasizing corn in the form of bread or hoecake, mush, hominy, and roasted ears.

This coiled grass basket is of a type traditionally used in many parts of West Africa, which enslaved Africans in South Carolina imported to the rice fields there. After rice had been pounded with a pestle in a mortar, the basket was gently tilted back and forth, tossing the rice upward and outward, allowing the husk to be blown away by the wind.

Stews, fried meat, rice, yams, fruits, and groundnuts were common in African diets, and when available were enjoyed by African Americans as well. Much of what has become identified as southern cuisine in America had its origins in kitchens presided over by African American cooks.

Just before the Revolution, Africans and African Americans had been in America for more than 150 years, and in the more densely settled coastal plantation areas, they had established slave communities. These communities persisted under extraordinarily adverse conditions. Planters required both men and women to engage in hard physical labor, and they worked in marshy rice fields, hot and humid tobacco fields, dusty wheat fields, and dangerous back-breaking lumbering camps. Workers on rice plantations spent days standing in the water of the rice field, prey to insects and disease, with a minimal diet to sustain them. Children were expected to work as soon as they were deemed old enough to be useful. Pregnant women worked, and after childbirth women returned to the fields quickly, with little time lost. All worked under the compulsion of the overseer's or slave driver's lash, and they were liable to be whipped for working too slowly. More fortunate workers labored on the boats engaged in river or coastal trade or worked as artisans, doing the carpentry, bricklaying, and other skilled work necessary for building and maintaining plantations and towns. Others performed domestic service, which was generally less physically demanding but brought its own risks. Household workers were continually under the eye of the slave owner, available for work both night and day, and women working in the owner's house were especially vulnerable to sexual exploitation.

People enslaved in the North were more likely than those in the South to live and work in small groups, often as part of their owners' households. Since they frequently worked side by side with their owners, working conditions for many in the North were less onerous than those of slaves on the large plantations of the South. Such close contact also led northerners to seek younger Africans for their slaves, especially young men whom they considered potentially useful workers but more easily managed and trained than older men. Africans in the North had more opportunity to learn the local language and customs and could learn more quickly how to negotiate their new society. Quasho, Pompey, Phyllis, and Prince lived in the household of Dr. Lazarus La Baron in Plymouth, Massachusetts, where they shared two rooms over the kitchen. In addition to her unpaid household labor, Phyllis, the cook, was able to earn money and was shrewd enough in her dealings that she earned a profit by investing in the cargo of a schooner sailing out of Plymouth. When Quasho joined the household, LaBaron wanted to give him a classical name to continue the theme begun with Phyllis's husband, Pompey. Quasho Quando, however, did not want to be called Julius Caesar, and neither whipping, withholding food, nor bribery would convince him. Finally, to restore peace to the household, LaBaron gave up the effort to make the African change his name.[45]

Although there were some advantages to being in the North, there were also important drawbacks. Northern slaves were more likely to be isolated from other blacks, particularly people from their own language groups and cultures. It was more difficult for them to find mates or to maintain regular contact with their families. Although they were less likely to live with people from the same cultural background, they did manage to find ways to preserve important aspects of their African backgrounds. Particularly in the cities and towns of the East Coast, Africans and African Americans built a rich shared tradition, preserving musical traditions, storytelling, and traditional religions.

Informal political structures with periodic festivals to elect or appoint local black "governors" or "kings" fostered cultural solidarity across ethnic lines throughout the Americas. These festivals sometimes lasted for a week and included parades, game competitions, a feast, and a fancy dress ball. During the middle of the eighteenth century, Negro election days, when African Americans gathered to choose these black informal authorities, became very popular even in New England, where there were relatively few blacks. Ceremonial black governors and kings, and sometimes other officials, did at times wield real power over their constituencies, and in some places, as in Rhode Island, actually operated a court system that paralleled the official courts. They held their power at the sufferance of the slave masters, but masters often found it convenient to work through the slave hierarchy. At the same time, these political structures were a way for African Americans to become a part of the culture in which they were located. In royal colonies with appointed white governors, the black officials were called kings; in New England, where white governors were elected, blacks elected black governors.

The week-long Pinkster, or Pentecost, holiday celebrated in New Amsterdam, became a predominantly black celebration attended by all races in New York and New Jersey by the late eighteenth century. Presided over by a black patriarch, the elaborate festivities included a parade, music and dancing, vendors of crafts and food, and exotic animals. Other festivals in the South carried on African and Latin American traditions, often combining them with European holidays. These too included parades with baton twirling, feasting, sometimes athletic competitions, and always African music and dance. For Africans and their descendants, music and dance were not simply frivolities and escape from routine labor. They were also an integral part of African and African American religious expression. Both the informal political positions and the festivals were important ways that Africans in America could preserve their cultural heritages, reaffirm the status of families who were important in Africa, reinforce communal values and beliefs, recall tribal customs, and remember shared traditions.

During the seventeenth and eighteenth centuries, the vast majority of black people in America maintained traditional African beliefs. The religion of the African Creoles who came early to the Americas reflected their mixed heritage. They were generally Christian, combining a form of Roman Catholicism with Islam and traditional African religions. By the 1700s there had been African Christians in the Kongo for more than two hundred years, and many fugitives attracted to Spanish promises of freedom in Florida for converts were already Christian. As slave traders brought more Africans from the interior to the British colonies in the mid-1700s, however, traditional African beliefs were strengthened in slave communities. Although the vast majority adhered to traditional African religions until well into the nineteenth century, evangelical Christianity found converts, particularly in the Chesapeake region of the Upper South and in urban areas of the North and South, during the religious revivals known as the First Great Awakening that began in the late 1730s. For many blacks in contact with this emotional outpouring of religious fervor, the principles of these revivals had great appeal. Evangelical missionaries preached the equality of all, regardless of race or economic status. They also put this egalitarian ideal into practice, supporting lay clergy, accepting women and blacks as preachers and exhorters, and admitting people to worship and to some aspects of church governance, regardless of their rank or condition. Moreover, many preachers were outspoken in their opposition to slavery. As American leaders developed their political philosophy to support independence from England, their republican rhetoric of liberty and equality combined with the religious principles of the First Great Awakening to give African Americans a powerful argument against the institution of slavery.[46]

Paul Revere's engraving of the Boston Massacre of 1770 was designed to gain sympathy for Boston's "martyrs." In some copies, the skin of the fallen figure in the center is colored brown to depict Crispus Attucks.

Slavery: From the Revolution to the Cotton Kingdom

On the afternoon of March 5, 1770, forty-seven-year-old Crispus Attucks, a fugitive slave, was drinking in a Boston pub with some other sailors when a British soldier entered and asked about local employment. Perhaps the soldier was new to the city and unaware that tensions between local workers and the British soldiers had erupted into minor disturbances all winter. Surely he knew about the long-standing resentment American sailors had toward impressment, and he should have known that local sailors would resent the British soldiers who had come to enforce England's Navigation Acts. These acts, with their limitations on American trade, had created hard times for the sailors gathered in the pub. To make matters worse, British soldiers often took part-time jobs to supplement their military pay at wages that undercut local workers and worsened the tight job market. When the soldier entered the pub that afternoon, he faced a hostile crowd. The patrons chased him out into the street with insults and angry exclamations about the kind of work he could do, one sailor suggesting the soldier might clean his outhouse.

That evening, violent confrontations erupted between soldiers and civilians in the city. In one case, a soldier stabbed a boy. At the same time, Crispus Attucks led a mob of boys, Irishmen, blacks, mulattoes, and other sailors in confronting the guard at the Boston Customs House. Attucks had worked as a crewman on a whaling ship sailing out of Boston for twenty years. His extraordinarily long tenure on the whaling crew may have been what made it possible for him to escape capture as a runaway slave. Part African and part Nantucket Indian, Attucks had run away from his owner in Framingham, Massachusetts, in 1750. Even in his youth, muscular and six-feet-two-inches tall, Attucks had a commanding physical presence. After many years at sea, he was accustomed to both danger and adventure.

With Attucks at the head, the club-wielding mob of twenty or thirty, began to taunt the soldiers. The whistling and yelling mob threw snowballs and chunks of ice, and bystanders joined the fray, tossing whatever they could pick up in the streets at the British soldiers. Attucks exhorted the attackers: "The way to get rid of these soldiers is to attack the main-guard. Strike at the root: this is the nest."[1] Finally, the captain of the guard ordered his harassed soldiers to fire on the crowd. At first they did nothing, and then the captain exclaimed, "Damn you, fire, be the consequence what it will." The soldiers' musket volley killed three and wounded two. Among the dead was Crispus Attucks. He was shot twice and was the first to die in what many considered the first battle of the American Revolution. Huge crowds attended the funeral services for the American martyrs. "A vast multitude" of people on foot and a long line of carriages accompanied their funeral cortege to the prominent Park Street cemetery near the Boston Common where they were buried.[2]

African American slavery in British America profoundly affected the course and tone of colonial politics and was deeply implicated in growing concerns about American liberty. During the last half of the eighteenth century, Americans voiced their fears about losing their freedom to British authorities. Increased taxation, enforced by the sizeable standing army of British troops stationed in the colonies, was an irritating reminder of the subordinate status of local American officials. The colonies had never been self-governing, but in the first half of the eighteenth century Britain had been occupied with conflict in Europe. One war after another between the major continental powers had distracted the crown and prevented its

In this 1789 announcement signed by its president, Benjamin Franklin, the Pennsylvania Abolition Society declared that its goal was "To instruct; to advise; to qualify those who have been restored to freedom, for the exercise and enjoyment of civil liberty. To promote in them habits of industry; to furnish them with employments suited to their age, sex, talents, and other circumstances; and to procure their children an education calculated for their future situation in life."

close scrutiny of colonial affairs. But in 1763, with the defeat of France in the Seven Years' War (known as the French and Indian War in America), and with the conclusion that Britain needed to raise funds to pay for that war, the mother country turned its attention to closer management of the American colonies. Many Americans, however, interpreted this increased supervision as an encroachment on their rights as British citizens, with some viewing such taxation as the unjustifiable tyranny of English authority over free Americans. Deeply influenced by the writings of British philosopher John Locke, American leaders demanded the rights and liberty they believed came directly from God, rights no temporal government could morally deny them. Revolution was justifiable, they argued, in the face of tyranny where governments prevented the operation of civil and natural law. They chose their words carefully for maximum rhetorical impact. "We will not be the slaves of England," they announced, and the irony of their language was not lost on American slaves.

Black Americans participated along with whites in organized protests against British tax policies in the 1760s. Black sailors and laborers were in the mobs crying, "No taxation without representation" that took to the streets in Boston, New York, Newport, Rhode Island, and other colonial towns protesting the 1765 Stamp Act. They agreed when the *Boston Gazette* ran a poem addressed to George Grenville, the British prime minister, expressing the determination of Americans to maintain their freedom:

> To make us all Slaves, now you've lost Sir! The Hope,
> You've but to go hang yourself.—We'll find the Rope.

Massachusetts lawyer James Otis also recognized the inherent hypocrisy in America's professed commitment to freedom. Among the earliest to publicly express some of the central themes of the Revolution, arguing during the 1760s that liberty was a God-given right and that governments had no right to tax people without their consent, he also believed that blacks were rightfully a part of the American citizenry. "The colonists," he said, "black and white, born here, are free born British subjects, and entitled to all the essential civil rights of such." Slavery must be ended, Otis argued, since "all men...white or black" were "by the law of nature free born."[3] Other influential colonials agreed. During the late 1760s Nathaniel Appleton, another New Englander, pointed to the inconsistency of white Americans' demanding freedom for themselves while denying freedom to other human beings.

Slaves were well aware of the contradiction their enslavement posed for the commitment to freedom that their masters publicly professed. They also realized the potential influence of whites sympathetic to the abolition of slavery, even though some were slaveholders, and continually appealed to these abolitionists' sense of justice. With the assistance of such prominent allies, many of whom were lawyers, slaves continued petitioning for general emancipation and brought suits asserting claims that they were illegally held in bondage. Acting through petitions to government officials and through court cases, for example, the Pennsylvania Society for the Abolition of Slavery, which counted Benjamin Franklin among its members, developed a complex legal and political strategy that chipped away at the legal foundations of slavery and the slave trade. Blacks from Pennsylvania and from outside the state sought their legal aid and in the process pushed the society's strategies toward a campaign against slavery.[4]

Slaves also found other allies. Although more likely to work within their own communities rather than fighting against slavery through the courts or the political system, such Quakers as Anthony Benezet, John Woolman, Joshua Evans, and John Hunt in Pennsylvania and western New Jersey, were among the first white Americans to urge the abolition of slavery. Before 1730 some crusading Quakers had criticized slavery as incompatible with their faith. In 1758 the Philadelphia Yearly Meeting of Friends condemned the importation, trading, buying, or holding of slaves by their members and took steps to remove slaveholders from leadership positions within the church. In 1759 Benezet published a number of antislavery and anti–slave trade pamphlets.[5] Individual Quaker meetings in the colony often financed the support of freed slaves who could not support themselves as one means of encouraging manumission, the freeing of slaves, by their members. Starting in 1773 in New England and spreading to other regions in the North, Quaker meetings began disowning members who refused to emancipate their slaves. The antislavery Quakers gradually convinced the others, and finally by the last decade of the century, Friends were no longer slave masters.[6]

Also in 1773, three years before Thomas Jefferson penned the Declaration of Independence, a group of enslaved African American men in Boston wrote to the governor and the general court of Massachusetts protesting their state of unfreedom. Identifying their communique as "the humble Petition of many Slaves, living in the Town of Boston, and other Towns in the Province," they complained of their oppression: "We have no property, We have no wives! No

Children!, We have no City! No Country!"[7] Understanding the precariousness of their situation as slaves petitioning powerful colonial officials, these African Americans went out of their way to cloak their protests in humility and the rhetoric of Christianity. They assured the governor and the court, "We desire to bless God, who loves Mankind," and observed that slavery, "is in itself so unfriendly to Religion, and every moral Virtue except Patience." Although, they said, "We presume not to dictate to your Excellency and Honors," theirs was a plea for freedom, the same freedom that white Americans were demanding from England. The slaves also offered the same argument—freedom was the right of human beings, and it was God's will. As one free black man asked, "Do the rights of nature cease to be such, when a Negro is to enjoy them?"[8]

Recognizing the development of antislavery sentiment in the colonies

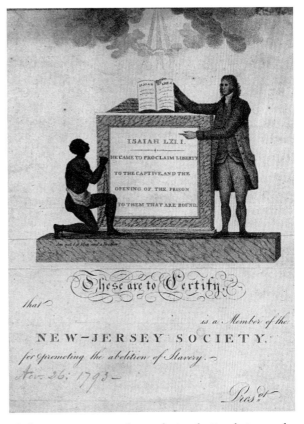

Abolition in New Jersey began during the Revolution, and the New Jersey Society for Promoting the Abolition of Slavery was founded with the goal of achieving "the immediate abolition of slavery from our whole land." In 1804 the New Jersey Legislature passed "An Act for the Gradual Abolition of Slavery."

and in Britain, the petitioners argued that God had "lately put it into the Hearts of Multitudes on both Sides of the Water, to bear our Burthens, some of whom are Men of great Note and Influence; who have pleaded our Cause with Arguments which we hope will have their weight with this Honorable Court."[9] A few months later, four Massachusetts slaves followed this petition with a printed letter addressed to the Boston town delegates and the colonial assembly. With more than a hint of sarcasm, they commented on the hypocrisy of American slaveholders' appealing for American freedom. "We expect great things from men who have made such a noble stand against the designs of their fellow-men to enslave them," they said. Yet, their request was not for immediate emancipation. It was much more modest, only to be allowed to work one

Massachusetts Slaves Petition the Governor, Council, and House of Representatives for Their Freedom

As leaders of the colonies were discussing the doctrine of natural rights and beginning to argue that they had a right to be freed from the oppression of English rule, black people held in bondage took their arguments to heart. In this petition to the Massachusetts governor and House of Representatives, African slaves use the patriots' own beliefs, including Christianity and natural rights, to argue for their own freedom.

---

25 May 1774

The Petition of a Grate Number of Blackes of this Province who by divine permission are held in a state of Slavery within the bowels of a free and christian Country

Humbly Shewing

That your Petitioners apprehind we have in common with all other men a naturel right to our freedoms without Being depriv'd of them by our fellow men as we are a freeborn Pepel and have never forfeited this Blessing by aney compact or agreement whatever. But we were unjustly dragged by the cruel hand of power from our dearest frinds and sum of us stolen from the bosoms of our tender Parents and from a Populous Pleasant and plentiful country and Brought hither to be made slaves for Life in a Christian land. Thus are we deprived of every thing that hath a tendency to make life even tolerable, the endearing ties of husband and wife we are strangers to for we are no longer man and wife then our masters or mestreses thinkes proper marred or onmarred. Our children are also taken from us by force and sent maney miles from us wear we seldom or ever see them again there to be made slaves of for Life ... By our deplorable situation we are rendered incapable of shewing our obedience to Almighty God how can a slave perform the duties of a husband to a wife or parent to his child How can a husband leave master and work and cleave to his wife How can the wife submit themselves to there husbands in all things. How can the child obey thear parents in all things. There is a grat number of us sencear ... members of the Church of Christ how can the master and the slave be said to fulfil that command Live in love let Brotherly Love contuner and abound Beare yea onenothers Bordenes ... We therefor Bage your Excellency and Honours will give this its deu weight and consideration and that you will accordingly cause an act of the legislative to be pessed that we may obtain our Natural right our freedoms and our children be set at lebety at the yeare of Twenty one for whoues sekes more petequeley your Petitioners is in Duty ever to Pray.

Benjamin Rush of Philadelphia, signer of the Declaration of Independence, exemplified American inconsistency on the slavery question. Although he argued for the moral and intellectual equality of blacks and whites and joined the Pennsylvania abolition society in 1784, he was himself a slaveholder.

day a week to earn the money to purchase their own freedom and that of their families.[10]

That same year white Philadelphia physician Benjamin Rush published one of the strongest antislavery statements of the period. Africans, he wrote, were the moral and intellectual equal of whites. He argued for an important distinction between enslaved Africans and free Africans. It was only slavery, he contended, that brought on the mental and moral deprivation that had been mistaken for racial inferiority. Thus, slavery and the slave trade must be ended so that Africans might become educated and useful citizens and so that America might become the beacon of freedom it professed to be. God, he argued, would not allow the sin of slavery to go unpunished. Yet, like many in the eighteenth century who condemned slavery, Rush himself was a slaveholder. Three years after his condemnation of slavery, as the Revolution began in 1776, he purchased William Grubber. Even though Rush joined the Pennsylvania Abolition Society in 1784 and later was one of its officers, he continued to hold Grubber in slavery until the 1790s.[11]

The commitment to freedom exhibited by slaves in the colonies gave rise to rumors of violent conspiracies. Abigail Adams wrote to her husband, John, in the fall of 1774 about the anxiety such rumors caused among her New England neighbors, exclaiming, "I wish most sincerely there was not a slave in the province." She also expressed her concern at the contradiction posed by the existence of slavery among a people who held to the ideal of freedom. "It always seemed a most iniquitous scheme to me," she wrote, "to fight ourselves for what we are daily robbing and plundering from those who have as good a right to freedom as we have."[12]

Massachusetts slaves continued to petition for freedom throughout the pre-Revolutionary years, arguing their "naturel [sic] right to be free and without molestation to injoy [sic] as property as they may acquire by their industry, or by any other means not detrimental to their fellow man." Less than one year before the April day in 1775 when seventy Massachusetts militiamen faced British troops on Lexington Green in Massachusetts, slaves petitioned for their freedom. They also asked for "unimproved land" on which to settle their families, "that each of us may there quietly sit down under our own fig tree [to enjoy] the fruits of [our] labour." None of the slaves' petitions was granted, but colonial authorities were well aware of the African Americans' determination to be free.[13]

As a small but growing number of white Americans questioned the compatibility of slavery and the ideal of freedom during the 1760s and 1770s, enslaved and free African Americans continued to join the protests for liberty. In New York City, they were among the Stamp Act rioters who demolished the house of a British officer, who said he "would cram the stamps down American throats at the point of his sword." Joseph Allicocke, an office clerk whose mother was mulatto, was a leader of the New York Sons of Liberty, the major protest group in the city. After relentless attacks on British taxation policies and on those who attempted to enforce them prompted their repeal, Allicocke was honored for his service to the cause. On May 21, 1766, as New Yorkers celebrated their victory, the young clerk was given a twenty-one gun salute and dubbed general of the Sons of Liberty.[14] "Black Sam" Fraunces, a West Indian mulatto, operated one of New York City's most notorious centers of revolutionary activity, the Queen's Head tavern at Broad and Pearl Streets. In this pub, black and white New Yorkers drank, socialized, and planned much of the protest against the Stamp Act. In 1774, the Queen's Head was the staging area for New York's counterpart of the Boston Tea Party.[15]

Though he was one of Virginia's most prominent slaveholders, Thomas Jefferson had long been ambivalent about slavery. His father, Peter Jefferson, had held slaves, and Thomas had grown up with slaves as his companions. Later, he claimed that his first memory was of being carried on a pillow by one of his father's slaves. Thomas formed lasting relationships with some slaves. Jupiter, one of Peter Jefferson's slaves, was born in the same year as Thomas, and the two grew up together. Thomas was the plantation heir; Jupiter became the coachman and hostler who managed the plantation stables. When his father died, Jefferson inherited almost 3,000 acres of land and more than fifty slaves including Jupiter. As an adult, Jupiter, an expert stonecutter, served as Thomas Jefferson's personal servant. It was he who crafted the columns at the eastern entrance of Jefferson's mansion at Monticello.

In 1770 Jefferson expressed his discomfort with slavery by assisting a Virginia slave, Samuel Howell, in his attempt to gain his freedom. Jefferson's argument that under nature's law "all men are born free," did not convince the Virginia court, which ruled against Howell's bid for freedom.[16] In the end, however, Howell took his own freedom. He and his younger brother Simon escaped within a few months of the verdict.[17] Years later when Jefferson was drafting the Declaration of Independence, he struggled with the contradiction slavery posed to the argument that God had given all people the right to personal liberty. In an early version of the document, Jefferson attacked the Crown for forcing slavery upon the colonies. Directly indicting Britain's role in the Atlantic slave trade, he wrote that the King had violated the "most sacred rights of life and liberty in the persons of a distant people who never offended him." The Crown had kid-

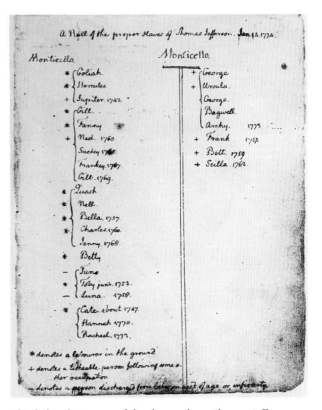

This ledger lists some of the slaves whom Thomas Jefferson owned in 1774. Yet he once wrote that slavery "is a perpetual exercise of the most boisterous passions, the most unremitting despotism on the one part, and degrading submissions on the other."

napped these African people, Jefferson claimed, and had bound "them into slavery in another hemisphere" or caused their deaths on the journey across the Atlantic. His fellow slaveholders forced him to strike this section from the final declaration, but its appearance in the first draft demonstrated Jefferson's life-long anxiety about this most un-American of American institutions.[18]

Jefferson was one of a number of Revolutionary patriots who were uncomfortable with slavery, an institution so abhorrent to the basic human values expressed in support of American independence. In his case the close personal contact he had with some blacks must have made his slaveholding particularly emotionally troubling. One can only speculate about the emotional and psychological impact on both Jefferson and Jupiter, once childhood companions, becoming slave master and slave. Even more striking in attempting to understand Jefferson, the slaveholder who penned the declaration against slavery, is

The Declaration of Independence. The original draft included an attack on the British king for having assaulted a "distant people" and "captivating and carrying them into slavery in another hemisphere." Southern delegates insisted that this clause be removed.

that he was also almost certainly the father of some of his own slaves born to Sally Hemmings, also a Jefferson slave. Perhaps a less self-reflective man might have been able to ignore these contradictions in his life and relationships, but it is unlikely that one of Jefferson's intelligence and thoughtfulness could have easily dismissed the obvious hypocrisy of his situation. Try as he might, he, like America and the Revolution itself, would in many ways come to be defined by the contradiction of the rhetoric of freedom and the tolerance of slavery.

While some blacks saw their best hope for freedom with the Revolutionary cause, others turned to the mother country. The majority of white Americans did not equate their freedom from the arbitrary British authority that they denounced with the freedom American slaves sought. Consequently, many African Americans saw England as the land of liberty, believing that England had outlawed slavery in 1770. This belief was based on a common misreading of the British court decision in the famed Somerset Case. James Somerset, a Boston slave, had been transported to London by his master Charles Stewart in 1770. Two years later, Somerset escaped, but he was recaptured and ordered to be sold into slavery in Jamaica. British abolitionists, led by Granville Sharp, won a suit to prevent Somerset from being taken from England in June of 1772. Although the British court under London's Lord Chief Justice Mansfield ruled only that Somerset could not be forced to return to slavery in the colonies, leaving him technically still a slave in Britain, many people, including British slaves, interpreted this decision as the end of slavery in England. Slaves in Britain, particularly in London, walked away from their masters, and many masters, who believed that the government had effectively abolished slavery, made little protest. As historian Gretchen Holbrook Gerzina concluded, "England took on the aura of a land whose soil was too free to abide slavery, and whose air was too free to breathe it."[19]

Although the British court ruling was not a clear-cut denunciation of slavery, apparently some American slaves were aware of and even acted on the news of the Somerset decision. When one Virginia slave fled his master, some speculated that he would probably "board a vessel for Great Britain . . . from the knowledge he has of the late Determination of the Somerset Case." Another master believed his runaway slave couple was on the way to Britain "where they imagine they will be free," he said, adding, "a Notion now too prevalent among the Negroes."

Thus, as American protest of British authority turned to military resistance, African Americans were divided over where they should stand in the hostilities. Through most of the colonial period, regulations had generally barred slaves and even free blacks from inclusion in the militia, but during time of war these rules had often been disregarded. African Americans had served in every colonial war from the 1690s through the French and Indian War, which ended in 1763. They enlisted in interracial military units as soldiers, scouts, laborers, wagoners, and sailors and generally received the same pay as whites. Even slaves were usually paid, although they were often forced to surrender their pay or a share of it to their masters. By the time of the Revolution, blacks were serving in many militia units in the northern colonies, and when the Continental Congress designated Massachusetts's militia as minutemen in 1775, such African Americans as Peter Salem of Framingham, Prince Estabrook of Lexington, Samuel Craft of Newton, and Cato Wood and Cuff Whittemore of Arlington were among them. Black minutemen stood at Lexington Green and attacked British troops along the road to Concord. One named "Prince the Negro" was among those wounded in the battle. More than a hundred black soldiers, including Peter Salem, Titus Coburn, Salem Poor, and Grant Cooper, helped defend American positions at the battle of Bunker Hill. Despite their valorous service, by the summer of 1775, commander George Washington and the Continental Congress, under pressure from southern planters, opposed the further enlistment of free blacks and slaves. Once the enlistments of blacks already under arms expired, Washington decided, no other blacks would be permitted to serve the American cause. In the face of abundant and widely known historical evidence to the contrary, they

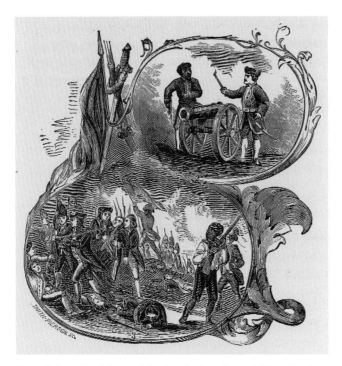

Peter Salem, black hero of the Revolution, shoots Major Pitcairn at the Battle of Bunker Hill. Edward A. Johnson, a school principal in Raleigh, North Carolina, published this illustration in 1890 in A School History of the Negro Race in America, from 1619 to 1890. *He believed black children should learn about black heroes.*

argued that slaves were too servile to make good soldiers. In reality, planters were well aware of the passionate desire of African Americans for freedom, and most feared insurrection should slaves gain access to guns.

The Americans' reluctance to include black troops in the army, the British identification with black freedom, and oppressive conditions for white servants and black slaves combined to convince many to side with the British. From the beginning of the Revolution, rumors abounded about servants and slaves joining British troops to strike against southern plantations. As one southerner explained, "malicious and imprudent speeches of some among the lower class whites...induced [the slaves] to believe that their freedom depended on the success of the King's troops." South Carolina newspapers reported that large bands of "the most infamous banditti and horse thieves [which included] a corps of Indians, with negro and white savages disguised like them" were raiding settlements and "stealing slaves" throughout the region. These banditti were groups of fugitive slaves, indentured servants, Cherokees, poor farmers, and "backcountry tories," who worked both independently and with British forces. Commanded by such men as "Captain" Jones, the "Colored Power Man," or the mulatto William Hunt, these guerrilla bands burned and looted plantations, stole horses, and attacked continental forces in many regions. One band in New Jersey was commanded by a 22-year-old runaway slave named Titus, who became known as Colonel Tye. Early in his career as a guerrilla leader, Tye captured a captain in the New Jersey militia. His large band, reportedly including up to eight hundred blacks, attacked American fortifications and large slaveholding estates, freeing slaves and indentured servants. Black guerrilla bands calling themselves The King of England Soldiers continued to raid plantations and to free slaves for fifty years after the end of the Revolutionary War.[20]

Lord Dunmore, the royal governor of Virginia, recognized the slaves' desire for freedom and realized the strategic advantage to be gained by attracting slaves and indentured servants to the British cause. He well understood the psychological value of recruiting American slaves to fight against their former masters. A victory by black troops would be both humiliating and infuriating to the Americans. As Dunmore explained to his superiors in England, "by employing them you cannot desire a means more effectual to distress your Foes."[21] In November 1775 he issued a proclamation offering freedom and a small payment to all slaves and servants who would fight for the British. Many slaves were attracted by the rhetoric of the American fight for freedom, but many others believed the English promised a more reliable route out of slavery. Hundreds of slaves joined Dunmore's Ethiopian Regiment. As successful as it was in the colonies, Dunmore's effort to raise an army of slaves was not universally accepted in Britain. Member of Parliament Edmund Burke warned against "the horrible

THREE POUNDS Reward.

RUN away from the subscriber, living in Shrewsbury, in the county of Monmouth, New-Jersey, a NEGROE man, named TITUS, but may probably change his name; he is about 21 years of age, not very black, near 6 feet high; had on a grey homespun coat, brown breeches, blue and white stockings, and took with him a wallet, drawn up at one end with a string, in which was a quantity of clothes. Whoever takes up said Negroe, and secures him in any goal, or brings him to me, shall be entitled to the above reward of *Three Pounds* proc. and all reasonable charges, paid by

Nov. 8, 1775.   §   JOHN CORLIS.

In November 1775, the day after Dunmore's Proclamation was issued, the young slave Titus fled from his master, John Corlies, in New Jersey, seeking refuge with the British. In this advertisement for his return, Corlies correctly predicted that Titus "will probably change his name." Three years later Titus, then known as Captain Tye, the pride of Dunmore's Ethiopian Regiment, led a guerrilla campaign against Monmouth County slaveholders.

By His Excellency the Right Honorable JOHN Earl of DUNMORE, His Majesty's Lieutenant and Governor General of the Colony and Dominion of Virginia, and Vice Admiral of the fame.

A PROCLAMATION.

AS I have ever entertained Hopes, that an Accommodation might have taken Place between GREAT-BRITAIN and this Colony, without being compelled by my Duty to this moſt diſagreeable but now abſolutely neceſſary Step, rendered ſo by a Body of armed Men unlawfully aſſembled, firing on His Majesty's Tenders, and the formation of an Army, and that Army now on their March to attack His Majesty's Troops and deſtroy the well diſpoſed Subjects of this Colony. To defeat ſuch treaſonable Purpoſes, and that all ſuch Traitors, and their Abettors, may be brought to Juſtice, and that the Peace, and good Order of this Colony may be again reſtored, which the ordinary Courſe of the Civil Law is unable to effect; I have thought fit to iſſue this my Proclamation, hereby declaring, that until the aforeſaid good Purpoſes can be obtained, I do in Virtue of the Power and Authority to ME given, by His Majesty, determine to execute Martial Law, and cauſe the ſame to be executed throughout this Colony: and to the end that Peace and good Order may the ſooner be reſtored, I do require every Perſon capable of bearing Arms, to reſort to His Majesty's STANDARD, or be looked upon as Traitors to His Majesty's Crown and Government, and thereby become liable to the Penalty the Law inflicts upon ſuch Offences; ſuch as forfeiture of Life, confiſcation of Lands, &c. &c. And I do hereby further declare all indented Servants, Negroes, or others, (appertaining to Rebels,) free that are able and willing to bear Arms, they joining His Majesty's Troops as ſoon as may be, for the more ſpeedily reducing this Colony to a proper Senſe of their Duty, to His Majesty's Crown and Dignity. I do further order, and require, all His Majesty's Leige Subjects, to retain their Quitrents, or any other Taxes due or that may become due, in their own Cuſtody, till ſuch Time as Peace may be again reſtored to this at preſent moſt unhappy Country, or demanded of them for their former ſalutary Purpoſes, by Officers properly authorized to receive the ſame.

GIVEN under my Hand on board the Ship WILLIAM, off Norfolk, the 7th Day of November, in the sixteenth Year of His Majesty's Reign.

DUNMORE.

(GOD ſave the KING.)

The earl of Dunmore, British colonial governor of Virginia, issued this proclamation in 1775 offering freedom to all slaves and indentured servants willing to serve the British cause during the Revolutionary War. The Virginia Gazette warned slaves to "Be not then…tempted by the proclamation to ruin your selves" and urged them to "cling to their kind masters."

consequences that might ensue from constituting 100,000 fierce barbarian slaves, to be both the judges and executioners of their masters."[22] The British prime minister, Lord North, agreed that Dunmore's proclamation should be tabled, awaiting further information and discussion. The overwhelming response of slaves to the British offer of freedom, however, put pressure on Dunmore to follow through on his proposal, as thousands walked off the plantations seeking the protection of the crown. Although it is impossible to be certain how many sought freedom by going to the British, estimates range as high as 100,000. Planters in South Carolina and Georgia were convinced that at least twenty thousand slaves would join Dunmore "in a fortnight." By 1778 Thomas Jefferson estimated that at least thirty thousand Virginia slaves had run away to the British, and at least thirty of these were from Jefferson's own Monticello plantation. Historians have placed the number of South Carolina's runaways at 25,000 or more between 1775 and 1783, while in Georgia more than 12,000 of the state's 15,000 slaves set out for freedom.[23] Even many slaves who did not manage to escape found greater independence, at least temporarily, as the Revolution drew many white southern men away from plantations. In 1781 Jack, a Virginia slave, was tried and found guilty of attempting to poison a white man and intending to raise a troop of slaves to lead into battle against Virginia forces.[24]

By January 1777 British success and the Americans' escalating need for manpower convinced General Washington to sanction the recruiting of free blacks, but still he would not enlist slaves. Within the month, however, with a Continental Army numbering only 3,000 men, Congress was forced to institute a draft. Meanwhile, the continuing loss of slaves to British offers of freedom for service, convinced American authorities of the need for dramatic measures. Rumors abounded that plantation slaves, having heard the British promise of freedom, were becoming unruly.[25] In Philadelphia one black man was reported to have threatened whites with retribution for any injustice when Lord Dunmore and his black troops captured the city.

Reacting to the mounting pressure, George Washington predicted that Dunmore's proclamation to servants and slaves would make him, "the most dangerous man in America." Many Americans were driven to such distress that they began to see the wisdom and expedience of following Dunmore's example. One northern state after another acknowledged the practical necessity of enlisting its slaves as a way of filling the manpower quotas set by the federal government. In early 1778 a Rhode Island general suggested to Washington that the state raise a battalion of blacks that might include slaves. Washington presented the proposal to Rhode Island's governor who in turn queried the state legislature on the matter. In February the legislature authorized the enlistment of slaves to form two battalions of the state militia. The slaves were promised freedom in return for their service.

New Hampshire, Massachusetts, and New Jersey soon followed suit, and although stiff opposition at first prevented New York from enlisting slaves, the need for men forced its legislature to pass a similar measure in 1781. In 1779, after the enlistment of slaves was generally accepted in the North, the Continental Congress urged Georgia and South Carolina to raise a slave army of three thousand "able-bodied negroes" to be commanded by white officers. Congress promised to compensate masters at a rate of $1,000 for each "standard size" man less than 35 years of age. Black soldiers would not be paid, except for receiving uniforms and food during their service and fifty dollars each and freedom at the end of the war.

Southern states remained reluctant to enlist slaves, especially in areas with large slave populations, despite the need. Even after the British captured Savannah, Georgia, and threatened to push into South Carolina, South Carolina refused to endorse either Congress's suggestion or a more specific plan proposed by

This African American was every inch the Revolutionary soldier in his full dress uniform. Equipped with back-pack, plumed hat, sword, and bayo-neted musket, he and his brothers fought valiantly for the patriot cause.

John Laurens, son of a South Carolina planter and former slave trader, to raise a black battalion to defend the state against the expected British invasion. The state legislature briefly considered the proposal, but the slaveholder-dominated body steadfastly refused. "We are much disgusted here at the Congress recommending us to arm our Slaves, it was received with great resentment, as a very dangerous and impolitic Step," they declared. Apparently, South Carolinians were more afraid of the consequences of arming their majority slave population than they were of a British invasion.[26]

Thus, very few African Americans served in southern units. Of the southern states, only Maryland armed slaves and integrated them into its militia. Virginia allowed a few free blacks to serve, and masters passed off some slaves as free so that they could serve in their masters' places or in place of the masters' sons. Tacitly acknowledging the fact that slaves were indeed serving in the Virginia forces, the state legislature passed a law in October 1783 guaranteeing freedom to any slave who served in place of his master. Yet, Virginia authority would not openly admit the enlistment of slaves. Even when General Lafayette personally appealed to Governor Thomas Jefferson, Virginia slaveholders refused to provide 150 slaves to replace losses in his ranks. Virginia masters did use their slaves in defending the state by sea, however. The legislature voted to enlist a thousand Virginia slaves in naval service, and while their actual numbers never approached that figure, black Virginians and others from Georgia and South Carolina, most of them slaves, did provide valuable service to the American navy.

The vast majority of African Americans in the American army and navy fought in integrated northern units. Only a few all-black or predominantly black units fought for the American cause: the Bucks of America, from Massachusetts; Rhodes Island's black regiment; companies of Connecticut's forces, and a unit consisting of six hundred to eight hundred Haitian blacks provided by America's French allies. Ironically, these Haitian soldiers played an especially important role in the southern states. In the fall of 1779 Haitian troops took part in an unsuccessful American action against British troops at Savannah, Georgia.

According to the official account of the battle, the legion of Haitians, "saved the army at Savannah by bravely covering its retreat."[27] One of the Haitian soldiers was Henri Christophe who would later serve under Toussaint Louuverture in the revolution that freed Haiti from French colonial control. Christophe later became the first ruler of an independent Haiti, the first independent black-ruled nation in the Western Hemisphere.

White soldiers in the militia often served as little as three months and generally insisted on staying close enough to home to defend their communities. The resulting high troop turnover became a major problem for American forces. Almost 400,000 men enlisted in the American army, but only 35,000 were on active duty at any one time. As historian Lorenzo Greene speculated, "had even half of the enlisted men been available regularly, the Americans should easily have overwhelmed the British" who never had more than 42,000 men under arms in America.[28] Blacks serving in the American army were more likely to serve in the Continental line than in state militia units. Thus, they were more likely to serve long enlistments of three years or more and to serve farther from home than the militiamen. Peter Salem, the hero of Bunker Hill, fought for seven years in the Continental army. Blacks' involvement in military action ranged over nearly the entire nation. Black New Englanders Prince Whipple and Oliver Cromwell were among those who manned the oars of the boat carrying George Washington across the Delaware River to Trenton, New Jersey, on Christmas night in 1776 to surprise the Hessian forces allied with the British. In 1777 Samuel Coombs became a hero at the Battle of Lake Champlain in New York State where, though wounded himself, he tended the wounds of others in his unit. Black soldiers endured the snow and freezing temperatures in the winter of 1778 as part of Washington's 11,000-man force at Valley Forge, Pennsylvania. At Valley Forge, Cato Cuff suffered frostbite from which he never fully recovered. Decades after the war he was

Governor John Hancock of Massachusetts presented this flag to the Bucks of America, a black unit in the Revolutionary War, in recognition of bravery and honorable service. The gold stars represent the original thirteen colonies.

Blacks who had served on merchant ships, as well as in the British and colonial navies, were recruited by the Continental Navy from the early days of the Revolution. Many served as pilots, others as laborers and carpenters.

not able to work outdoors in cold weather. In the fall of 1781 African-born Prince Bent and other blacks of the Rhode Island regiment served with Washington at the siege of Yorktown, where British forces under Cornwallis surrendered.[29]

Cornwallis's defeat was the turning point of the war. When the news reached London a month later, Prime Minister Lord North was reported to have said, "Oh God . . . It is all over."[30] King George wanted to continue the war, but the Parliament and British public opinion was against it. Lord North resigned early in 1781, and peace negotiations between Britain and the new United States of America began the following summer.

By the end of the war, more than five thousand African Americans had served in the American forces, and more than a thousand black men and women had served with the British armed forces. Many black women, generally slaves, had served as nurses and cooks. The records of the Royal Artillery, for example, listed fifty-five "Negro Wenches" as having served the British cause. Black women also worked in hospitals and served as camp domestics and laborers for the American forces.[31] In all, 20 percent of all those who fought on both sides of the Revolution were black.

The end of the war brought freedom to thousands of slaves, most of those who fought with the Americans, some who left with America's French allies, and many more who left with the withdrawing British troops or with the Tories who fled to Canada. In the fall and early winter of 1783, most of the passengers aboard the ships sailing from the United States to Nova Scotia were black Revolutionary War veterans and their families, former slaves, and white former indentured servants. Former slave Charles Dixon left New York on the week-long voyage with his wife, Dolly, and their five children. They settled in Port Roseway, Nova Scotia, where Dixon found work as a carpenter with the British army engineers. Life was not easy there, but they were free, and Dixon was able to support his family. Racial intolerance increased in Canada as the number of blacks settling there rose, and most of the resettled blacks were desperately poor. [32]

Before the Revolution, abolitionists in England and America had considered the feasibility of establishing a Christian colony in Africa where blacks might be resettled. After the war, the destitution of the black refugees in Canada and England, the renewed interest among Quaker abolitionists, and the recruitment of hundreds of volunteer settlers gave new impetus to this humanitarian and evangelical venture. The establishment of a site in Sierra Leone on the West African coast and the hiring of African seaman and former slave Gustavus Vassa, or Olaudah Equiano, in 1787 as the clerk supervising the outfitting and loading of the emigrant ship encouraged blacks' interest. Troubles arose, however, when newspapers printed rumors that convicts would also be sent to the colony and when the committee fired Equiano who had complained that provisions for the colony were inadequate. The British did establish the colony, however, and in the 1790s they relocated many of the former American blacks from Canada to Sierra Leone. Not all left, however, and scattered black settlements with descendants of Revolutionary-era American immigrants survived in Canada's eastern provinces.

Probably more slaves gained their freedom through their association with the British than by fighting with the Americans. After the Treaty of Paris ended the Revolution in 1783, British ships left the port of New York with at least three thousand fugitive slaves aboard, and British vessels took away at least twice that number from Charleston. In all, more than fourteen thousand blacks went with the British troops when they withdrew, but not all of these people were freed. Some who had sought asylum with the British but had not actually served in the British armed forces remained slaves. For them, Jamaica or some other British West Indian colony became the new site of their bondage. Moreover, during the next ten years, British slavers continued a brisk trade, sailing more than eight hundred slave-trading ships out of Liverpool alone. Between 1783 and 1793, Liverpool traders transported at least three hundred thousand slaves worth more than fifteen million pounds sterling. Slave trading remained a brutal and ugly business. The captain of the slave ship *Zong*, for example, was questioned in 1783 about why he had thrown 133 slaves overboard. He explained that the slaves were sick, and rather than have his backers suffer the possible loss of their deaths aboard ship, he threw his human cargo into the sea where their loss would be covered by insurance. Despite the continuation of this inhumane trade under British auspices, however, some former slaves who left with the British did find a measure of freedom in the West Indies or in Europe. [33]

Elizabeth Freeman, called Mum Betts, won her freedom by suing in the Massachusetts courts in 1780. Her case set the legal precedent that slavery was incompatible with the state constitution.

During the war, many white Americans, particularly in the northern states, had become convinced that slavery had no place in a new nation being built on the principles of freedom. Vermont outlawed human bondage in its state constitution in 1777, echoing the Declaration of Independence in declaring "all men are created equally free and independent." Other New England states also wrote the abolition of slavery into their constitutions, but it sometimes took the determined action of slaves themselves to make it effective. In 1780 Elizabeth Freeman, known as Mum Betts, sued for freedom from her owner John Ashley of Sheffield, Massachusetts. As a slave, Freeman had been injured attempting to defend her younger sister from being beaten by Ashley's wife. Acting partly in response to hearing a reading of the Declaration of Independence and to a discussion of the 1780 Massachusetts state constitution, she asked lawyer Theodore Sedgwick to challenge slavery in court on the grounds that it violated both the spirit and letter of the law. Sedgwick argued before a jury in the Great Barrington Court of Common Pleas that the state constitution required the abolition of slavery and won the case. In 1781, the jury awarded Elizabeth Freeman thirty shillings, court costs, and her freedom. Although this was only a lower court ruling, it established the critical precedent that slavery was incompatible with the guarantees of freedom in the state constitution.

Two years later, in 1783, the Massachusetts state supreme court confirmed the lower court's ruling in the case of Quock Walker, a slave who ran away from his master, Nathaniel Jennison, after suffering a brutal beating. Walker sued for and won his freedom on the grounds of slavery's illegality under the state constitution. The jury awarded Walker 150 pounds in damages, and Jennison was then tried and convicted of assault and battery. Thus slavery was abolished in Massachusetts in 1783. By 1784 when Rhode Island and Connecticut established emancipation programs, all of New England had prohibited slavery either by state constitution or by legislation providing for its gradual abolition. At the same time, New Jersey moved to ensure that owners free all slaves who had served the American cause in the Revolution, and a Congressional committee chaired by Thomas Jefferson recommended that slavery be outlawed in the territory that would later become the states of Kentucky, Tennessee, Mississippi, and Alabama. Only one vote prevented Congress from adopting the measure that would have prevented the introduction of slavery in those areas after 1800. George Washington, the new U.S. president and owner of more than two hundred slaves, expressed his desire to see the institution die away and his confidence that it would in time. Washington had a decidedly long view, however, hoping that slavery could be abolished by "slow, sure, and imperceptible degrees."[34]

Antislavery sentiment on both sides of the Atlantic was stimulated in 1789 with the publication in England of Olaudah Equiano's powerful autobiography, *The Interesting Narrative of the Life of Olaudah Equiano; or Gustavus Vassa.* Equiano told the absorbing story of his life in slavery, his struggle to achieve freedom, and his adventures as a sailor. Selling in at least eight editions in the first five years, his narrative was a ringing indictment of the institution of slavery in Christian society. Equiano settled in England and, a few years after the publication of his story, married an English woman with whom he eventually had two children. His time on the lecture circuit promoting his autobiography also promoted the cause of antislavery. In the United States, by 1804 all states north of Maryland had either abolished slavery outright or had enacted plans for gradual emancipation. Although the Revolution had not begun as an antislavery crusade, it had nonetheless brought freedom to vast numbers of slaves. No other event in American history until the Civil War—almost a century later—would result in freedom for more slaves.

Such developments convinced many that slavery was a dying institution. In 1778 Virginia had prohibited the importation of slaves, and in 1782 the state encouraged masters to free their slaves by removing all restrictions on manumission. Other southern states soon followed Virginia's example. By 1787 South Carolina closed its overseas and domestic slave trade, North Carolina placed a heavy tax on slaves imported from Africa, and Delaware passed laws protecting free blacks from being kidnapped into slavery. Also in 1787 Congress passed the Northwest Ordinance prohibiting slavery in the northwest territories. But there were signs that year that not all believed in slavery's demise. The Constitutional Convention in Philadelphia was riven with disagreements over the issue. Some delegations wanted the complete abolition of slavery, but South Carolina and Georgia made it clear that they would not join the federal union should slavery be attacked. Thus, fearing dissension that would prevent their establishing a unified government, delegates' debate on slavery at the national convention was muted. As an indication of the volatility of disagreements on this issue, the words *slavery* and *slave* did not appear in the finished document. In fact, neither word would appear in the Constitution until they were included in the Thirteenth Amendment, which abolished slavery in 1865 after the Civil War. Yet slavery cast its shadow over the Constitution in many ways. Referring only to "those not free" or "those owing service" the Constitutional framers wrote in a fugitive slave provision, later bolstered by congressional law, and prohibited federal restrictions on the international slave trade for at least twenty years. In a complex calculation, the Constitution also furnished slaveholders with additional representation in Congress by allowing them to count three-fifths of their human property in the population numbers that determined the representation of state districts in the U.S. House of Representatives. Slavery not only produced wealth for slaveholders; now it also increased their political influence, helping them to defend the institution.

Even so, slavery remained a precarious and dangerous undertaking, as rebellions and rumors of rebellions were constant reminders of the slaves' determination to be free. A slave rebellion begun in 1791 in the French West Indian colony of St. Domingue had become a full-scale protracted war for Haitian independence, and American slaveholders were terrified that the spirit of that revolution would spread to the U.S. mainland. There was good reason for their fears. When news of events in Haiti reached New York City, slaves there celebrated the revolt by erecting a "Liberty Pole" flying a pennant that read "Freedom to Africans." In Philadelphia, authorities reported groups of blacks roaming the streets declaring their support for the Haitian rebels, and a black boat crew took over a vessel in the harbor, urging other black boatmen to follow suit as part of a freedom struggle. The tales told by the approximately ten thousand French slaveholders who fled St. Domingue for the safety of the United States fueled planters' fears. Virginian John Randolph claimed to have overheard his plotting slaves using the Haitian revolt as a model, and the *Richmond Register* reported that one runaway Virginia slave had taken the name Liberty before escaping his master.[35]

In 1792 local governments in Virginia demanded additional weapons against slave revolts, and shortly thereafter, North Carolina executed three slaves for an attempted uprising. The next year, slaves set several fires in Albany, New York. Virginia, fearing the influence of free blacks, prohibited entrance to any African American who was not a slave. A grand jury in Charlotte, North Carolina, blamed the Quakers for encouraging a growing number of slave uprisings, citing unrest in Charleston, Savannah, Baltimore, New York City, and Elizabeth, New Jersey. Fears of slave rebellion continued throughout the eighteenth century. In 1799 slaves struck out against their masters in Fredericksburg and Richmond, Virginia, starting a series of fires. That same year a number of slaves were executed for attacking and killing two slave traders in Southampton, Virginia.

Contrary to the hopes of such leaders as George Washington, slavery did not die away in the generations following American independence, despite its threats to peace and slaveholders' security. In 1793, under President Washington's administration and with his support, Congress passed the nation's first fugitive slave law to enforce the Constitutional provision protecting slave property. The law imposed a fine of $500 on anyone who aided a runaway slave. It also recognized the role that Native Americans played in assisting fugitives by providing that representatives of the Delaware Nation and representatives of Congress would meet to decide appropriate trial procedures for people accused of violating this law. The same year, Eli Whitney's invention of the cotton gin revolutionized the processing of cotton, making it far easier and more profitable to produce a variety of short staple cotton that could be grown inland where it did not compete with the more established rice crop. Whitney, a teacher educated at Yale University who traveled to South Carolina, was tutoring planters' children when he noticed the tedious task of hand separating the seed from the fiber to process short staple cotton. He developed a simple machine, essentially a box containing a rotating cylinder with protruding nails, that combed through the cotton and separated out the seeds. One slave with this device could do the work of fifty slaves removing the seeds by hand. The potential for cotton profits rose dramatically, and slave labor became more valuable.

Slave revolts and rumors of revolts persisted. In 1800 the French sent more troops to St. Domingue and lured Toussaint Louverture, the leader of the revolt, to promised peace talks where they captured him. Nonetheless, the revolution continued. In the late summer of that year, Virginians discovered plans for a massive slave revolt just outside their capital. The plot had been devised by Gabriel and his brothers Solomon and Martin, all slave blacksmiths owned by Thomas Prosser. It centered on the plantation of William Young near Richmond but had spread to the city and the surrounding countryside as news of the plan was carried by slaves whose work brought them in contact with slaves from other plantations. More than a thousand slaves, many armed with bayonets, scythes, and guns met secretly outside Richmond, Virginia, and made plans to capture Richmond and the firearms stored in its arsenal. They intended to take Governor James Monroe prisoner; kill all the whites in the city except Quakers, Methodists, and Frenchmen; strike alliances with poor whites, artisans, and Indians; and set up a new Virginia government. Another slave betrayed Gabriel's plan before the plotters acted, and the governor mobilized the state's forces to arrest them. After a trial that revealed the extent of the planned uprising and further inflamed whites' fears, Gabriel, his brothers, and twenty-four other slaves were convicted and hanged for their part in the conspiracy.[36]

Slave rebellions and the Haitian Revolution continued into the nineteenth century. Congress hoped to block the spread of strikes for freedom in 1803 by restricting immigration from the West Indies, but people continued to be arrested for slave conspiracies. Twenty blacks were convicted of arson in New York City in 1803, others continued to be jailed for arson throughout the South, and twenty slaves were executed for poisoning white people in Georgia, Virginia, and South Carolina. The growing profits from using slave labor, however, more than counterbalanced the danger, and planters moved to increase their slaveholdings, replacing some of their losses from the Revolution. Between 1790 and 1810 the number of slaves in the U.S. rose from fewer than seven hundred thousand to more than one million. After years of restricting the importation of slaves into the state, South Carolina relaxed its regulations in 1802, permitting increased numbers of slaves to be imported for personal use. That year, the U.S. Congress defeated efforts to bar slavery from the Mississippi territory, and in 1803, South Carolina reopened the slave trade with South America and the West Indies. The proportion of African-born slaves in South Carolina's slave population more than doubled to 20 percent in the twenty years between 1790 and 1810.[37]

With more efficient cotton processing, planters only needed sufficient land, fertile soil, and an appropriate climate to expand the cotton production that, in the late eighteenth century, had centered in a few inland areas of South Carolina. Soon President Thomas Jefferson and the Congress provided cotton planters with exactly what they needed. In 1803, the year before Haiti finally achieved its independence, France sold the United States an immense tract of land extending westward from the Mississippi territory to the Rocky Mountains and northward from the Gulf of Mexico to the border of Canada. Although

Jefferson, a believer in small and restricted federal government, was uncertain that the Constitution gave the President the right to make such an acquisition, he moved ahead with the Louisiana Purchase in the belief that it was good for the nation. The addition of this territory doubled the land size of the nation. In its southern region, it provided the dark rich soil and the climatic conditions ideal for the production of short staple cotton.

Like most American slaveholders, Jefferson feared the existence of the independent black nation of Haiti in the West Indies. Planters used its violent beginning as an effective argument against the post-Revolutionary antislavery movement in America, and such fears weakened the influence of those organizations. Despite his stated belief in revolutionary struggles for liberty, his administration moved diplomatically against Haiti and refused to recognize the new nation. Jefferson signed a trade embargo against Haiti in February 1806 at the request of French.

The Louisiana Purchase provided eastern planters with new opportunities to make their fortunes in cotton production. Large and small planters moved thousands of slaves southwestward into the new territory. Slave traders made a profitable business buying slaves cheaply in the northeastern South and selling them at much higher prices in the new "Cotton Kingdom." Slave labor in the new area of the South was far more valuable for producing cotton, and the crop rapidly became the nation's most valuable product. During the first two decades of the nineteenth century, cotton increased from representing slightly more than 7 percent of American exported goods to being the single most valuable export of the entire nation.[38] As the value and economic importance of cotton production grew, so did the political power of cotton planters and the value of slave labor. The expansion of the plantation South and the rise of the cotton kingdom dashed the hopes of those who had believed that slavery would die out in the aftermath of the Revolution.

The main house of the Kingsley plantation near Jacksonville, Florida, built about 1798. Zephaniah Kingsley's African-born wife, Anna, did not live in the main house, perhaps out of respect for her Senegalese culture, where men and women did not share living quarters.

It was during this expansion of the plantation South in the United States and the seemingly insatiable market for African slaves in the Americas that Kajor's warriors abducted young Anta Majigeen Njaay. She could not remember how long her captors held her in the windowless cell on Goree island off the West African coast before they rowed her to the vessel bound for Cuba in 1806. At the Cuban slave market, her life took another unexpected turn. There, instead of being sold to one of the immense sugar plantations attempting to replace exports from the newly independent Haiti, she caught the eye of Zephaniah Kingsley, Jr. Kingsley was a sea captain, African slave trader, and plantation owner from Spanish Florida. The son of a Quaker merchant and loyalist, he had been born in Bristol, England, raised in Charleston, South Carolina, and had lived in Nova Scotia after the American Revolution. He had also resided in Haiti, St. Thomas, and Florida, living essentially in an African society. He had several sea captains working for him, but when he captained the ship, the crew was composed entirely of African slaves. Slaves managed his plantation holdings, and he functioned as the patriarch of a family with more than one wife, a pattern familiar to Anta among wealthy men in her homeland. Kingsley had come to Cuba to sell a cargo of forty-three male slaves. He then bought three female slaves who had just arrived from Africa, including Anta and Sophie Chidgigine, another young girl from Anta's village.[39]

Zephaniah Kingsley then took an unusual step. He married thirteen-year-old Anta, thirty years his junior, in a ceremony, as he said, "celebrated and solemnized by her native African custom." He then carried his three new acquisitions to his Laurel Grove plantation up the St. Johns River in Florida. Laurel Grove contained a shipyard, a farm, cotton fields, and citrus groves and was populated by more than a hundred slaves from a variety of African nations. Abraham Hannahan, a mulatto slave born and raised in Kingsley's father's household in Charleston, South Carolina, supervised its large and complex operations. Sophie Chidgigine would become Hannahan's wife. Upon their arrival at Laurel Grove, Anta was taken to Kingsley's plantation house, rather than to the slave quarters. Already pregnant with Kingsley's child, Anta would live as Kingsley's wife for the next thirty-seven years. In her new life she became known as Anna Madgigine Jai Kingsley.

Slavery on the Kingsley plantation of Spanish Florida was undoubtedly more flexible and a more complex arrangement than on most of the plantations of the United States developing to the north. The Revolution and American

An African American Day of Thanksgiving

On January 1, 1808, minister and former slave Absalom Jones preached an inspirational sermon in the African Episcopal Church in Philadelphia to celebrate the end of America's involvement in the Atlantic slave trade.

Having enumerated the mercies of God... it becomes us to ask, What shall we render unto the Lord for them? Sacrifices and burnt offerings are no longer pleasing to him: the pomp of public worship, and the ceremonies of a festive day, will find no acceptance with him, unless they are accompanied with actions that correspond with them.... Let the first of January, the day of the abolition of the slave trade in our country, be set apart in every year, as a day of publick thanksgiving for that mercy. Let the history of the sufferings of our brethren, and of their deliverance, descend by this means to our children to the remotest generations; and when they shall ask, in time to come, saying, What mean the lessons, the psalms, the prayers and the praises in the worship of this day? Let us answer them by saying, the Lord, on the day of which this is the anniversary, abolished the trade which dragged your fathers from their native country, and sold them as bondmen in the United States of America.[2]

independence had profoundly affected the lives of American slaves. The spirit of American liberty with its rhetoric of freedom and philosophy of natural rights inspired all Americans, especially those denied the benefits of the rights America professed to celebrate. In the wake of independence, and in light of black participation in the war to achieve it, there appeared to be cause for hope. Slavery declined in the northern states, some influential American leaders took antislavery stands, and Congress abolished the Atlantic slave trade at the earliest possible time, given its twenty-year constitutional protection. Elated African Americans gathered in churches and public meetings on January 1, 1808, to celebrate a day of thanksgiving for the end of the slave trade.[40]

Yet as the eighteenth century drew to a close, there was cause for doubt about the future of slavery, and events of the early nineteenth century seemed to confirm those doubts. The western extension of the United States into the new land of the Louisiana territory and the steady rise in the economic importance of cotton encouraged the forced migration of eastern slaves into the newly available southwestern lands of the Mississippi delta. For slave families broken by the move southwestward where the strong backs of young men were in great demand for clearing and preparing the land, the opening of the cotton kingdom continued and accelerated the misery of slavery. By the end of the first decade of the 1800s, slaves in the upper and eastern South lived in constant fear of being "sold down the river" to a land of massive cotton plantations where slave life was harsher and shorter, where it was more difficult to create families, and where communities were more difficult to maintain.

Even some free blacks and slaves in the northern states faced the danger of being kidnapped or illegally sold to the voracious new southern market. Isabella Baumfree was born into slavery in Hurley, New York, north of New York City in 1797. Unluckily, this was two years before the state's emancipation law went into effect, and she remained a slave rather than becoming an indentured servant who could look forward to freedom. New York had not belonged to the Dutch for more than a century, but it retained much of its Dutch heritage, and many in the area were Dutch, including the Ardinburgh family who enslaved Isabella. Isabella had been raised in Dutch culture, and she spoke English with a heavy Dutch accent. As a child, she shared living quarters with her father, James, mother, Betsey, and about ten other Ardinburgh slaves, both males and females, in the cellar of her master's hotel. The cellar was dimly lit by only the light that could seep in through a few tiny glass panes. In wet seasons water and mud from the earthen foundation oozed between the floor boards, bringing with it a chill and a noxious odor that Isabella never forgot. Had she been born two years later she would have been freed after twenty-five years of indentured service under the plan of gradual emancipation New York State adopted in 1799. This plan left the thousands of blacks born before the law's enactment in bondage well into the nineteenth century. Although their numbers dwindled year by year, as late as 1820, there were more than 500 slaves in New York City and 190 slaves in Brooklyn.

Isabella had experienced the horror of slavery early in her life. She had been too young to remember when several of her ten or twelve siblings were sold away, but she did remember her mother Mau-mau Bett's reaction when her master died. With tears in her eyes, knowing that the remaining members of the family would soon face sale on the auction block, the slave mother told her young daughter to have faith in God. Isabella, only ten years old at the time, remem-

bered that her mother tried to ease the pain of their impending separation by explaining that no matter where they might be sent, the family would always be under the same moon and stars, and God would always be looking out for them. When times were bad, she told Isabella, she must pray to God to make her new masters good. The auction that separated her from her mother and youngest brother severely tested Isabella's faith, and sometime later, she became discouraged. When it was obvious that her prayers were not working, and her masters "didn't get good," the pragmatic young Isabella spoke to God again. This time she said, "God, maybe you can't do it. Kill them."[41]

One of the leading slave-trading firms kept surplus slaves from the Upper South and Mississippi Valley in this holding pen in Alexandria, Virginia, near Washington, D.C., before selling them to new owners.

Isabella was a slave until New York's legislature finally abolished slavery completely in the state in 1827. By then, she was thirty years old, a wife, and the mother of four children. On the eve of her emancipation, however, she learned that her master had sold her five-year-old son, Peter. The buyer then gave the boy to his brother who, skirting the law, had given Peter as a wedding present to another relative, a man named Fowler, who was leaving New York for Alabama. Isabella feared that once in the South, her child would be beyond the reach of New York's emancipation provision and face a lifetime of slavery. She was away from home when her son was sold; when she returned, he was gone. The distraught Isabella confronted her mistress, but the woman dismissed her concerns. "A fine fuss to make about a little nigger!" she told Isabella. "Why, haven't you as many of 'em left as you can see to?" Isabella was furious. In her grief, she became determined. "I'll have my child again" she vowed.[42]

Isabella soon gained the aid of Quakers who directed her to go to the Court House and tell her story to the grand jury. She received a sympathetic hearing at the Court House, and a judge issued a writ for the man who had given Peter away, but the writ was served erroneously on the man's brother. In the meantime, after finding that he might face a one-thousand dollar fine and fourteen years in prison, the man who had evaded the writ made his way to Alabama to retrieve Isabella's son. He returned about six months later, but kept the boy instead of giving him up to his impatient mother. She sued for his release, but as the court system was working its way slowly, she appealed to another lawyer whom she was told would work quickly and doggedly for her. She raised what money she could and gave it to the lawyer who sent a bounty hunter after her son and his master. The following day, the lawyer called her to identify her son.

The boy had been so abused and badly beaten in slavery in Alabama that, afraid to displease his master, he denied having a mother in that area. When she saw him, Peter refused to acknowledge her, and claimed that his scars had been caused by accidents. The terrified boy pleaded not to be taken from his master, but the judge ruled that he should be returned to his mother. When she was finally able to quiet his fears, Isabella found that her child's body was covered with sores and scars. Fowler had beaten him, he said. When she asked how Fowler's wife, Eliza, her master's sister, had reacted when he was abused in this way, he replied: "Sometimes I crawled under the stoop, mammy, the blood running all about me, and my back would stick to the boards; and sometimes Miss Eliza would come and grease my sores, when all were abed and asleep." The painful memories of slavery, of temporarily losing her son, and of Pete's brutal treatment in the South fueled the power and passion of Isabella's later work as an antislavery speaker and women's rights advocate. By then she had changed her name to Sojourner Truth.[43]

Truth's experience on the eve of northern emancipation was not an isolated incident. Even as slavery was ending in the North, the inhumanity of slavery continued, and many former slaves carried painful memories into freedom. Others were sold South ahead of emancipation in contravention of the law. Conditions were worse for African Americans in the South, where freedom became less and less likely. As the eighteenth century closed, the institution of slavery was changing. It had existed in every colony before the Revolution, from the rocky shores of New England to the swampy coast of South Carolina. In the after-

This carte de visite *with a photograph of Sojourner Truth bore the caption "I sell the Shadow to Support the Substance." Such cards were sold to support the abolitionist cause.*

math of independence, however, slavery became more regional, increasingly confined to the South. As the South expanded westward into the lower regions of the Louisiana territory in the first decades of the nineteenth century, slavery moved with it, becoming the major labor system of the area.

Charles Ball was born into slavery in Calvert County, Maryland. His grandfather Ben had been a warrior in Africa and was captured and brought to Maryland as a slave in about 1730. He remembered his grandfather as an elderly man who was devout in the religion of his people, praying every night and adhering to his faith's rigid principles of morality, "love of country, charity, and social affection." Charles lived with his mother and several brothers and sisters, while his father and his grandfather lived on different nearby plantations. In the mid-1780s, when he was only about four years old, Charles's master died, and his mother and her children were sold to different buyers. Seeing her small child sold away from her, Ball's mother begged her new owner, "Oh, master, do not take me from my child." His only reply was to tear the child from her arms, hand him to his new master, and hit her with his whip to quiet her. The child's

new owner lifted the boy onto his saddle, assured her that he would be a good
master, and spurred his horse away. As they left, her son saw the driver drag-
ging his distraught mother off to be transported to Georgia. Fifty years later that
horrible scene remained vivid in Ball's memory.[44]

With the loss of his wife to Georgia and most of his children to Carolina,
Ball's father became depressed, but he continued to visit his remaining child
every week. Ball remembered that his father always brought a small gift when
he visited, sometimes apples, melons or sweet potatoes, but Ball later recalled,
the food always "tasted better...because he had brought it." His father's continued despondency made his owner suspect that he planned to run away.
Trying to avoid any difficulty and knowing the man always carried a large knife,
the owner hatched a plan to have his slave falsely arrested for theft, put in jail,
and then sold to Georgia. Charles's grandfather Ben overheard the constable,
who had come to his plantation to enlist the aid of the overseer there, discussing the master's plans. Late that night, Ben walked the three miles to the
other plantation and warned his son, who ran away to Pennsylvania, where
antislavery sentiment was strong. In a short time, the child had lost both his
mother and his father.

It was not until about 1800, when he was twenty years old, that Charles
Ball had an opportunity to think about gaining his own freedom. Because there
was not enough work on the Maryland plantation, his master hired him out to
the Washington Navy Yard not far away. There his life improved dramatically.
Working as a cook on the frigate *Congress,* for the first time in many years he
had enough to eat. He had clothes and even some money, gifts from the ship's
officers. Most importantly, he met two black men from Philadelphia, one a slave
and one free, who worked on another ship in the yard. The free man regaled
him with tales of life in Pennsylvania, by then a free state, and Ball became
determined to escape. With the help of his new friend, he laid plans to stow
away on a Philadelphia-bound ship, only to find that the ship's destination was
changed to the West Indies. It sailed without him, and shortly thereafter, after
he had spent two years in Washington, Ball's owner returned him to Maryland
and sold him to another local owner. Charles married Judah, a slave woman
from a nearby farm. During the next six years he visited her every week, and
they had three children.[45]

One day, Ball's master arranged to meet him in town and, with no fore-
warning, sold Ball to a Georgia slavetrader. The new owner tied Ball's hands

behind his back. He answered his entreaty that he be allowed to say goodbye to his wife and children with the assurance that he could get another wife in Georgia. Ball was fitted with a padlocked iron collar, handcuffed to another man, and chained from his collar to the other thirty-two men whom his purchaser intended to march south. The buyer tied together the nineteen women he had purchased by looping ropes around their necks. After crossing Virginia and North Carolina, just over the border of South Carolina, the trader was approached by a man who said he was looking for some "breeding wenches." Observing that two pregnant women were having trouble keeping up with the rest, the trader extolled their virtues. One was twenty-two years old and reportedly already had seven children; the other was nineteen and had four children. They were sold for $1000 for the pair.

After nearly five weeks of walking, they arrived at a farm near Columbia, South Carolina, where the trader removed their chains, reasoning that they were now too far from home to attempt escape. Three weeks later, better fed and rested, the fifty slaves and their owner made their way into Columbia, where the crowds celebrating the Fourth of July presented a good opportunity for a slave auction. Ball later remembered the people gathered outside the jail yard, drunkenly singing and shouting "in honor of free government, and the rights of man." The day's slave auction was interrupted for a dinner for about seven hundred served under the trees on plank tables. Politicians made speeches reiterating the claim that "all men were born free and equal." Finally Ball was sold to an elderly wealthy planter who lived outside Columbia and was the owner of more than 260 slaves.[46]

Charles Ball spent the next four years in slavery in South Carolina and Georgia, passed to other family members and finally sold for a term of seven years to a man who was to establish a plantation on the Georgia frontier. When this man died, Ball found himself under the control of an abusive mistress and became determined to run away. He set out on foot in August when the corn was ripe, hoping to make his way back to his wife and three children in Maryland. On his long journey, he traveled sometimes on roads, at other times through the woods and swamps, navigating by the stars, fording and swimming across freezing rivers and streams when he could find no handy boat, and camping in the woods or in a barn during cloudy or snowy weather. He was helped by a planter friend of his old master early in his trip and encountered another runaway along the way, but he was alone for most of the seven months that it took him to make his way back to Maryland. Finally in Maryland, he was confronted by a slave patrol, shot with buckshot, beaten, bound, and put in jail. About a month later, after his wounds had healed, he pried the chain from his feet, dug the jail door lock from a rotten post, escaped from jail, and continued on his way. Ball was reunited with his wife, reacquainted with his children, and on the advice of his wife's master, hid for a time and then worked for wages as if he were a free man.

In 1812 the United States fought a second war with Britain to defend its independence. Its army initially numbered only 6,000 white men, since black men had been excluded from the militia. African Americans volunteered at the beginning of the war, as they had in the Revolution, but at first the service of most was refused. Some communities were willing to use slaves and free black laborers to build defense fortifications, but few were willing to arm them. The Americans did not fare well in the early years of the war, and in 1814 British troops captured Washington, D.C., burning the White House and driving federal officials from the capital. Even then, some authorities were reluctant to employ black troops. Philadelphia, just a few days' march from Washington, refused the offer of a defense force of 2,500 black volunteers and even sought to segregate the workforce on defense fortifications. New York authorized recruiting free and enslaved black military units only in the last year of the war, and Philadelphia waited until the very end of the war to assemble a black unit. African Americans, however, contributed significantly to the war effort and served in some of the key battles of the conflict.

The British army burned the U.S. Capitol after it captured Washington, D.C., in 1814. Though black men volunteered throughout the war, in most cases their service was refused—even after the burning of Washington, nearby Philadelphia rejected 2,500 black volunteers.

More African Americans fought at sea than on land during the War of 1812. In the early years of the nineteenth century, blacks had constituted between 10 and 20 percent of the crews in American naval forces. Although varying under the command of different officers, the harsh, cramped conditions aboard ship generally militated against segregated facilities and forced a degree of interracial association and even camaraderie not common ashore. Commodore Oliver Perry, who commanded a crew in the Battle of Lake Erie in 1813, praised the African Americans who were a quarter of his crew for their bravery under fire, observing that they seemed "absolutely insensible to danger."[47] Charles Ball was one of those who served on a ship. He was a member of the crew of a river ship until the British blew up the flotilla. After that, he manned a cannon and marched with the militia.

It was common, Ball remembered, as it had been in the Revolution, for slaves to seek their freedom by escaping to the British. Thousands of slaves, he believed, left the Chesapeake area during the summers of 1813 and 1814. One fall the British sent a boat and carried away 250 blacks, including all 100 slaves of one plantation mistress, except for one who had a family nearby. Ball heard that they had been transported to Trinidad. During the war at least 3,500 slaves sought sanctuary with British forces, and many settled in Nova Scotia, Canada.[48] The British also armed and supplied some three thousand African Americans and Seminoles who manned the "Negro Fort," a Spanish garrison in northern Florida, along the Apalachicola River. From this stronghold, blacks and their Native American allies raided the plantations of South Carolina and Georgia, freeing hundreds of slaves. American gunboats retaliated by attacking and destroying the fort and killing or capturing most of its forces.[49]

General Andrew Jackson issued a call for black troops early in the fall of 1814, promising free blacks the same wages as white troops and promising slaves their freedom. While enlisting blacks to meet the British in New Orleans, Jackson visited a Louisiana plantation owned by Calvin Smith and, with Smith's permission, went into the fields personally to select his recruits. Speaking with a slaveholder's understanding, he asked the slaves, "Had you not as soon go into battle and fight, as to stay here in the cotton-field, dying and never die?" Then he promised, "If you will go, and the battle is fought and the victory gained on Israel's side, you shall be free." James Roberts, one of the slaves who heard Jackson's words explained that they seemed like "divine revelation." He expressed the feelings of many of his fellow slaves: "In hope of freedom, we would run through a troop and leap over a wall."[50] Jackson departed with 500 of Smith's slaves, a costly contribution of valuable property. Smith encouraged the general to emphasize the promise of freedom as an incentive to faithful and courageous service and was relieved that his slaves, not his sons, were enlisted. "If the [N]egroes should be killed," Smith reasoned, "they are paid for; but if my children should go and get killed, they cannot be replaced." Jackson's officers understood this perspective and encouraged planters to provide black troops for the war. "I glory in your spunk," Captain Brown, one of Jackson's assistants told Smith. "Let us have as many [N]egroes as you can spare, for we are sure that those [N]egroes you give us will gain the victory."[51]

Ironically, the most celebrated African American service of the war came two weeks after a peace agreement had been signed. Not aware of the war's end, six hundred blacks serving under Jackson battled British forces at New Orleans in early 1815. At the suggestion of one of the black soldiers, Jackson had the men erect a fort of cotton bales. The furious fighting pitted American troops, including hundreds of African Americans just days from the plantation and with very limited training, against armored British military professionals. The bravery of the African American force in defeating the British at New Orleans became legendary. Jackson personally commended his troops on their heroism, but he reneged on his promise of freedom for the slave soldiers. Realizing that he was not to be freed as promised, James Roberts boldly confronted the general, "I did fight manfully and gained the victory, now where is my freedom?" Jackson was shocked. "I think you are very Presumptuous," he told Roberts, but the slave was undaunted.

White soldiers and New Orleans townspeople, hearing this exchange, suggested that Roberts be shot for his insolent tone. Later, Roberts reflected, "Two days before, I had, with my fellow soldiers, saved their city from fire and massacre, and their wives and children from blood and burning." Yet, the people of New Orleans would have had him shot "simply for contending for my freedom, which both my master and Jackson had solemnly before high heaven promised before I left home." This was a particular travesty because Roberts, who was more than sixty years old, had been similarly disappointed forty years earlier. During the Revolutionary War he had accompanied his master, an American officer, into combat. Roberts had expected his freedom, but his master was killed in battle, and when the war was over Roberts was separated from his wife and four children and sold at auction. In 1815, still enslaved after having served the

The invention of the cotton gin greatly increased the efficiency of cotton processing. Before the cotton gin, it took a slave a day to clean a pound of cotton; with a gin, the slave could clean as much as fifty pounds a day.

cause of America's freedom for a second time, James Roberts was furious at having been once again "duped by the white man."[52]

The war had not brought freedom to Roberts or millions of other slaves; it merely secured the western frontiers of their captivity. British forts and Indian alliances no longer hindered America's western expansion. General Andrew Jackson's defeat of the Creek Indians further cleared the way for population growth in the Deep South, where land-hungry planters established frontier communities to serve the growing demand for cotton. Planters introduced sugarcane into the southernmost sections of the area carved from the Louisiana Purchase, and sugar production became highly profitable in the newly emerging state of Louisiana.

Cotton, however, overwhelmed all other cultivation and became the dominant crop of the Deep South. Planters and their slaves, aided by the new technology of Eli Whitney's cotton gin, poured into the new territory, where the soil and the climate were ideal for growing cotton. National cotton exports grew from less than 140,000 pounds in the years just before the invention of the cotton gin to more than 17 million pounds in 1800, seven years after its introduction. As the demand for cotton increased, the value of the slave labor that produced it rose dramatically. The growth of New England textile manufacturing after 1810 and steadily increasing demand from British textile mills accelerated the growth of cotton production in the Deep South. By 1812, American growers supplied at least half of the 63 million pounds of the raw cotton these mills processed each year.

Robert Brown escaped from his owners in Martinsburg, Virginia, on Christmas night of 1856 by crossing the half-mile-wide Potomac River on horseback. The Underground Railroad leader William Still asked of Brown's escape, "Where could be found in history a more noble and daring struggle for Freedom?"

Westward Expansion, Antislavery, and Resistance

3

In Spanish Florida, Anna Madgigine Jai Kingsley became a free woman in 1811. By then, she was eighteen years old and the mother of three children, George, Martha, and Mary. In granting her and the children their freedom, Zephaniah Kingsley made manifest his memoir's claim, "She has always been respected as my wife and as such I Acknowledge her."[1] He also freed Abraham Hannahan, manager of his Laurel Grove plantation. By this time, Anna was taking a larger role in her husband's affairs and managed the plantation when Hannahan was away. Anna exercised her new freedom in 1812 by moving across the river and establishing her own farm on a Spanish homestead land grant, living there with her children and twelve slaves of her own.

Growing profits from cotton in the United States fueled planters' desire to extend their holdings and encouraged the country's expansionist aims. Conflict along Florida's northern border erupted into open warfare in 1812. American guerrillas from Georgia and South Carolina, aided by dissident Spanish soldiers and covertly financed by President James Madison and Secretary of State James Monroe, crossed the border to support a group of Spanish insurgents and besieged the northeast corner of the colony. The rebels, who hoped to throw off Spanish rule, held Zephaniah Kingsley hostage until he signed a pledge giving them his support. They also conducted raids on area plantations, and the Americans took hundreds of slaves and free blacks back to Georgia with them. Meanwhile, the Spanish governor enlisted the aid of the Seminole Indians, who also conducted raids, destroying most of Kingsley's Laurel Grove plantation. Forty-one Africans left Laurel Grove with the Seminoles.[2]

The rebels attacked Anna's farm in late 1813, but she was prepared for them. Warned of their approach by a Spanish gunboat crew, she put her furniture in the woods, hid her children and her slaves near the shore, and to deny the rebels a base of operations, set ablaze her home and the slave cabins. The gunboat then took Anna, her family, and her slaves down river to the Spanish fort. For her heroism in the face of danger, Anna was later rewarded with a 350-acre land grant from the Spanish government. Early the next year, Kingsley, Anna, and their children moved to nearby Fort George Island, where they established the Kingsley plantation on land abandoned by one of the insurgents. There, Anna was mistress of the household and partner in the management of the plantation, where she had her own house.

Kingsley's holdings in land and slaves grew until eventually he was the master of more than two hundred slaves who worked his plantations of more than thirty-two thousand acres. Kingsley's familial situation was not unique in Spanish Florida. As in the West Indies, white planters often took African wives or mistresses, some of whom they freed. Anna and Zephaniah Kingsley had established their lives and their relationship very much in the African style of family and slaveholding. Kingsley had more than one wife, and Anna presumably enjoyed the prerogatives of the first wife. Though Anna had been a slave, after receiving her freedom she too became a slaveholder. Kingsley's management of his plantations was somewhat unusual for the Americas. He used the task system for slave labor, which meant that rather than working from sunup to sundown, slaves' time was generally their own after they completed their assigned tasks. He also permitted his slaves to purchase their own freedom for half the market price.[3]

By 1815 cotton had become America's largest and most valuable export. As the power of cotton-producing slaveholders increased, some prominent whites who were still uneasy with slavery but unwilling to directly confront the slave system established the American Colonization Society. A disparate group of ministers, politicians, and businessmen met in the U.S. Capitol in Washington, D.C., in 1816 to organize the society, whose goal was to promote emancipation by providing for the resettlement of freed American blacks in West Africa. The Society's founders included some of the era's most prominent white Americans, Quakers, Protestant missionaries, northern businessmen, and slaveholders. Virginian Charles Fenton Mercer, New Jersey minister Robert Finley, and Francis Scott Key, who penned the words of "The Star-Spangled Banner," were the organizers. Supreme Court Justice Bushrod Washington became the new organization's president, and such powerful political figures as U.S. Representative Henry Clay from Kentucky, U.S. Representative Daniel Webster from New Hampshire (later senator from Massachusetts), Secretary of State and President-elect James Monroe from Virginia, U. S. Representative John C. Calhoun from South Carolina, future President John Tyler from Virginia, and General Andrew Jackson from Tennessee were members. The society's advocacy of removing free blacks to Africa placated slaveholders seeking a slave system more secure from the dangers posed by free blacks. The American Colonization Society could also reassure northern white workers who were becoming increasingly concerned about competition from black labor, and it could use the language of freedom and opportunity to recruit blacks for colonization.

Members' motivations were as varied as the members themselves. Many shared Thomas Jefferson's concern that wronged and possibly vengeful former slaves could not be safely integrated into white society. Removal of free blacks also appealed to those who feared the consequences of the continued close association of blacks and whites, or "race mixing," as Jefferson had called it. Separation was necessary, he had written in *Notes on Virginia* in the 1780s, for the preservation of the "dignity" and the "beauty" of the white race.[4] Some colonization society members sought to Christianize Africa but believed that white men could not survive the tropical climate. They hoped to supplement African missionary efforts by sending American blacks, freed and educated for the purpose. Still others believed that African Americans would never be accepted in American society and hoped to encourage free blacks to emigrate to West Africa, where they might be partici-  pating members of society.

The idea of colonizing American blacks in West Africa was not new. Many freed slaves who left North America with British forces at the end of the Revolution had settled in the British West African colony of Sierra Leone at the end of the eighteenth century. Black Massachusetts sea captain Paul Cuffe, son of an African father and a Native American mother, promoted African colonization more than a decade before the founding of the American

Paul Cuffe of New Bedford, Massachusetts, was one of the few blacks in the whaling industry to rise to the position of captain. In 1815 he transported a number of black families from America to Sierra Leone in West Africa.

Colonization Society. In 1810 he and his all-black crew sailed to Sierra Leone. The settlement of some 3,500 residents, including blacks from the British West Indies, Africans rescued from slave ships by patrols enforcing Britain's 1807 ban on the Atlantic slave trade, native-born Africans, and American black immigrants impressed him. He hoped to establish a profitable trade with the colony in order to demonstrate the feasibility of commercial relations between Africa and America that did not include trading slaves.

Cuffe's plans had been interrupted by the outbreak of war with Britain in 1812, but he resumed his efforts when the war ended three years later. Free blacks whom he contacted in Boston, New York City, and Philadelphia were enthusiastic, and a London antislavery group agreed to help finance the venture.[5] In December 1815 Captain Paul Cuffe set out for Sierra Leone in his brig *Traveller*, loaded with cargo for trade, a black crew, and thirty-four black settlers who ranged in age from eight months to sixty years. Cuffe himself had considered moving to Sierra Leone, but he was unable to convince his American Indian wife to leave Massachusetts. He did, however, invest $8,000 in the colony and in goods to trade but was unable to obtain the necessary trade authorization from the British government.

Paul Cuffe's activities encouraged the American Colonization Society, and they hoped to draw on his experience in their campaign to convince the U.S. Congress to help finance their colonization plans. They also wanted him to return to Africa to explore the Guinea coast for a suitable location and to contribute his knowledge of West Africa and Sierra Leone to their efforts to set up an American colony.[6] Cuffe was able to convince several black leaders in New York and Philadelphia to encourage black emigration, the African Institution groups he had helped organize provided organizational support, and prominent white leaders addressed large crowds promoting the society. Most black community members in northern cities, however, rejected any association with the American Colonization Society, even when Cuffe himself spoke in black churches extolling the wonders of Africa and the opportunities opened by colonization. Although most African Americans wanted nothing to do with an organization led by slaveholders, some northern blacks were attracted by the prospect of settling in Africa. For African-born blacks, colonization offered the opportunity to return to the home they had been forced to leave behind years before. Boston Crummel, originally from the region of Sierra Leone and enslaved in New York for many years, was anxious to go home, but Crummel's wife who had been born on Long Island in New York was far more skeptical about emigration.

During the late eighteenth and early nineteenth centuries, there were many African-born blacks in America. As blacks established themselves in freedom, the names they gave to their organizations and community institutions expressed their identification with an African homeland. In 1780 in Newport, Rhode Island, they founded a mutual aid society called the African Union Society. Also in the eighteenth century, Philadelphia blacks established the Free African Society, the African Church of St. Thomas, Bethel African Methodist Episcopal Church, and the African Humane Society. Boston blacks began the African Society and the African Masonic Lodge, and black children in New York City were educated in the African Free School. African memories and African identities remained strong in the early nineteenth century. African-born blacks in the North still gathered by ethnicity and nationality on the old Dutch holiday of Pinkster, or Pentecost, on governors' election days, and on other festive occasions. Well into the nineteenth century, African ethnicities were still apparent in some places, particularly in the South. William Wells Brown, who had been born a slave in Kentucky in 1814, recognized "Kraels, Minahs, Congos and Mandringas, Gangas, Hiboas, and Fulas," among dancers gathered by ethnic group in a New Orleans square during the early 1830s.[7]

After Congress ended the African slave trade in 1808, however, the numbers of African-born blacks in America dwindled. In the North, where abolition prohibited the introduction of new slaves, there were few African-born blacks by the 1820s. American-born blacks were linked to Africa only through the memories and stories of older family and community members, and they were more likely than earlier generations to see themselves as Americans. Northern free blacks claimed their rights as Americans, even though they were well aware that in most free states they were not regarded as full citizens. Blacks in New England were able to vote and could appeal to the law for the protection of their civil rights, but in the Midwest they faced ubiquitous racial restrictions. Ohio's state constitution of 1802 prohibited free blacks from voting, holding political office, or testifying against whites in court. After 1804, any black person wishing to reside in Ohio was required to register with the county as a prerequisite to employment. A few years later the law required blacks to post a $500 bond. Similar laws or state constitutional provisions were enacted in Michigan, Illinois, Indiana, Iowa, and Wisconsin. These regulations were not always rigidly

The First Bryan African Baptist Church of Savannah, Georgia, claimed to be the first African American Baptist church in America. This early church was an example of the adaptation of African religious practices and beliefs to an emerging American religious form.

enforced, but they made free black life precarious in those states. John Malvin, a freeman who migrated from Virginia to Ohio in the late 1820s, expressed his disappointment. "I found every door closed against the colored man," he reported, "except the jail and penitentiaries, the doors of which were thrown wide open to receive them."[8]

Northern free blacks were committed to establishing their rights as Americans, and they were suspicious of the American Colonization Society, particularly because it disavowed any interest in improving the condition or rights of blacks in America. Three thousand blacks met at Philadelphia's Bethel Church in 1817 to denounce the society's plans. They claimed that black military service in the Revolution and the War of 1812 gave them rights as Americans and expressed their unwillingness to leave friends and relatives in southern bondage. They believed that slaveholders wanted to remove free blacks from the nation because they were the strongest voices against slavery. They also had strong suspicions that if colonization became federal policy, the government would coerce free black people to emigrate. The meeting unanimously adopted resolutions denouncing the society and rejecting its plan. Black supporters of colonization could not withstand the strength of the people's sentiments. James Forten, who chaired the meeting at Bethel Church, doubted that blacks could ever freely progress in America. As he wrote to Paul Cuffe, "my opinion is that [black people] will never become a people until they come out from amongst the white people." Fierce opposition to colonization among Philadelphia's blacks prevented Forten from speaking out on the issue.[9]

African Americans in the Upper South, particularly in Baltimore and Richmond, were among those most attracted to the program of the American Colonization Society. In the Upper South states, under the influence of the principles of the Revolution and following the example of such prominent planters as George Washington, many slaveholders had freed their slaves during the late eighteenth and early nineteenth centuries. So many had done so that the Virginia legislature took steps to limit the size of the free black population and discourage further emancipations with an 1806 law that required emancipated slaves to leave Virginia or face re-enslavement. A few years later the state imposed a tax on all free blacks within its borders. Maryland and other Upper South states also passed measures calculated to discourage emancipation and the growth of the free black population. In these areas colonization was attractive both to some emancipated blacks and to slaves who might trade their bondage in America for freedom in West Africa.

One reason that southern whites found the possibility of removing all or at least most of the free black population from the country attractive was because they believed that the presence of free blacks made slaves more difficult to control. Whites saw free blacks as likely troublemakers and potential subversives in the slaveholding society. Their freedom of movement and inevitable association with slaves were continual reminders to the slaves of the possibility of freedom. Louisiana planters believed that Charles Deslondes, a free mulatto from Haiti, led the uprising by some four hundred slaves in St. Charles and St. John the Baptist parishes in 1811. Slaves formed into military companies moved towards New Orleans, beating their marching cadence on drums and burning plantations as they moved through the countryside. They killed at least two whites and sent hundreds of others fleeing to New Orleans. State and local militia suppressed the uprising, killing sixty-six African Americans in the process. Even after authorities had the bodies of some of those killed dismembered and their heads placed on poles along the Mississippi River as a warning to would-be rebels, continued slave unrest and rumors of rebellion kept whites in a state of high anxiety.

Planters also faced threats to their slave property from the marauding bands of free blacks and fugitives called maroons. Maroon communities of runaway slaves were common throughout the Caribbean and the southern United States. They established themselves in inaccessible areas, often in the mountains, from whence it is believed they derived their name from the Spanish *cimarron*, from *cima* (mountaintop). From their strongholds they conducted raids on plantations, attempting to free slaves from bondage. In 1818 planters in Virginia and the Carolinas increased local patrols in an effort to defend themselves against people from isolated maroon settlements who periodically attacked plantations, freeing slaves and wreaking havoc on local communities. They also lobbied Congress for a new, stricter fugitive slave bill, which passed in the U.S. House of Representatives but was defeated in the U.S. Senate.[10]

In the 1820s, events in Charleston confirmed whites' worst fears. South Carolina authorities discovered a massive slave conspiracy conceived and led by Denmark Vesey, a free black man. Vesey, probably born in the West Indies, was the former slave of a sea captain. He had purchased his freedom in Charleston in 1800 with money he won in a lottery. Vesey was a skilled carpenter, and he settled comfortably into Charleston's free black community. For twenty years Vesey worked as a carpenter and studied the Bible, memorizing passages, he argued, that proved that slavery was counter to God's law. In the fall of 1820 he began to sketch out an elaborate plan to destroy slavery in the city and the surrounding region. He enlisted five slaves in his scheme, among them two trusted servants of South Carolina's governor, and engaged one of the city's African American blacksmiths to fabricate weapons. Vesey and most of his top leaders were religious men associated with the African Church of Charleston, and their faith encouraged a powerful commitment to the plan that would put their religious principles into action. Galvanized by Vesey's sermons on freedom, they saw blacks as God's chosen people and were determined to stage a bold frontal attack on the bondage that held them. In June 1822 at an appointed time at the end of the work week, hundreds of slaves from nearby plantations converged on Charleston to continue preparations for the rebellion. Several free African Americans who worked with horses stood ready to provide mounts for the insurgents.

Part of Vesey's inspiration for the rebellion was the Haitian Revolution thirty years before, and he wrote a letter appealing to the black government in Haiti for assistance. He set the date for the uprising as July 14, 1822, the anniversary of the storming of the Bastille at the start of the French Revolution. It was also a Sunday, a day when masters generally did not require slaves to work, and some rural slaves were allowed to come into Charleston for church services and social gatherings. Their plan was to attack the city arsenal to secure firearms and then to assault the guardhouse, killing as many of the city guards as possible before burning the city and conducting raids in the surrounding countryside. Finally, the rebels would seize ships in Charleston harbor and all would sail for the safety of Haiti. Six weeks before the target date, however, word of the plot reached authorities; they mounted a full investigation and arrested one of Vesey's lieutenants. Realizing the gravity of the situation, he moved the attack date forward to June 16, but before the uprising could begin, planters deployed a local military force to discourage any rebel action. The plotters went into hiding, but Vesey and most of his followers were captured. Denmark Vesey and seventy-one other blacks were convicted of plotting insurrection, and thirty-five, including Vesey, were hanged. Their bodies were dissected by local surgeons and displayed as a warning to any who might consider them heroes. Most disturbing to some slaveholders was the discovery that at least four white men had been indirectly involved in the plot by purchasing guns and ammunition for the insurgents. They were fined and sentenced to prison.

The actual number of slaves who took part or planned to take part in the conspiracy is unknown, but Denmark Vesey's plot was certainly one of the most elaborate in nineteenth-century America. It further alarmed a slaveholding South already fearful of slave uprisings. Charlestonians were so anxious about creating a general panic that many dared not speak publicly of the plot. One woman who lived in the city wrote to a friend that at the height of the excitement, "twenty-five hundred of our citizens were under arms to guard our property and our lives," but then she warned, "unless you hear it from elsewhere, say nothing about it."[11]

The fact that Vesey was a free man confirmed suspicions that contact between free blacks and slaves was dangerous. In response, South Carolina tightened its slave code and restrictions on free blacks, instituting curfews and requiring that all black gatherings be supervised by whites. Free blacks were required to have white guardians, and if they left the state, they could not

Rolla's Testimony in the Trial of Denmark Vesey Slave Plot Conspirators

Rolla Bennett was a participant in Denmark Vesey's plot against slaveholders in Charleston, South Carolina, in 1822. He was a slave of the governor of South Carolina, and, along with Vesey, was executed for his role in the conspiracy.

I know Denmark Vesey. On one occasion he asked me what news, I told him none; he replied we are free but the white people here won't let us be so, and the only way is to rise up and fight the whites. I went to his house one night to learn where the meetings were held. I never conversed on this subject with Batteau or Ned—Vesey told me he was the leader in this plot. I never conversed either with Peter or Mingo. Vesey induced me to join; when I went to Vesey's house there was a meeting there, the room was full of people, but none of them white. That night at Vesey's we determined to have arms made, and each man put in 12 1/2 cents toward that purpose. Though Vesey's room was full I did not know one individual there. At this meeting Vesey said we were to take the Guard-House and Magazine to get arms; that we ought to rise up and fight against the whites for our liberties; he was the first to rise up and speak, and he *read to us from the Bible, how the Children of Israel were delivered out of Egypt from bondage.* He said that the rising would take place, last Sunday night week, (the 16th June) and that Peter Poyas was one.

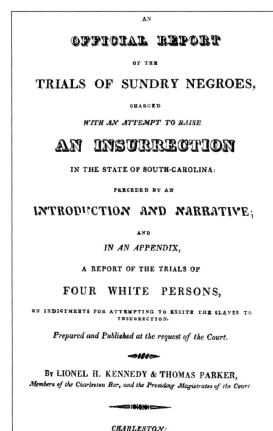

AN

OFFICIAL REPORT

OF THE

TRIALS OF SUNDRY NEGROES,

CHARGED

WITH AN ATTEMPT TO RAISE

AN INSURRECTION

IN THE STATE OF SOUTH-CAROLINA:

PRECEDED BY AN

INTRODUCTION AND NARRATIVE;

AND

IN AN APPENDIX,

A REPORT OF THE TRIALS OF

FOUR WHITE PERSONS,

ON INDICTMENTS FOR ATTEMPTING TO EXCITE THE SLAVES TO INSURRECTION.

Prepared and Published at the request of the Court.

By LIONEL H. KENNEDY & THOMAS PARKER,

Members of the Charleston Bar, and the Presiding Magistrates of the Court.

CHARLESTON:

PRINTED BY JAMES R. SCHENCK, 23, BROAD-STREET.

1822.

The city of Charleston, South Carolina, required blacks to wear tags identifying their occupations. After 1848, these tags were required for free blacks as well as slaves; ironically, this one bears the design of the Revolutionary-era liberty cap.

return. Some people suspected that Vesey had been encouraged by northern antislavery forces, and to guard against such outside influences, the state of South Carolina passed the Negro Seaman Act. This act required authorities to place any African American seamen who arrived in any port in the state in the local jail for the duration of their stay. Contact between such northern free blacks and South Carolina's slave and free black population was considered particularly dangerous. The Supreme Court declared the law invalid in 1824, but South Carolina continued to jail black sailors and attempted to discourage any emancipation that might enlarge its free black population.[12]

Some American blacks saw African colonization as a viable alternative to enduring the racial restrictions that grew more rigid as southern whites felt more threatened, and in 1820, with financial help from the federal government, the American Colonization Society sent its first settlers to its colony of Liberia, just south of Sierra Leone. Eighty-six African Americans led by Daniel Coker, the prominent minister of Baltimore's African Methodist Church, set sail on the *Mayflower of Liberia* for a new life in the West African colony. Lott Cary, a former slave who had bought his own freedom, was one of several blacks from Richmond, Virginia, who set off with another group in 1821. Cary's emigration was sponsored by Richmond's First Baptist Church, an interracial congregation that sent him as a missionary to the African people. Like many settlers, Cary had many reasons for emigrating. "I am an African," he declared, explaining that he wanted to regain his heritage and hoped to develop his talents without the restrictions burdening black people in America. During the first decade fourteen hundred blacks, most already free, followed the original settlers from America to Liberia.[13]

The expansion of American slavery and the political changes that accompanied it reached beyond the country's borders. In 1819 Spain sold Florida to the United States, and the life that Anna and Zephaniah Kingsley had built in

Spanish Florida was threatened. A few years later American forces gained control of the territory, bringing the promise of economic stability but threatening the fluid race relations that had existed under the Spanish. President James Monroe appointed Zephaniah Kingsley to the Territorial Council, where he urged the assembly to encourage manumissions and argued for the utility of alliances between whites and free blacks in a slaveholding society. Kingsley's fears about the vulnerability of his family situation were realized when the council passed laws restricting manumission, requiring freed blacks to leave the territory, prohibiting interracial marriage, and making mixed-race children ineligible to inherit a parent's estate. Although they were generally protected from these new laws by the fact that they had lived in Spanish Florida before it became United States territory, the rights of Anna and Zephaniah's last son, born after American acquisition of Florida, were not so clear. In 1828, Kingsley published a pamphlet explaining his objections to the new laws and his fears for the future. "Our laws to regulate slaves are entirely founded on terror," he charged, "constructed for the protection of whites, and vexatious tyranny over the persons and property of every colored person."[14]

In 1831, Kingsley deeded much of his holdings in Florida to Anna, his children, and another wife, Flora, the daughter of Sophie and Abraham Hannahan, but he was still not assured of their security. Between 1835 and 1837, Kingsley consulted with President Jean Pierre Boyer and bought land in Haiti, where he established two estates. He settled his three wives, his sons, and about sixty freed slaves on these estates, promising the freedmen a share of the crop and land of their own after nine years of labor. Anna Kingsley left Fort George Island and the land she owned there, where she had lived for nearly twenty-five years. She left her married daughters behind in Florida. In Haiti, Kingsley hoped his family could find a "land of liberty and equal rights, where the conditions of society are governed by some law less absurd than that of color."[15]

Thousands of African Americans accepted President Boyer's invitation to settle in Haiti during the 1820s, but African colonization remained controversial. In 1827 Samuel Cornish and John Russwurm founded *Freedom's Journal*, the first African American newspaper in the nation, specifically as an antislavery and anticolonization paper. In naming the newspaper, the editors were careful to assert their American, not their African, heritage to further dissociate themselves from the American Colonization Society. The debate among African Americans over the use of the term "African" intensified by the 1830s. Some argued that "oppressed Americans" was most descriptive of their status, and others even objected to the term "colored" unless accompanied by the word "American." When New York City's *Weekly Advocate* changed its name to the *Colored American* in the 1830s, the editor explained the appropriateness of the new name. "We are Americans," he argued, "colored Americans."[16]

By that time, the society had sent almost fifteen hundred American blacks to Liberia, but it was under increasing attack from northern free blacks. When African Americans gathered for a Fourth of July celebration in 1830 at St. Philip's Episcopal Church in New York City, Peter Williams, the black rector of that church, condemned the treatment of native-born black Americans, which he said was worse than the treatment of newly arrived immigrants. He left no doubt, however, about his

The publishers of Freedom's Journal, the first African American newspaper in the United States, declared, "We wish to plead our own cause. Too long have others spoken for us. Too long has the public been deceived by misrepresentations, in things which concern us dearly."

identification with the nation. He asserted, "We are NATIVES of this country; we ask only to be treated as well as FOREIGNERS." They had a right to claim their rights, he reminded his black audience, since "not a few of our fathers suffered and bled to purchase [America's] independence."[17]

While relatively few African Americans migrated to West Africa, a much larger forced migration of African Americans was taking place. As more states were carved from the territories of the western South and admitted to the union, an ever-increasing demand for labor increased slave prices in the lower South and stimulated a burgeoning internal slave trade. Despite the nation's first economic depression in 1819, the region's population, production of cotton, cultivation of sugar, and profits continued to expand. After Louisiana (1812), Mississippi (1817), and Alabama (1819) gained statehood, a portion of the slave trade already flowing into Tennessee and Kentucky was diverted to satisfy their demands. Between 1810 and 1820 an estimated 120,000 slaves were moved to the new states of the Deep South. Largely because of the interstate trade, Alabama's slave population rose almost 150 percent, from 47,000 to almost 120,000 in the single decade of the 1820s.[18] The pressures to extend slavery's boundaries affected black families all over the South, as thousands of family ties were splintered by sale and migration. Slaveholders in the new cotton- and sugar-producing states placed a premium on young strong slaves who could tolerate the long hours of work under the harsh work conditions of the Deep South summers. One Alabama planter directed his brother in Virginia to send only slaves forty-five years of age or younger, "excepting 2 or 3 healthy old women to cook and a trusty old man to attend to the hogs."[19]

New Orleans became the major seaport for the worldwide distribution of the crops, and a major slave depot as well. Prior to 1820 a southern planter or a planter's son anxious to start his own plantation was likely to move west with many of the slaves from the family's eastern plantation, often moving slave families together to the new site. The opening of the Deep South and the immense profits to be made by selling slaves into the expanding cotton and sugar markets changed this pattern. Although slave prices fluctuated yearly, during the 1820s young men between eighteen and thirty years old who sold for $500 to $700 in Virginia brought as much as $1,600 in Natchez and New Orleans. Slave-trading fever gripped many whites, who saw in these profits their opportunity to get rich. Many borrowed money at exorbitant interest rates to buy slaves in the Upper South and sell them in the markets of the Deep South. "My object," remarked one such trader who had brought slaves from Virginia in 1835, "is to make a fortune here as soon as possible by industry and economy, and then return to enjoy myself." By 1820, 70 percent of the slaves who were taken South were moved by slave traders.[20]

Potential profits also encouraged slaveholders to treat their slaves more like animals than human beings. Travelers through the Upper South testified to the breeding of slaves for the Deep South market. In 1833 the English observer Edward S. Abdy reported that Virginia planters "bred slaves as graziers bred cattle for the market." Also in the early 1830s a relatively poor farmer and "slave breaker" in Maryland named Edward Covey bought a slave named Caroline

A group of slaves perform chores in their quarters in Georgia. Slave quarters were no substitute for a home: so-called "slave patrollers" would search these settlements at random, hunting for stolen goods and escaped slaves.

because she was said to be a "breeder." Caroline was his only slave, but he had hope that she would help him increase his holdings. To this end, Covey rented a male slave from a neighbor and tied him to Caroline each night. By the end of the year's rental, Caroline increased Covey's holdings by giving birth to twins.[21] In the 1850s William Chambers, a Scotsman visiting in Richmond, observed that Virginia "as a matter of husbandry, breeds [N]egro labourers for the express purpose of sale."[22] Frederick Law Olmsted, another traveler, commented on the increased worth of a slave woman who could be counted on to produce children, and sale advertisements often designated young female slaves as "good breeders." Georgia slaveholder James Roberts claimed to keep fifty or sixty slave women solely as breeders and to have twenty or twenty-five children bred each year on his plantation.[23]

Slaveholding was becoming an even more profitable venture in the nineteenth century, but being a planter required a substantial financial investment. Slave trading, on the other hand, presented great opportunities for white

Americans of more modest means. With just a small sum of money, many whites could start trading businesses that eventually netted them substantial gains, but the trade was the source of untold misery for slaves and their families. Illiterate horse trader and backwoodsman Nathan Bedford Forrest struggled to make a living in Mississippi, but his fortunes changed after he moved to Memphis and took up a new trade in human beings. During the 1850s he became one of the wealthiest men in the South, propelled to affluence by the enormous profits of the infamous trade.[24] The business partners of Franklin and Armfield were others who made their fortunes in the trafficking of human beings. Located in a quiet section of Alexandria, Virginia, theirs was one of the nation's largest slave-trading companies. Its high, whitewashed walls surrounding a series of buildings gave it the appearance of the prison that it was.

Ethan Allen Andrews, a New England teacher and author, toured the Franklin and Armfield slave pens in 1835 and published a detailed description of his visit. Inside the walls Andrews found two fenced yards, each with a padlocked gate. The first held sixty or seventy black men, most between eighteen and thirty years old, but also a few boys as young as ten. In the other fenced yard were thirty or forty black women, with a few children among them. Andrews's guide, a company employee, assured him that the proprietors treated the slaves well and took care not to separate families. Indeed, Andrews saw evidence that the slaves had recently enjoyed a "wholesome and abundant" dinner, and they appeared to be reasonably healthy, clean, and "neatly and comfortably dressed."[25]

This pleasant picture painted by the guide was covertly challenged, however, by one of the slaves, "a young man, of an interesting and intelligent countenance." The man looked directly at Andrews each time the guide turned away, "shook his head, and seemed desirous of having [Andrews] understand, that he did not feel any such happiness as was described, and that he dissented from the representation made of his condition." Andrews never got a chance to speak with this daring young slave, but he was sure that given an opportunity, this captive "could a tale unfold." Andrews later concluded that the seeming care with which the slaves were fed and clothed was dictated only by the fact that their market value was dramatically improved when they appeared "in good order and well conditioned."[26]

The slaves gathered at Franklin and Armfield and elsewhere in the eastern Upper South were eventually moved to the Deep South for sale. The *Virginia Times* reported that in 1836 Virginia exported 40,000 slaves southward, and it placed the value of these exports at $24 million. Many went by water, in boats specially built for the trade, down the Atlantic Coast, through the Gulf of Mexico, to New Orleans. Others traveled overland, chained together and forced to march up to 1,000 miles, southwestward through the Carolinas, Georgia, and Alabama, and on to Natchez, Mississippi, where the Alexandria firm and other Upper South traders operated Deep South branch offices. In 1836 alone, *The Natchez Courier* estimated the number of slaves imported into Mississippi, and the surrounding states of Louisiana, Alabama and Arkansas at 250,000. Many of these fractured slave families had been settled in the Virginia and Maryland Chesapeake area for more than a hundred years. This second middle passage, as historian Ira Berlin has termed this internal slave trade, devastated thousands of families, leaving wives without husbands, children without fathers, and parents without sons.[27]

Charles Ball was one of those enslaved in frontier Georgia during the mid-1820s. This was the second time he had been enslaved there. After his agonizing first escape and service in the War of 1812, he had been discharged from the army in the fall of 1814 and had returned to Baltimore to work. His wife died a few years later, but he continued to live and work in Maryland. In about 1818 he had married a free black woman, and they eventually had four children. He saved his money, bought a small farm, and supported his family by selling his produce and dairy products at the Baltimore market. One day in the mid-1820s, after the fugitive Ball had lived for nearly twenty years without a master, the sheriff and two other men came to his door. They said they had a writ for his arrest, bound him, and took him to jail, where he was confined with other blacks who told him they had been purchased by a Georgia trader. Although Ball at first had not recognized him, one of the men who came for him was his former mistress's brother. She had remarried and moved to Louisiana, and her brother had decided to claim ownership of Charles Ball. The brother took Ball to his plantation in Georgia, and one day Ball overheard him contending that he had bought Ball in Maryland. Understanding then that the man had no legal claim to him, Ball sought out a lawyer and sued for his freedom. Unfortunately, as a slave, Ball could not testify in court, and after hearing the master's story, the judge decided the case in the master's favor.

Feeling doubly aggrieved, Ball awaited his chance for escape. As punishment for questioning his master's claim to him, he was given extra work, whipped often, and locked in a cabin by himself each night. One especially dark night, the overseer neglected to properly latch the door, and Ball seized his opportunity. Hiding in a swamp, he was confronted by a slave patrol, bound, and taken to a tavern. When his master arrived to reclaim him, he decided to offer Ball for sale to the gathering at the tavern, and he was sold for $580 to a man with a small plantation at a distance of two-days' walk. His new owner, saying he did not whip his slaves, soon demonstrated his own method for them. He required Ball to watch as a woman was stripped, tied to a post under a high pump, and had cold water poured over her. After she became unconscious, the master had her removed to her bed, where she would recover after a few days. Watching this torture, Ball decided not to wait to suffer a similar fate. One night shortly thereafter, he ran away, hoping to go south and join the Seminoles in Florida.

Once again Charles Ball found himself traveling at night, this time following the road east toward Savannah. Deciding that no one would suspect a man heading to Savannah of being a runaway, he took a ride with a black man carting a load of cotton to town and hired himself out at the waterfront. He managed to get a job loading a Philadelphia-bound ship and confided in a black crew member from New York, saying he had been kidnapped from Baltimore and was a fugitive. The man was reluctant to help him, for fear of trouble from the captain, but assured Ball that he would not betray him should he stow away. As he loaded the ship, Ball prepared a place for himself in the hold, and just before the ship sailed, hid among the cotton bales.

Reaching Philadelphia, Ball was aided by a Quaker who recognized him as a runaway, took him to a home in the black community, and provided him with

Slave catchers often used dogs to hunt fugitives. In this 1861 oil painting by the English artist Richard Ansdell, entitled The Hunted Slaves, *runaways who have taken refuge in the Dismal Swamp of North Carolina defend themselves from canine attack.*

a suit of clothing and some money. After two weeks in Philadelphia, Ball decided to return to Maryland, sell his farm, and bring his wife and children to the North. In Maryland he found a white man living in his house. Questioning the man and a black neighbor, he pieced together the story of what had happened to his wife and children. Shortly after Ball had been taken to Georgia, a small group of white men disguised in blackface appeared at their cabin door late at night. They tied up the neighbor who was staying with the family and kidnapped Ball's family. Ball had no idea where they had been taken and knew his master had offered a $150 reward for his capture. All Charles Ball could do was return to Philadelphia, imagining the hardships his wife and children endured as they were sold and joined the growing stream of slaves traded farther south.

In 1834 British geographer George W. Featherstonhaugh happened upon traders moving about three hundred slaves from Virginia south to Natchez. It was early morning when he saw them, and the people were preparing to break camp for the day's journey. The white slave drivers stood around the dwindling fire laughing and smoking cigars, while slave women stood or sat on nearby logs and children warmed themselves by the fire. Some two hundred slave men stood chained together in double file at the front of the forming procession. There were horses for the drivers, a horse-drawn carriage, and nine wagons to transport supplies and any slaves unable to walk. The traders, Featherstonhaugh observed, were well dressed, and some had their broad-brimmed white hats wrapped in black mourning crepe. The crepe was in honor, they said, of the death of General Lafayette, revered for his assistance in gaining American liberty during the Revolution. The Englishman was sympathetic to what he saw as the predicament of planters. As he saw it, the abolitionists were calling on the planters to bankrupt themselves by setting free the labor source that made their wealth possible. Nevertheless, the scene of human despair he witnessed appalled him. "I have never seen so revolting a sight before," he wrote. He wondered at the "monstrous absurdity" of those who could subscribe to "the spirit of the Declaration of Independence" while engaging in "such a horrid trade."[28]

Not all Americans thought that the immense profits from the slave crops justified slavery's movement westward, and political conflict accompanied slavery's expansion. As thousands of Americans moved into the western territories in the aftermath of the war of 1812 and as new states entered the Union, proslavery forces and antislavery advocates clashed over how far slavery should be allowed to spread. When the residents of Missouri petitioned for statehood in 1817, there were almost ten thousand slaves in the territory. The controversy emerged full blown after Alabama was admitted to the union in 1819, balancing the eleven free states with eleven slave states. As Missouri became a state that same year, some in Congress attempted to fix boundaries for slavery with a view toward its gradual abolition. The compromise that resulted from the acrimonious debate set the boundary between future slave states and future free states. Except for the state of Missouri, slavery would not be allowed north of a line drawn from Missouri's southern border.

Thomas Jefferson saw a dangerous principle in the division established by the Missouri Compromise. It was, he said, "like a fire bell in the night" that should arouse the nation. He foresaw mounting regional tensions over the issue of slavery that would lead to more serious conflict. Though Jefferson could see no way of safely doing away with slavery, he viewed maintaining slavery as a dangerous balancing act. It was, he said, like holding a "wolf by the ears, and we can neither hold him, nor safely let him go." He knew that slavery was wrong, but feared black anger and retribution should slaves be freed from slaveholders' control. "Justice," he said, was "in one scale, and self-preservation in the other."[29]

Great profits in the burgeoning Cotton Kingdom translated into increasing political power for southern slaveholders, power that supported slavery's continued existence. The profits to be made in the markets of Mississippi and Louisiana continued to spur the internal slave trade and kept the slave traders in business.

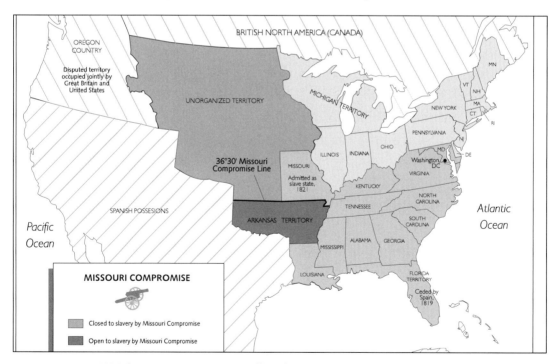

In 1820 the Missouri Compromise allowed Missouri to enter the nation as a slave state and brought in Maine as a free state. It restricted slavery in future states carved from the Louisiana territory to the area south of the southern border of Missouri. Congress hoped this compromise would settle the question of the extension of slavery once and for all.

In the mid-1830s novelist Joseph Holt Ingraham visited "Forks of the Road," a group of rough wooden buildings that constituted a slave-trading settlement about a mile outside of Natchez, Mississippi. He found a thriving business with a substantial number of well-dressed white men in attendance. Slaves were lined up in order of height from the tallest, about five feet nine or ten inches tall, to the smallest, a young boy of about ten years of age. The slaves were dressed in "strong shoes and white cotton shirts" and were freshly scrubbed in preparation for their sale. The auctioneer stepped forward to address the potential buyers. "Good morning, gentlemen! Would you like to examine my lot of boys?" he asked. "I have as fine a lot as ever came to market."[30]

Patrons looked the slaves over closely, examining their teeth, their tongues, and their hands and checking their bodies for telltale scars of the lash, scars that might indicate a rebellious nature in need of violent restraint. This process was particularly humiliating for slave women, who had to endure physically intrusive examinations of their bodies by strange men attempting to ascertain their abilities to bear children. Potential buyers questioned slaves about their backgrounds, their skills, and their attitudes. George, a slave from Virginia who called himself a "full blood Wirginny," was about twenty years old and a skilled coachman. He admitted to having a temper but claimed never to take out his anger on his horses.[31] He also explained that he had been sold away from his wife, who was left behind in Virginia. On the two-month trek to Mississippi, George had taken a new wife, and he asked that any buyer also purchase his new wife, an eighteen-year-old whom he described as a good seamstress and nurse. The buyer promised nothing but agreed to present the young girl to his wife, who would make the decision. Thus, even in the most dire circumstances, as their lives were shattered by the trade in human cargo, slaves might try to shield themselves and their loved ones from further harm as best they could. Ingraham did not report whether George's attempt to stay with his new wife was successful.

As these sales south often destroyed slave family life, some made the dangerous decision to attempt escape. Slaves often made this decision at critical moments of change in their lives when their circumstances were likely to worsen significantly, such as when a master died or was about to sell them. Generally, slaves held in the Upper South and border states were more likely to attempt escape than those in the Deep South. Being closer to the free states where they were likely to find help and shelter made escape a more practical proposition than it was in the interior of the lower South. From some places in the Upper

$100 REWARD

WILL be given for the apprehension and delivery of my Servant Girl HAR-RIET. She is a light mulatto, 21 years of age, about 5 feet 4 inches high, of a thick and corpulent habit, having on her head a thick covering of black hair that curls naturally, but which can be easily combed straight. She speaks easily and fluently, and has an agreeable carriage and address. Being a good seamstress, she has been accustomed to dress well, has a variety of very fine clothes, made in the prevailing fashion, and will probably appear, if abroad, tricked out in gay and fashionable finery. As this girl absconded from the plantation of my son without any known cause or provocation, it is probable she designs to transport herself to the North.

The above reward, with all reasonable charges, will be given for apprehending her, or securing her in any prison or jail within the U. States.

All persons are hereby forewarned against harboring or entertaining her, or being in any way instrumental in her escape, under the most rigorous penalties of the law.

JAMES NORCOM.

Edenton, N. C. June 30

James Norcom of Edenton, North Carolina, offered a $100 reward for the return of Harriet Jacobs. After escaping in 1835, Jacobs spent seven years in hiding in Edenton before arriving safely in the North.

South, slaves could gaze across state lines toward a not-too-distant freedom. Looking northward from the southern shore of the Ohio River in Kentucky, the free state of Ohio beckoned. In winter, when the river was frozen, some fugitives did attempt to escape across the ice floes, a feat depicted in Harriet Beecher Stowe's *Uncle Tom's Cabin*, the nineteenth century's best-selling novel. Many a slave who faced being sold to the Deep South must have considered such a dramatic attempt for freedom.

Initially in the internal slave trade, the call was for young men to work clearing the fields for new plantations, to establish new cotton crops in Georgia and Alabama, and to plant cotton and sugarcane in Louisiana and the Mississippi Delta. The resulting gender imbalance on many of the plantations made it difficult for arriving slaves to establish families. Historian Ann Patton Malone found that only about half of the slaves in the rural Louisiana parishes she studied were able to establish two-parent or couple households because of the shortage of female slaves. Most of the young male slaves brought from Kentucky to work on Walter Bashear's plantation in Louisiana, for example, never married.[32]

The presence of many young single slave men, without local family ties could pose particular problems, and planters were well aware of the dangers. From the slaveholder's point of view, a slave without a family was a slave with little to lose. Common wisdom among the planter class was that family ties could make slaves easier to control and discouraged them from running away. Some planters attempted to form their slaves into family groups, even pairing male and female slaves who had been parted from their original families. One Louisiana planter was so certain of the quieting effect of marriage on his slaves that he required any slave seeking to sever a spousal relationship to first suffer

25 lashes. By the mid-nineteenth century, natural increase and more importations of women had created greater balance between the number of slave women and slave men in the lower South.[33]

Planters' realization of the power of family ties and community relationships among slaves contradicted the contentions of some slaveholders that African Americans did not suffer from the family separation that was an increasingly common part of slavery with the ever-expanding internal slave trade. Many slaveholders answered charges that the trade was inhumane by arguing that slaves were limited in their ability to form human attachments and thus were not affected by being separated from other family members. Clearly their use of family as a means of slave control contradicted such assertions, and these claims were rendered ludicrous by plainly visible evidence to the contrary. Even casual observers who witnessed the reactions of slaves torn from their loved ones understood the absurdity of this rationalization. Time and time again, the obvious pain of separation and the extraordinary security measures taken to prevent wholesale revolt made it obvious that slaveholders and traders knew better, regardless of what they said.

Some whites acknowledged being troubled by the inhumanity of breaking up marriages and families, but their moral unease was generally silenced by the huge profits that resulted from these sales. In a perverted attempt to accommodate Christian morality to the immorality of the trade, the Savannah River Baptist Association debated whether the church should accept a slave's new marriage after his old marriage had been broken by sale. The church elders decided that such remarriage must be allowed because a spouse's sale was equivalent to her death, and thus the new marriage was acceptable in the sight of God. This decision was merely a curiosity, since at the time, southern laws did not recognize any slave marriages.[34]

Rationalizations about the relative unimportance of family among slaves were further contradicted by the everyday experi-

Slave traders separate a slave mother from her infant in an illustration from the American Anti-Slavery Almanac *for 1840. The abolitionist press sold many almanacs illustrated with provocative woodcuts demonstrating the brutality of slavery.*

ences of most white slaveholders and their families. Unlike northern society, where the African American population was small and regular interracial contact was relatively rare, whites on southern plantation associated daily with African Americans. During his travels through the South in the decades before the Civil War, northerner Frederick Law Olmsted was surprised by what he called "the close cohabitation and association of black and white." He was fascinated by the scene of a white mother and daughter sitting with a black mother and daughter on a train. The women "talked and laughed together; and the girls munched confectionery out of the same paper, with a familiarity and closeness of intimacy that would have been noticed with astonishment, if not with manifest displeasure" in the North.[35]

Throughout the South such casual, even comfortable, interracial relationships often occurred, as the children of slaveholders and the children of slaves grew up together, played together, and frequently became best friends. Slave women sometimes nursed white babies, and many white adults looked back fondly on an "old black mammy" who served as a surrogate mother for much of their childhood. Slave men, too, were sometimes remembered warmly as "old uncles" who taught white children to fish or carve. Although slaves' vulnerability complicated matters considerably, they sometimes formed genuinely affectionate relationships with the white children in their charge. Yet all these associations, no matter how intimate, became complex as the white children grew to adults, often becoming the legal owners of their old mammies or uncles or their best childhood friends. Slaves often remembered the heartbreak of encountering their former friends and charges as white adults in the racially stratified society of the slaveholding South. Their disappointment often turned into intense anger as they were forced to act out their part as the acknowledged inferior.

Charles, for example, was a handsome mulatto Virginia slave who was a hero to his master's young white sons whom he was charged with conducting to school. The boys admired Charles's stories and songs, his bravery, intelligence, and knowledge. As the boys learned in school and gained white school friends, they gradually abandoned Charles, who was forbidden to learn reading and writing. One of the boys later remembered the impact of this change on Charles. "His temper, from being mild, became bitter; his bravery became fierceness; and by his recklessness the whole family was kept in perpetual panic. Punishment only made him defiant." At age nineteen, Charles set fire to a house, and his owner, believing him uncontrollable, sold him to the Deep South.[36]

Although there is less evidence of the impact of these relationships on southern whites, the romanticization of race relations in the plantation South was undoubtedly affected by their childhood experiences. The unrealistically idyllic pictures of the old South painted in the writing, music, and art of many white southerners may have been an attempt to cope with the emotional impact of confronting the inhumanity of slavery on people whom they knew personally and even cared about. Thomas Jefferson, who in adulthood became the owner of Jupiter, his best childhood friend, argued that, from his point of view, one of the worst things about slavery was its corruption of whites. According to Jefferson, the relationship between master and slave was characterized by "the most unremitting despotism on the one part, and degrading submissions on the other." The master's child imitated his parent, he argued, and was "nursed, educated, and daily exercised in tyranny." Even for those whites who attempted to act humanely toward their slaves and toward African Americans in general, the system of bondage and white supremacy on which the southern way of life was based limited their ability to do so.[37]

There is much yet to be learned about the way race relations shaped southern white culture, but there is no question about the significance of slavery to the expanding southern economy. Slaves not only cultivated the land that enriched the slaveholding community; they also built the towns and the grand plantation homes that housed the growing white population. The increasing slave population also made it possible for people to create slave communities in the relatively newly settled areas, sometimes forming family groups from unrelated individuals whose families had been shattered by the internal slave trade. In Tennessee, the number of slaves rose from 3,000 in 1790 to more than 140,000 by 1830 and Mississippi's slave population jumped from just over 3,000 in 1800 to almost 66,000 by 1830. Both women and men were worked mercilessly on Deep South plantations, where strong hands and backs were required and expected of all slave laborers.

Solomon Northup, a free man kidnapped into slavery, explained the labor needed to operate the cotton plantation where he was enslaved. During the early spring months of March and April, slave women and men drove oxen or mules pulling immense ploughs that churned the soil to make it ready for seeding. During the heat of the late spring and summer, men and women hoed and plowed to thin the new plants and to keep the grass and weeds away from them. Cotton picking began in late August, when slaves filled huge cloth bags that

Born free in New York but kidnapped into slavery in Louisiana, Solomon Northup published Twelve Years a Slave *in 1853, after regaining his freedom. Publication of the book led to the arrest, but not the conviction, of his kidnappers, and it ultimately earned him $3,000.*

became heavier and heavier as they moved down the seemingly endless rows. Novices were recognized by their hands, bloodied from the sharp thorns of the cotton plant, while heavy calluses helped protect the hands of veteran pickers. A field hand working from sunup to sundown was expected to pick from 50 to 150 pounds of cotton a day; an exceptional hand could pick 200 pounds in a day.[38]

Growing sugar was even more physically demanding than cotton cultivation. Workers prepared the fields in a similar fashion, but sugar planting began in January and continued until April. Planting sugar was necessary only once every three years. As Northup described the process, slaves formed three gangs, one gang following the other as they worked their way down the rows. The first gang cut the cane stalks, leaving healthy short pieces from which the new plants would grow, while the second gang set the stalks in place. The last gang covered them with three inches of soil to complete the planting process. Then came the hoeing season, which lasted until August, followed by cutting and stacking of cane to be used as seed. By October slaves commenced the general cane cutting and begin milling the cane. Cutting and milling continued until the fields were completely harvested or until heavy frost ended work. Generally, in an attempt to beat the frost, slaves were worked very long hours, sometimes working around the clock by the light of a full moon. Usually the frost occurred only a few weeks before the January planting began.

In the summer, workers in the delta and low country did this heavy labor under a blazing sun and in strength-sapping humidity, facing the dangers of dehydration, malaria, and yellow fever. In the winter, they suffered from cold and frostbite. These conditions took a heavy toll on the slaves of the Deep South, where slave life expectancy was lower and the rate of illness was considerably higher than in the Upper South. These extreme circumstances were worsened by the often-brutal treatment by overseers, who were largely unsupervised during the summer months, when many planters sought the more healthful climates of the North or Upper South. Tales of the inhumane conditions of life in the Deep South combined with the fear of family separation, made the prospect of being "sold down the river" a dreaded horror among the slaves.[39]

During the 1820s, as the power of the cotton planter grew in the South, antislavery sentiment, always important in the free black community, was growing stronger in the northern states and taking on a more radical tone. In 1826, free blacks in Boston established a new abolitionist group they called the Massachusetts General Colored Association, dedicated to providing for the needs of free blacks and fighting for an immediate end to slavery in the nation. That year David Walker, a black shopkeeper from North Carolina who had recently moved to Boston, addressed the association and called for open slave rebellion.

Walker's public endorsement of a violent attack on slavery and the publication of his remarks as *Walker's Appeal in Four Articles* in 1829 exacerbated southern fears. His was a militant statement of racial pride hurled against white assertions of black inferiority. Walker attacked African colonization and claimed blacks' rights as Americans. "Let no man of us budge one step," he commanded, "and let slave-holders come to beat us from our country. America

Slaves perform the hot and backbreaking labor of boiling sugarcane juice in a Louisiana refinery. This illustration appeared in Frank Leslie's Illustrated Newspaper *in 1871, but the refining methods shown here had changed little since well before the Civil War.*

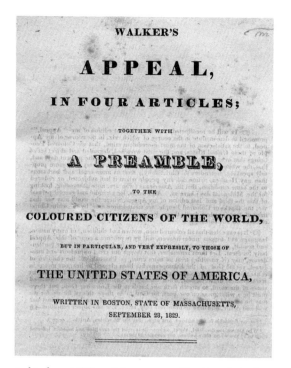

In his fiery 1829 antislavery pamphlet, David Walker wrote, "the Blacks or Coloured People, are treated more cruel by the white Christians of America, than devils themselves ever treated a set of men, women and children on this earth."

is more our country, than it is the whites'—we have enriched it with our *blood and tears.*"[40] Walker condemned the nation's hypocrisy and excoriated those Americans, including Thomas Jefferson, who employed the rhetoric of freedom while supporting human bondage. He disparaged Jefferson's speculations on black inferiority and argued that such charges could only be effectively refuted by blacks themselves. To drive the point home, he called for immediate and direct actions by slaves. "You [whites] are not astonished at my saying we hate you, for if we are men, we cannot but hate you, while you are treating us like dogs."[41] Walker's fiery appeal signaled a new, more combative era in the northern struggle against slavery.

Nat Turner was a slave on the Travis plantation in Southhampton County, Virginia, seventy miles from Richmond. He was not a preacher in any formal sense, but he was a deeply religious man. He saw visions and interpreted signs—blood on the corn and strange human figures in the air—and he became convinced that he had been chosen to be a prophet and the deliverer of his people. "I saw white spirits and black spirits engaged in battle," he reported, "and the sun darkened—thunder rolled in the heavens, and blood flowed in the streams."[42] He believed it was a sign from God. He and four others planned an insurrection, initially to take place on July 4, 1831, but at the last minute Turner was uncertain of God's command, and they suspended their plans. Soon, however, Turner again saw the vision and, convinced of its command, he set the attack for late August. The rebels, then numbering seven, started their assault in the early morning at the Travis plantation house. They killed the five whites in the household and took guns and ammunition. After this attack, Turner drilled his troops near the barn before moving on to the next plantation, where their number grew to fifteen. They attacked one plantation after another, killing as they went and enlisting more and more followers.

By midmorning Turner's band had grown to forty. They continued their attacks, acquired horses, more guns, swords and axes, and by late afternoon had a small army of more than sixty mounted insurgents. They halted on the outskirts of the county seat, Jerusalem, to recruit more men for an attack on the town, and there a small contingent of white militia confronted Turner's divided forces. During the ensuing fight, Turner and his men routed the militia but then themselves were attacked by white reinforcements from the town. What remained of Turner's forces scattered into the nearby woods with the intention of regrouping again near the place where they had started out. Turner hid in the woods until he became convinced that he had been betrayed. Finally, he made his way back to the Travis plantation, dug a hollow under a pile of fence railings, and hid there for six weeks.

While Nat Turner was in hiding, whites, stunned and panicked by the magnitude of the rebellion, began to take general revenge on area slaves. The rebels had killed sixty-one whites, making this the bloodiest slave revolt in U.S. history, and all African Americans in the region paid a heavy price. Newspapers reported a frenzy of killing. Many slaves, most of whom had no part in the rebellion, were tortured, burned to death, shot, or otherwise horribly murdered. In one day, whites killed one hundred and twenty blacks in retaliation for the revolt. One group of whites rode from Richmond through Southhampton County killing every African American they saw. They stopped to ask a free black man working in his garden if they were in Southhampton County, and when the farmer confirmed that they were, they shot him dead. A reporter interviewed one white man who bragged that he personally had killed between ten and fifteen black people.

Many whites assumed that Turner's attack was part of a general slave uprising, and the panic spread to the entire region. The governor of Virginia called out the state infantry, and the U.S. Navy offered assistance. Rumors that slaves were conducting racial warfare fed the general hysteria. Some terrified whites falsely claimed that two thousand blacks had burned Wilmington, North Carolina, and were marching on the state capital at Raleigh. When North Carolina uncovered an actual plot perpetrated by some twenty-four blacks in a number of counties, people's worst fears seemed confirmed. As in Virginia, North Carolina authorities called out the state militia and placed cities and towns under heavy guard. Harriet Jacobs, a young woman enslaved in Edenton, North Carolina, witnessed the widespread brutal assaults on black men, women, and even children in the town.

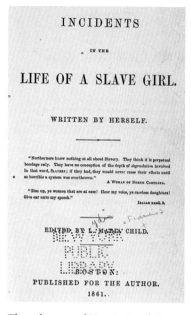

The title page of Harriet Jacobs's Incidents in the Life of a Slave Girl (1861). In the book she describes how she rejected an opportunity to buy her freedom. "The more my mind had become enlightened, the more difficult it was for me to consider myself an article of property," she wrote.

She remembered the quasi-official force that attacked blacks at random: "The citizens and the so-called country gentlemen wore military uniforms. The poor whites took their places in the ranks in every-day dress, some without shoes, some without hats." Upon the commander's order, these troops reacted like "wild scouts rushing in every direction, wherever a colored face was to be found." Jacobs watched from the safety of a window in her master's house as some of the men vandalized and robbed the homes of African Americans while others administered public whippings.[43] In South Carolina and Georgia, rumors of slave uprisings alarmed the white population, and officials mobilized the local guard. At one point, the entire white population of Macon, Georgia, was awakened in the middle of the night by a false report that area slaves were in revolt. As far as New Orleans, reports of the discovery of a stash of arms at the home of a local black man inflamed fears of plots.[44]

Some Virginians used the alarm over Nat Turner's insurrection to press the state to abolish slavery. Community meetings, especially in western Virginia, where slaveholding was not as widespread or as critical to the economy as in the eastern tidewater area, drew large crowds to openly debate the issue, something rarely done in the South. A group of white women sent a petition to Virginia's state legislature, expressing their concern that members could not concentrate on their duties knowing that their loved ones were not safe at home. "Perhaps when deeply engaged in his legislative duties," they suggested, "[the legislator's] heart may quail and his tongue falter with irresistible apprehension for the peace and safety of objects dearer than life." Some white Virginians turned to colonization as a solution to the danger of slave revolt. The citizens of Buckingham County asked the state to remove all blacks, slave and free, from the county, following the proposal Thomas Jefferson had endorsed in the latter years of his life. Charles City, Virginia, called for gradual emancipation, but powerful proslavery forces quashed challenges to the institution. Thus, Nat Turner's revolt raised significant questions about slavery, provoking the last serious debate on the subject in the state's government.[45]

Finally, ten weeks after Nat Turner's initial attack in Southhampton County, Virginia, authorities captured him, tried him, found him guilty, and hanged him, all within a period of two weeks. A huge crowd gathered to witness his hanging, after which surgeons skinned and dissected his body, parceling out portions as souvenirs of the occasion. Decades after his execution, it was possible to purchase purses fashioned from Turner's skin, and trophies made of his bones became southern family heirlooms. Nat Turner lived in the nightmares of white southerners for generations, but to African Americans, Turner became a legendary hero. He symbolized the determination of slaves to break their chains and a desire to avenge the cruelty they and their loved ones suffered at the hands of slaveholders. A Turner-like character was the central figure in the 1859 novel *Blake: The Cabins of America* written by Martin R. Delany, a free black abolitionist and community activist in Pittsburgh. In the novel, Henry Blake runs away from slavery and travels through the South urging slaves to rise up against their masters. The novel became part of African American folklore celebrating slave rebellion, comparing it to America's strike for liberty in the Revolution and equating Nat Turner with George Washington.

Meanwhile, in the South, whites attempted to protect themselves from future rebellions by placing more restrictions on the movement and the actions of African Americans. In his annual address to the state legislature in 1831, the governor of Virginia argued that state law should place stricter controls on all blacks, slave and free. He used Turner's religious motivations to urge particularly harsh restrictions on black preachers, whom, he said, should be "silenced." In the next few months the legislature passed a number of measures to address whites' fears of future slave revolts. Laws barred blacks from holding religious services or meetings at night without the written permission of masters or overseers and prohibited teaching slaves to read or write. Free blacks had had very little to do with Turner's rebellion, but most whites continued to believe that they were particularly likely to foment slave unrest. The Virginia legislature considered a bill to remove all free African Americans from the state, but the state senate, by a narrow margin, indefinitely postponed it. In 1834, Virginia did prohibit free blacks from entering the state.

In nearby Maryland, officials prohibited the sale of slaves or migration of free blacks into the state and provided funds to the state's colonization society to encourage free black residents to migrate to Liberia. Delaware, which had prohibited free blacks from voting in 1831, prohibited them from using firearms in 1832. The state also stiffened enforcement of the law forbidding black meetings held after 10 p.m. and preventing nonresident blacks from addressing African American audiences. States farther south also restricted the rights and movements of free blacks and made it difficult for masters to emancipate slaves and illegal to educate them. In Alabama, white anxieties about the potential dangers of slave literacy were heightened when Jacob Cowan of Mobile was caught distributing copies of David Walker's *Appeal* to his fellow slaves, who were suspected of plotting a rebellion. The city's lawyer, David Crawford, labeled this plot a "treasonable conspiracy." An 1831 North Carolina ordinance prohibited slaves or free blacks from acting "in any manner to officiate as a preacher or teacher in any prayer meeting." Missouri targeted itinerant preachers, not allowing blacks to enter the state to preach the gospel. [46] Turner's rebellion affected even the free states. In Ohio, for example, the governor, concerned about the potential dangers of African American migration to the state, urged stricter enforcement of early nineteenth-century black laws restricting black migration and legal rights. Several states in the Midwest with similar restrictions also tightened enforcement, hoping to prevent southern racial violence from spilling over into the North.

Since slavery was almost solely a southern phenomenon by the 1830s, the North was not likely to endure a slave rebellion, but northern communities sometimes were drawn into the conflicts. In the summer of 1839, the slave schooner *Amistad* arrived in New London, Connecticut, in the custody of the naval vessel the *USS Washington*. The *Amistad* had left Havana, Cuba, with fifty-three African slaves bound for a plantation in the province of Principe, also in Cuba. Once at sea, the captives, led by a strong, dignified, and manly African named Joseph Cinque, broke free of their chains, revolted against the crew, killed the captain, and took over the vessel. They attempted to return to Africa but were tricked by some of the crew and spent two months at sea before reaching the coast of Long Island, where they encountered the navy vessel.[47]

The vessel's captain, Richard Meade, set the white crew free and transported the Africans to New London, where they

Joseph Cinque led the rebellion aboard the slave ship Amistad.
Abolitionists commissioned and sold copies of his portrait to raise money for the Amistad *captives' defense.*

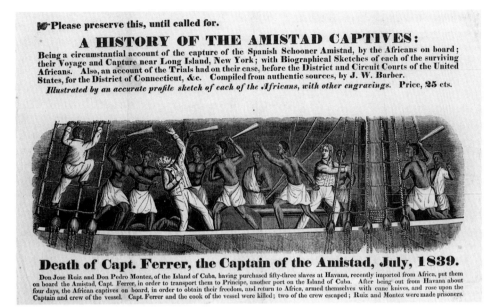

☛ **Please preserve this, until called for.**

A HISTORY OF THE AMISTAD CAPTIVES:

Being a circumstantial account of the capture of the Spanish Schooner Amistad, by the Africans on board; their Voyage and Capture near Long Island, New York; with Biographical Sketches of each of the surviving Africans. Also, an account of the Trials had on their case, before the District and Circuit Courts of the United States, for the District of Connecticut, &c. Compiled from authentic sources, by **J. W. Barber.**

Illustrated by an accurate profile sketch of each of the Africans, with other engravings.   **Price, 25 cts.**

Death of Capt. Ferrer, the Captain of the Amistad, July, 1839.

Don Jose Ruiz and Don Pedro Montez, of the Island of Cuba, having purchased fifty-three slaves at Havana, recently imported from Africa, put them on board the Amistad, Capt. Ferrer, in order to transport them to Principe, another port on the Island of Cuba. After being out from Havana about four days, the African captives on board, in order to obtain their freedom, and return to Africa, armed themselves with cane knives, and rose upon the Captain and crew of the vessel. Capt. Ferrer and the cook of the vessel were killed; two of the crew escaped; Ruiz and Montez were made prisoners.

This broadside advertised A History of the Amistad Captives *by J. W. Barber, an account published in 1840, just a year after African captives successfully rebelled aboard the Spanish schooner* Amistad. *The U.S. Supreme Court ultimately decided that the captives had exercised their right to self defense and should be freed.*

were imprisoned and charged with piracy and murder. The seizure of the *Amistad* quickly became an international incident, as Spain demanded the return of both the ship and its slave cargo. Abolitionists, on the other hand, argued that because the Atlantic slave trade had been outlawed by both the United States and England, and Spain had agreed to the prohibition, these Africans were actually kidnap victims, and the revolt amounted to self-defense. The incident became a celebrated abolitionist cause, and Joseph Cinque became an antislavery hero. Philadelphia black abolitionist Robert Purvis commissioned Cinque's portrait, and copies were sold for one dollar each to raise money for the Africans' defense.[48] Many African Americans hung Cinque's portrait in their homes, and black abolitionist William Wells Brown named his daughter Cinque. For the next two years the case worked its way through the courts. Finally in 1841, former President John Quincy Adams pleaded the Africans' case before the U.S. Supreme Court, and the Court ordered that the Africans be freed. Twenty-nine of the original fifty-three *Amistad* captives had died during the two years they were in jail. Only Cinque and twenty-four others survived to be released and transported to West Africa.

Harriet Tubman, who had escaped from a slave plantation in Maryland in 1849, and who returned to the South as an agent of the Underground Railroad many times to lead slaves to freedom. Maryland planters reportedly offered a total of $40,000 for her capture. William Still, black leader of Philadelphia's underground railroad, said that "in point of courage, shrewdness, and disinterested exertions to rescue her fellowman, she was without equal."

Troublesome Property: The Many Forms of Slave Resistance

Just three weeks before the *Amistad* Africans returned to Africa, the American ship *Creole* sailed out of Hampton Roads, Virginia, bound for New Orleans with one hundred thirty-five slaves aboard. As the vessel approached the British Bahamas, nineteen slaves, led by Virginia slave Madison Washington, staged a rebellion. The rebels killed a slave trader whose gun had misfired, wounded the captain, and took over the ship. They forced the crew to put into port at Nassau, where British authorities captured them. The British imprisoned the nineteen who had taken over the ship, and the American consul demanded that they be returned to the United States for trial. Black Bahamians, however, had other ideas. Fifty boats filled with local residents sailed to the *Creole*, surrounded it to prevent it from leaving port, and then threatened to free the slaves by force if necessary. The authorities succumbed to public pressure and released all of the slaves.[1]

The news of the *Creole* incident flashed back to the United States. The South was furious at the loss of its slave property, but Madison Washington joined Joseph Cinque as a symbol of black manhood and as a hero in the black community and among white abolitionists. Addressing a largely African American audience in Buffalo, New York, in 1843, black abolitionist Henry Highland Garnet called Washington "that bright star of freedom [who] took his station in the constellation of freedom" and included him in a list of slave revolutionaries along with "the patriotic Nathaniel Turner." Then, echoing David Walker a decade before, Garnet called for widespread slave resistance, urging slaves "from this moment cease to labor for tyrants who will not remunerate you." Anticipating the consequences of such action, Garnet added, "RATHER DIE FREEMEN THAN LIVE TO BE SLAVES. Remember that you are THREE MILLION."[2]

Whether or not they heard Garnet's call, black people continued to resist slavery. Violent resistance was common enough to generate white fear, but African Americans used many other, more common, more subtle, and less dangerous means of resistance. The frequency of violent revolts was limited by the remote possibility of success and by the unbridled brutality of the white response. More subtle resistance was less likely to evoke such an intense response. Most areas in the South maintained pass systems that required any slave not under the direct control of a white person to carry written permission to move about. Slaveholding and nonslaveholding whites participated in slave patrols, watching transportation routes and gathering places to ensure that unauthorized slaves were not off plantations and did not meet in unsanctioned groups. Holding millions of African people in bondage required a virtual police state, and southern society came to tolerate, and even honor, a military social climate that accepted violence as a necessity.[3] Additionally, slaveholders' right to human property was guaranteed by the Constitution, and slavery was ultimately protected by the military force of the United States. Any successful slave uprising would have had to defeat local white volunteers, state militia, and the U.S. military, an improbable occurrence.

Given the realities of slaves' lives, the direct violent confrontation of slavery generally was impractical. Confrontations were most likely to be spontaneous outbursts resulting from a specific situation. Slaveholders and overseers used violence to compel fear and obedience, but most understood that its excessive use was dangerous. John Quitman, a Mississippi planter with four plantations and more than five hundred slaves, believed that abuse made slaves stubborn and difficult to handle. This philosophy did not stop him from administering severe whippings to slaves for a wide range of infractions, including "picking trashy cotton" or not meeting the day's picking quota, but he prided himself on being fair to his slaves. His slaves recognized their master's self-image and used this to their advantage whenever possible. Rather than directly confronting Quitman's authority, the slaves were more likely to try to circumvent his control. They conducted general work slowdowns, feigning illness, breaking tools, and sabotaging equipment under the guise of clumsiness. They even set barns afire when they thought they could get away with it. The house slaves became particularly difficult to control whenever Quitman was away from the plantation, because they understood his wife Eliza's reluctance to admit to her husband that she could not administer the household. Apparently, the situation was completely out of hand when Eliza Quitman wrote to her husband: "I have never communicated any of my domestic troubles to you, since you left me, and I am not sure that it is proper for me to do so now... but I cannot help it." She reported that the slaves refused to work properly, remained away from the house, and one even had taken Quitman's carriage for his own amusement. She had not been able to attend church, she complained, because the slave did not return in time, "tho [sic] he had been told expressly that the carriage would be wanted."[4]

Despite her difficulties, Eliza Quitman usually maintained the fiction of the slaves' obedience and loyalty to the master's family. "The servants," as she called her slaves, "work and conduct themselves well," she wrote on another occasion. When the Quitman family vacationed in Newport, Rhode Island, they took their slave John with them, since the entire family was convinced of John's absolute loyalty. "He has alway[s] been as kind, attentive and faithful as anyone could be towards his master's family," remarked Quitman's son. "I myself have heard him say, that if it were in the power of these abolitionists to give him a thousand freedoms, he would not desert us." The Quitmans believed John's protestations and were not concerned when they stopped in Boston en route. Therefore, the family was shocked when John disappeared. John Quitman called the slave "ungrateful," while Eliza Quitman and their son supposed that John must have been kidnapped by Boston abolitionists. They fully expected that if John ever got the opportunity to escape, he would find his way back to the Quitman household.[5] Obviously many of John Quitman's slaves understood him and his family far better than the Quitmans understood their slaves. Southern slaveholders often boasted about knowing their slaves and assumed that slaves were ignorant and lacked

An idealized portrayal of American slavery produced by a northern apologist for the institution, the cartoonist E. W. Clay. A slave-owning white family visits the slaves on their plantation. While a group of happy slaves dance in the background, an old slave says, "God Bless you massa! you feed and clothe us. When we are sick you nurse us, and when too old to work, you provide for us!"

understanding. In reality, within slavery's power relationship masters had less need for understanding, while slaves often relied on their knowledge and understanding of the master and the slave system for survival.

Slaves also understood that the most effective and practical resistance could not be traced to its perpetrator. Such resistance often was supported by the system of ethics and morality they had developed to cope with the brutality and injustice of slavery. Slaves argued that almost everything slaveholders had was purchased with their stolen labor, and they believed that any deception or theft from the master was fully justified. Lying to and tricking masters or overseers was standard practice. Taking something from the master was not stealing, they reasoned, but simply redistributing his property, since they themselves were his property.

While stealing from the master was generally acceptable and even admirable among slaves, particularly if done with imagination and style, stealing from fellow slaves was not. Those within the slave community highly valued trustworthiness, justice, and mutual support. It was extremely important to slaves that their fellows could be counted on the keep their secrets, and those who proved untrustworthy were community outcasts. When Denmark Vesey was devising his revolt, he warned his fellow conspirators not to reveal their plans to house servants, even though house servants were often an important part of the slave intelligence network. As those privy to information overheard in conversations at the master's house, they could provide information useful to the other slaves in shaping their resistance, but their close association with slaveholders also made them suspect in the eyes of many of their fellow slaves. Indeed, it was a house servant who betrayed Denmark Vesey's plans.

House slaves were generally among those advantaged few whose treatment was superior to that of ordinary field workers. Often living in the plantation house, they had better living conditions and were sometimes supplied with second-hand clothing from the master's family. Abolitionist, novelist, and playwright William Wells Brown began his life as a slave in Kentucky and later became a house slave on a Missouri plantation. In his autobiography, he explained that working in the

The autobiography of fugitive slave William Wells Brown went through four American and five British editions within three years of its publication, and earned its author international fame.

master's house was "a situation preferable to that of a field hand, as I was bet-ter fed, better clothed, and not obliged to rise at the ringing of the bell, but about half an hour after."[6]

There were disadvantages to being a house slave, however. Lewis Clarke, the son of a Scotsman and a Kentucky slave woman, was a house slave who described his situation as little better, and in some ways worse, than that of slaves who worked the fields. "We were constantly exposed to the whims and passions of every member of the family; from the least to the greatest, their anger was wreaked upon us." The situation was especially dangerous for attractive young women. In her 1861 autobiography, fugitive slave Harriet Jacobs wrote of the constant sexual harassment she faced as a young girl living under her master's roof. "My master met me at every turn, reminding me that I belonged to him," she explained, "and swearing by heaven and earth that he would compel me to submit to him." It was so common for white men to prey on the female slave, Jacobs continued, that "if God has bestowed beauty upon her, it will prove her greatest curse."[7]

It was painfully ironic that slave women victimized by slave masters could find themselves the targets of the wrath of the master's jealous wife. The mis-tress, forced to turn a blind eye to mixed-race children on the plantation, often vented her anger on the female slaves to whom they were born. The antebellum plantation was governed by nineteenth-century gender rules, and the master's wife had little authority, except over her children and her household slaves. A planter's wife generally dared not confront her husband about his sexual liaisons. Though slave women had little choice but to submit to the master, as those with the least power on the plantation slaves often became the scapegoats for the mistress's frustrations. The planter's wife certainly had a better life and a great deal more power than did the slaves in her household, but she, too, lived in a society where white men ruled. The relationships between the white women and the black women on the plantation, and indeed among all those in the planter's household, were complex. Although vulnerable to abuse by the master, house slaves were more likely to have the master's ear than other slaves and sometimes even had a personal relationship with his family.[8]

It worked to a slaveholder's advantage to create a slave hierarchy headed by a group of privileged bondsmen who identified with the master's interests and acted as his eyes and ears among the other slaves. A handbook for planters pre-pared by James Henry Hammond of South Carolina described the head slave driver as the most important slave on any plantation. The driver was generally charged with maintaining the work pace, schedule, and discipline among the slaves and enforcing the rules of the plantation. The master supplied him with the trappings of status and power, including high boots, a better coat than other slaves, and a whip. The driver often administered whippings, so that slaves might direct their anger for such punishment toward him, and not the master. The slave driver worked directly under the authority of the overseer who served as the master's plantation manager. Although there were a few black plantation overseers, almost all overseers were white men. On plantations without an overseer, the slave driver might be second in authority only to the master himself.

The slave driver was also an important member of the slave community. He was often the person to whom slaves could turn to settle disputes among themselves, and his influence with the master could be very useful to other slaves. If, for example, a slave wanted to leave the plantation, to stay out after curfew, to begin work later, or to leave work earlier, the driver could sometimes arrange it. He could provide extra food or better clothing for the slaves or intercede with the master for better working conditions or to secure a special holiday. Solomon Northup, who was a driver on a plantation in Louisiana for eight years, wrote of how he was able to use the power of his position to aid his fellow slaves without his master knowing. He became so skilled with the whip that he was able to simulate whippings without, however, touching the slave being punished. Although it might not be possible if the master or overseer was at close range, at other times he was able to "[throw] the lash within a hair's breath of the back, the ear, the nose, without reaching either of them." Such subterfuge, of course, required the complicity of the people being beaten, who had to act as if they were in pain.[9]

The relationship between a slave driver and the other slaves generally depended on the extent to which he was willing or able to circumvent his master's wishes. A slave driver could also use his position to the detriment of the slaves, but he did so at his own peril. Although slaves had little power, they might exercise what collective power they had to punish a driver whom they thought was unfair. A notoriously brutal or unjust driver could find himself censured by his fellow slaves who refused to associate with him or even to talk to him. Other slaves might spread rumors about a driver's competence or his honesty to the master's house, undermining his authority, or he might have a work-related accident. The driver's position forced him to balance retaining the master's trust with having the respect and cooperation of his fellow slaves.[10]

Clearly, the slaves' world was much more complicated than most slave-holders understood. The slave community supported its members as they dealt with the institution of slavery and the human relationships within it. Under the power of the planters, slaves had to depend on ingenuity, imagination, and the creative use of information. They also used whites' racial stereotypes to their advantage whenever possible. Since slaveholders generally assumed that slaves' singing connoted contentment and passivity, the slaves used music to pass along messages, to control the pace of work, to placate a suspicious master, or to subtly comment on a person or a situation for the benefit or amusement of fellow slaves. When slaves sang "patter-roll round me. Thank God he no ketch me," most other slaves understood the humorous message. Slaves referred to the slave patrols, generally made up of poor white men who did not own slaves, as "patter rollers." This song was the story of slaves who eluded the patrol by cunning and guile. A song urging slaves to "Steal away to Jesus" could alert listeners to an upcoming secret meeting, while "Swing low sweet chariot, coming for to carry me home," might tell of the possibility of rescue from bondage. Other songs about seeking freedom announced "people get ready, there's a train a comin'," or told of the "dark and thorny" pathway "beyond dis vale of sorrow" leading to "de fields of endless days." Old Testament stories of deliverance from bondage and the triumph of good over a powerful evil often provided the themes for slave songs: The walls of Jericho that Joshua destroyed became a surrogate for the bonds of slavery. The message was subtle, but the words, musical inflection, pitch, and tone told the story of the slave's suffering and determination to be free.[11]

Most of the slave songs were group creations, as one person after another added lines, harmonies, and rhythms. In the fields, songs were group perfor-mances with a leader, informally selected for that position because of a strong voice, melodic ability, and good memory for tone and words. Expressing them-selves through their music, slaves also might exert some control over their labor. Plantation work often involved a gang of slaves moving through the fields planting, weeding, cultivating, or picking. They worked as a unit, with over-seers or drivers urging them on, and to keep up the speed, overseers often pun-ished the slowest worker. Slaves, however, sometimes established their own pace and protected the weakest laborers by working to the rhythm of field chants. With the entire gang moving in unison to the steady cadence of a work song, slaves both controlled the pace of work and appealed to white people's assumptions about their contentment.

While some forms of resistance involved group action, others were personal protests. Slaveholders wanted unconditional control of their slaves, and denying them that control could be a subtle form of protest. The actions of an African named Abd al-Rahman Ibrahima illustrate a form of resistance that did not involve open defiance or violence, that might be mistaken for submission, but that enabled the slave to maintain his sense of personal dignity and self-worth.

Rahman's father ruled the warlike West African Muslim Fulbe people from the interior of present-day Guinea, and Rahman was a military leader who wore the long braids of a respected warrior. In the late eighteenth century, Rahman's enemies captured him in battle and sold him into slavery, and in 1788 Thomas Foster, a farmer in the Mississippi territory then held by Spain, bought him and another Fulbe captive for $930. Foster soon realized that his new slave had been a person of some status, as Rahman offered Foster a handsome ransom for his release. Foster refused the offer, contemptuously named his new human property Prince, and had Rahman's braids cut, a process that required several men to overcome his resistance.[12] In the tradition of his people, the removal of his warrior locks was a humiliation that reduced a proud soldier to the level of a child.

Despite this insult, Rahman did what he could to preserve his dignity and honor. When Foster demanded that Rahman work in the fields, he refused, as any warrior would be expected to do, but savage whippings revealed the impracticality of this stance. He then ran away to the woods around Foster's farm, but not knowing the territory, this too proved untenable. He contemplated suicide, but could not bring himself to commit such a flagrant breach of the teachings of the Koran. After some time, Rahman returned to Foster's farm and found Foster gone and his wife, Sarah, alone. At first Sarah was frightened by the fugitive at her door, but in an act of acceptance that became Natchez area folklore, she extended her hand. Rahman took her hand, then knelt before her and, in a gesture understood in his warrior culture as one of surrender, placed her foot on his neck.[13] In this way, Rahman came to terms with his new status. He was no longer a warrior of high position but was a slave with little control over his own life. Yet by offering his submission, he was asserting his choice, however limited, and in doing so maintained a measure of personal dignity.

In his culture and in that of other West Africans, an important mark of manhood and personal honor was one's ability to maintain self-control. Foster believed Rahman's character suited him for leadership, and he made Rahman his slave driver. Although some people might have interpreted his distinguished bearing and quiet dignity as a sign of loyalty to his master and acceptance of the legitimacy of the system that held him in bondage for forty years, Rahman never stopped resisting slavery, nor did he stop searching for a means of escape.

Just before the turn of the nineteenth century, Foster bought Isabella, an American-born Christian woman whom Rahman soon married. In 1807, a chance encounter with John Cox, a white man whom he and his father had known in Africa, changed Rahman's life. Cox at first attempted to buy Rahman's freedom, but Foster refused to sell him. Cox then became Rahman's advocate, publicizing the story of the enslavement of an African nobleman and, finally in the 1820s, winning the sympathy and support of Secretary of State Henry Clay and President John Quincy Adams. Under political pressure, Foster agreed to sell Rahman, but only if he would return to Africa. Rahman readily agreed to return home when freed, and, aided by the American Colonization Society, he embarked on a one-year fund-raising tour to secure the money to purchase his own freedom and that of his family members. He and Isabella sailed for Liberia in 1829 and, a year later, two of their nine children and five of their grandchildren made the trip. Rahman had finally gained his freedom after more than forty years in slavery, but he never made it back to his home in West Africa. There was great rejoicing when news of his return reached his nation, but within a year of his arrival, before he could make it back to his people, he died in Liberia.

For millions of slaves like Rahman, resistance was more private and less violent than open rebellion. Running away was one common form of revolt, and although some escape attempts were well planned over time, often the decision was made suddenly, the result of some traumatic event. A slave suffering an unjust punishment, too ill to work at the required pace, or fearing sale and separation from family might choose to run away. One North Carolina slave attempted to escape with her two children after her master branded her face with a hot poker.[14] Spontaneous escapes, without preparation and often with limited information, were likely to end in failure. Sometimes fugitives went only as far as the nearby woods or swamps to evade slavery for a few days, but there were short-distance escapes that lasted longer. In the late 1820s, while hunting for birds, naturalist John James Audubon met a runaway slave in the swamps of Louisiana. The man had been camping in the swamp with his wife

A family of slaves escapes to freedom in a painting by Eastman Johnson. Since families were often split up when slaves were sold to different owners, the preservation of family unity was often a strong motivating force for escaping slaves. Johnson specialized for a time in genre paintings of black life in the South, and one writer commented that his paintings demonstrate "the affection, the humor, the patience and serenity which redeem from brutality and ferocity the civilized though subjugated African."

and three children for over a year. Seated in the camp after dinner, the man doused the fire and, in the darkness, told Audubon a tale that was typical of the reasons many slaves ran away. The slave family's master had suffered financial losses and put up his slaves for auction. The overseer had bought the man and a planter one hundred miles away had bought his wife. The children had been scattered on different plantations along the river, sold for high prices, it was said, because of their good breeding. One night during a storm, the man escaped to the swamp, and then he spent the next few weeks gathering his family. When Audubon discovered them, they were hungry and in desperate straits. Slave friends on their old plantation about ten miles away had generously given the family what little food they could spare and had provided them with ammunition for the ancient gun the man had found. Sympathizing with the family's plight, Audubon pledged his aid. He convinced the man to return with him to his first master, and prevailed upon the master to repurchase the family.[15]

Having a family made it much more difficult for slaves like the fugitives Audubon encountered to run away. A master angered by losing a slave might take retribution on the fugitive's family. On the other hand, attempting to escape with a family, especially with young children, made an already-difficult task nearly impossible. Thus, most of those who escaped from slavery were unmarried young men from their mid-teens to mid-twenties. Newspaper ads placed by masters indicate that runaways were most likely to be strong healthy, young men. By the time women had reached their mid- to late teenage years, they were likely to be mothers encumbered by children. Analyses of runaway ads indicate that some fugitives were mothers and their children, but they represented only a small percentage of those who attempted escape and an even smaller percentage of those who were successful. A mother's situation was often especially heartbreaking. Would she resign herself to remaining a slave or leave her children behind with friends or relatives? This was a dreadful decision for a mother, even if she knew that someone in the slave community would become her children's guardian if she were sold away or escaped.[16]

Sidney Steel remained a slave in Maryland after her husband managed to purchase his freedom. The couple planned her escape with their four children, but their hopes for freedom for the entire family were foiled when Sidney and the children were captured and returned to Maryland. For months Sidney's master watched closely to ensure that she would not attempt another escape. After a number of months she finally found her chance, but it was clear that a second attempt with all of the children would be impossible. This time Sidney decided to leave the two older children, Levin and Peter, in slavery, while she struck out for freedom with the two younger girls. As Sidney later told her family, on the night of her escape, she went to her sons' bed, and while they slept she "kissed them—consigned then into the hands of God and took her departure again for the land of liberty." She and the girls made it to freedom in New Jersey, but soon after her escape, the master sold her two sons to slaveholders in the Deep South.[17]

Slavery regularly forced parents into such heartrending decisions. Since slaveholders owned adult slaves and their children, slave parents could provide only limited parental protection. Their children might be mistreated, unjustly punished, worked mercilessly, or sold away, and there was little that slave par-

A female slave throws herself out of a window. Suicide was an extreme form of slave resistance throughout the institution's history, beginning when captured Africans threw themselves overboard to escape the horrors of the Middle Passage.

ents could do. Sometimes, in despair, they resorted to drastic measures. In 1856 Margaret Garner, her husband, and members of their extended family escaped from slavery in Kentucky. They crossed the frozen Ohio River to the free state of Ohio, where they joined nine other fugitives from Kentucky. The group then traveled to Cincinnati, where they stopped at the home of a free black relative. In Cincinnati, however, slave catchers trapped the party, and, not able to bear the thought of her children growing up in slavery, Margaret decided they would be better off dead. She managed to kill her baby before the slave catchers stopped her from killing the others. She later asserted that she would have killed all her children if she had had time.[18]

The vast majority of slaves were determined to survive the horrors of slavery, but for a few in utter despair, life seemed unendurable. Suicide was the most drastic means of denying a slaveholder's authority. It was so common among the newly enslaved during the Middle Passage from Africa to America that slave ship captains took special precautions, stringing netting on deck to keep slaves from jumping into the ocean. Masters of newly arrived Africans kept vigilant watch to ensure that they did not commit suicide during the first days of their enslavement in America. Charles Ball told the story of an African from the Congo named Paul whom he met in the swampy woods while he was enslaved in South Carolina. Paul told him how his capture had torn him from his wife, four children, and widowed mother in Africa. Severe whippings after two previous escape attempts had not diminished Paul's determination to be free, so his master had him fitted with an iron collar with bells attached to a bar over his head. This contraption was extremely uncomfortable, and the noise of the bells continuously marked his whereabouts. Still, Paul managed to escape again and had been wandering in the woods for almost a month when Ball found him. He was tired, weak, and almost starved, unable to catch game because the bells frightened animals away before he could reach them. Touched by Paul's plight, Ball promised to return on his next day off with a file to unlock the collar. When he returned a week later, Ball found that Paul had hanged himself. His body was protected from scavenger birds by the ringing of the bells.[19]

Suicide was rare among African American slaves; few gave up all hope. The vast majority managed some resistance to the dehumanizing and emotion-numbing impact of slavery. Relationships to family and community, humor, and music all became weapons of resistance. Sometimes escaping for a short time was a means of psychic survival, and many who ran away did so without intending more than a temporary respite. Thousands of slaves, however, sought a more permanent escape. Most were recaptured, but the prospect of freedom was a strong incentive. Some runaways found sanctuary with Native Americans in the southern interior, in the swamps of Florida, Louisiana, and North Carolina, or on the western fringes of the slave states. Others escaped to New Orleans, Charleston, or other southern port cities, where they stowed away on vessels sailing to the North or the West Indies. The temptation to strike out for freedom was strong, especially for those in the Upper South, where free states were close,

This engraving shows a number of slaves escaping from the Eastern Shore of Maryland and heading north to the free states. The Underground Railroad leader Harriet Tubman took this route to freedom and inspired countless others to escape by the same route.

sometimes just across the river. Nothing was more inspiring for slaves in Maryland and Virginia than knowing that the free state of Pennsylvania was close at hand or more thrilling for slaves in Kentucky or Missouri than seeing freedom on the opposite bank of the river in Ohio or Illinois.

The decision to attempt escape was never easy, even for those in the Upper South. The road to freedom was often obscure, and a fugitive needed information about travel routes, finding and identifying those willing to assist, and what to expect in the way of weather and social climate beyond the plantation. Escape often meant leaving family and friends behind and facing terrible punishment from an irate master if they were caught. In many communities in the free states, organized groups, often called vigilance committees, worked to shelter fugitives, but runaways first had to reach them. Vigilance committees were part of the legendary Underground Railroad. This movement dedicated to aiding fugitives from slavery took its name from recent technology, the railroad train that developed during the 1830s and 1840s. The terms associated with the new railroad became the code words used by these secret organizations. They called escape routes rails, safe houses stations, and the fugitives themselves passengers or packages. Those who assisted fugitives called themselves conductors.

An underground railroad station in Union City, Michigan. This area of central Michigan had a steady traffic of fugitives fleeing north toward Canada.

From the mid-nineteenth century into the twentieth century, the Underground Railroad became one of the most romanticized chapters in American history. As it was told, the story emphasized the role of organized groups, generally white and often Quakers, helping fugitives. People escaping from slavery were most often depicted as passive victims who were guided to freedom by the operators of the Underground Railroad. In reality, from the start, the fugitives played the most active role in the process risking escape and making their way to areas where they might contact organized assistance. Many of those blacks and whites who aided fugitives, especially in the slave states, were not part of any formally organized group but were simply compassionate human beings willing to take risks in order to help a fellow human being in need.

In the 1850s, Thomas Fitzgerald, a free African American in Chester County, Pennsylvania, informally became a part of the Underground Railroad, though he was never part of an organized group. Chester County, located in southern Pennsylvania near the border of Maryland, had a continual stream of fugitive slave traffic, and the Fitzgerald farm became a popular stopping place for those on the run. A Fitzgerald descendent wrote, "Great-Grandfather Thomas noticed that his barn began to attract a lot of strangers." Occasionally, when black travelers asked for overnight lodging in the barn, Fitzgerald offered them a room in the house, but the strangers never accepted. Nor did they remain for the morning breakfast he always offered, although after their departure, he always "thought one of his cows gave a quart less milk than usual."[20]

Fugitives often turned to fellow blacks, slave or free, for help, and while there were exceptions, they generally received aid. Reportedly, Thomas Fitzgerald and his family "were not joiners of reform movements but they were stubborn in what they believed to be right." They believed slavery was wrong, and like so many other little-known blacks, "without fanfare...met the issue squarely when it confronted them."[21] It was this kind of help that a slave named Fed depended on for his successful escape. Fed had been born in Virginia but was sold away from his mother when he was ten years old, weighed and sold "by the pound" to a Georgia trader because his owner needed money to help construct his new house. Fed was cruelly used by his Georgia master, who punished him for one infraction by kicking him in the face, breaking his nose and dislocating his eye. As he grew older, Fed made two unsuccessful escape attempts before he managed to evade capture and make his way by foot through the Louisiana swamps and up the Mississippi River to St. Louis, Missouri.[22]

STATE of SOUTH-CAROLINA.

KNOW ALL MEN by these Presents, That I Stephen Tinker of the City New York Mariner

for and in Consideration of the Sum of Fifty one Guineas

to me in Hand paid at and before the Sealing and Delivery of these Presents, by William Gibbons Junior of the State Georgia — the Receipt whereof I do hereby acknowledge, have bargained and sold, and by these Presents, do bargain, sell, and deliver unto the said William Gibbons

One Negroe Man Slave named Ceasar

TO HAVE AND TO HOLD the said Negroe Man Ceasar

unto the said William Gibbons his

Executors, Administrators and Assigns, to his and their only proper Use and Behoof for ever. And I the said Stephen Tinker my Executors and Administrators, the said bargained premises unto the said William Gibbons his Executors, Administrators and Assigns, from and against all Persons shall and will warrant and for ever defend by these Presents. In witness whereof, I have hereunto set My Hand and Seal, Dated at Charleston on the Fifteenth Day of July in the Year of our Lord One Thousand Seven Hundred and Eighty Five and in the Tenth Year of the Independence of the United States of America.

Signed, Sealed and Delivered, in the Presence of

Stephen Tinker

Tho Ham Sen

A 1785 contract from Charleston, South Carolina, gave one Joseph Gibbons the power to search out and return an escaped slave, Caesar, to his owner, William Gibbons.

In St. Louis, a black cook on a river steamer gave Fed food and information about the city. He took refuge in the outhouse of a black minister, afraid to make himself known to the minister lest he place him in danger. After crossing the river to Illinois, Fed found a black man named Caesar who lived in the neighborhood. Caesar gave him food and shelter for the night, advised him about the countryside, and told him what to say if confronted by a white man. He also gave Fed the name and location of a black friend from North Carolina farther along his escape route who would give him assistance. After a few close calls, he arrived at the home of Caesar's friend, who took him in and wrote out a "free pass" for him in the name of John Brown.

After traveling another week, Fed, now Brown, happened upon the brother of the minister whom he had met in St. Louis, who took him home, gave him some food, and directed him to a rural black community where he would be safe for a while. Brown spent two weeks there and then set off for Indianapolis. In that city, a black man looked closely at him, recognized him, and told him that he was in great danger. His master had covered the region with advertisements for his apprehension, complete with a drawing that was a good likeness of him. Though it was dangerous, the man took Brown home with him and told him about the local Underground Railroad. Finally after more than nine months of travel and much informal aid, the man directed Brown to one of the station managers of the Underground Railroad thirty miles away. Reaching the town the following morning, Brown sought out the black man who was his contact, and the man directed him to his

This sketch of John Brown was the frontispiece to Slave Life in Georgia, *his autobiography of his thirty years as a slave in Virginia, North Carolina, and Georgia. The book was first published in London in 1855 by the British and Foreign Anti-Slavery Society.*

first stop on the Underground Railroad. The Quaker family to which he was directed hid him for a few days and then escorted him to another safe house. In this way, he was passed along until he found safety in Michigan. Brown worked in Michigan for a few years, settled briefly in Canada, and then made his way to England and the antislavery lecture circuit, where he told enthusiastic audiences about the trials of slavery and his adventures on the Underground Railroad.[23]

The more organized efforts that more closely fit the romantic legend of the Underground Railroad were frequently interracial activities. Blacks, especially those who had been slaves and had critical knowledge of slavery, often formed partnerships with white abolitionists who brought important social and political contacts and crucial financial resources to the movement. Ripley, Ohio, about fifty miles east of Cincinnati, was a small Ohio River town with a reputation for sheltering fugitives who could make their way across the river. It was in an area partly populated by Virginia slaves who settled in the free state of Ohio after being freed by their masters' wills. Ripley's free blacks and a few white allies ran an active Underground Railroad operation, and one of the most dedicated of the white abolitionists was a Presbyterian minister named John Rankin. Rankin's home on the bluffs, one hundred wooden steps above the Ohio River and a little more than two hundred yards from the Kentucky shore, became a station on Ohio's Underground Railroad. John Parker, a former slave born in Norfolk, Virginia, worked with Rankin and financed much of the Underground Railroad

The John Rankin house, an important stop on the Underground Railroad in Ripley in southern Ohio. Rankin, his wife, and their neighbors sheltered more than two thousand slaves on their escape to freedom.

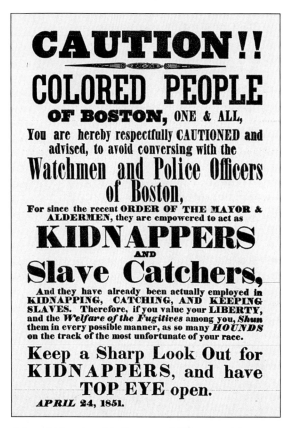

CAUTION!!

COLORED PEOPLE
OF BOSTON, ONE & ALL,
You are hereby respectfully CAUTIONED and advised, to avoid conversing with the
Watchmen and Police Officers of Boston,
For since the recent ORDER OF THE MAYOR & ALDERMEN, they are empowered to act as
KIDNAPPERS
AND
Slave Catchers,
And they have already been actually employed in KIDNAPPING, CATCHING, AND KEEPING SLAVES. Therefore, if you value your LIBERTY, and the *Welfare of the Fugitives* among you, *Shun* them in every possible manner, as so many *HOUNDS* on the track of the most unfortunate of your race.

Keep a Sharp Look Out for KIDNAPPERS, and have TOP EYE open.
APRIL 24, 1851.

A broadside printed in Boston in 1851 warned free blacks as well as escaped slaves to be aware of the danger posed by kidnappers. The draconian Fugitive Slave Act of 1850 had abolished many basic safeguards, meaning that it was easy for free black people accused of being escaped slaves to be captured as fugitives.

activity in Ripley with the profits from his successful foundry business. Working to shelter fugitives was always dangerous, but it was especially so for a black man; yet Parker risked his own freedom by traveling into slave territory to lead fugitives to safety. Ripley was an important center of Underground Railroad activity because it was only eight miles upriver from Maysville, Kentucky, a trading center for grain, hemp, tobacco, and slaves. One Lexington, Kentucky, newspaper in the late 1830s blamed abolitionists in Ripley and other Ohio River towns for the depreciation of slave property by "twenty percent in all the counties bordering the Ohio River." After Kentucky revoked its ban on the importation of slaves in 1849, slave traders brought a steady stream of enslaved African Americans into the state to be sold or traded to the lucrative markets farther South.[24]

The determination of slaves to be free and the success of the Underground Railroad in border areas spawned the distasteful but lucrative trade of slave hunter. Slave hunters roamed the countryside in search of runaways, hoping to collect the rewards offered for the capture and return of runaways. Free African Americans were also vulnerable to slave hunters and opportunists with few scruples about kidnapping northern blacks and selling them into slavery. Blacks could be in danger if they ran afoul of virtually any white person with authority. Edwin Heathcock, a black workman in Chicago, had a disagreement with his employer in 1842 and found himself under arrest as a potential fugitive. Illinois state law provided that any black person unable to prove his or her free status must be arrested and held until claimed. A city ordinance instructed police officials to sell at auction the labor of a suspected fugitive unable to pay the cost of board for the period of incarceration. Heathcock was penniless and thus was placed for auction. Initially, the crowd sympathized with Heathcock, and no one offered to buy him. Then the sheriff, pleading the crowd's forgiveness for being forced by the law to engage in the distasteful business of "man selling," explained that if no one bid for Heathcock, he would be put in jail until the cost of his imprisonment was paid. At that point white abolitionist Mahlon Ogden stepped forward to offer the sum of 25 cents, and the deal was concluded. As Heathcock's legal owner, Ogden promptly set the man free.[25]

Philadelphia was another active area for the Underground Railroad, and black abolitionist William Still led the vigilance committee there. Still was born in New Jersey, but both his parents had been slaves. His mother, Sidney, had changed her name to Still after her escape from slavery in Maryland. One day in his office, William encountered a former slave from Alabama who called himself Peter Freedman. Freedman was searching for his family, and as the two talked, it became clear to William that Peter was his own older brother whom his mother had left behind in slavery when she escaped. Peter told William that their other brother, Levin, had died nearly twenty years before, and that Peter

had managed to buy his own freedom. He had then begun to earn the money to buy his wife and three children, who were still in slavery. Meanwhile, he had set out to find his mother and father. William listened to Peter's story with intense emotion and then took him to be reunited with their mother and to meet his five brothers and three sisters.[26]

Harriet Tubman, perhaps the most famous conductor on the Underground Railroad, worked closely with William Still. Tubman had escaped from slavery on the Eastern Shore of Maryland in 1849, when she was in her twenties. She had heard rumors that she was about to be sold away from her husband, a free black man, and the rest of her family, who were also enslaved. Rather than face the auction, she ran away. A local white woman gave her directions to a house where she would be safe and wrote the names of two people who would help her on a paper. Helped by these strangers, she made her way to Philadelphia, where she met William Still and learned

William Still, for fourteen years a leader of the Underground Railroad in Philadelphia, assisted and interviewed hundreds of fugitives making their way north. After hiding his illegal notes, he published the interviews in book form in 1873.

about the area's Underground Railroad. Two of her sisters had been sold south, and Tubman became determined to rescue her other family members before they, too, were lost to her. Beginning in 1850, she made many trips back to Maryland, risking her own freedom to bring out her relatives and many other slaves.

Tubman was so successful that she became notorious in the Upper South, and a reward was offered for her arrest. Among black people, she became known for her daring rescues, complicated plans, and determination. As she walked down the road, she would sing slave spirituals, like "Steal Away" or "Bound for the Promised Land," with coded meanings to inform her charges about their impending escape. If her pursuers were close behind, she sometimes would take a train going south, on the theory that the slaveowner would not look for runaways heading in that direction. She was a small woman who was very strong but had the ability to look old and decrepit—not the person southern slaveholders would suspect of being the legendary Harriet Tubman. Although she suffered from short lapses of consciousness as the result of a head injury suffered when she was young and rewards for her capture were widely advertised, no one she helped ever was caught.[27]

Tubman performed some of the Underground Railroad's most daring rescues, using an extensive network of stations through Maryland, Delaware, New Jersey, Pennsylvania, and New York. One time she brought a large group of eleven people, including her brother and his wife, out of Maryland to safety in Canada. After her father was implicated in helping escaping slaves by a man who ran away but became afraid and returned, she extricated her elderly parents from slavery by constructing a crude one-horse–drawn buggy to take them to the railroad station. During her dangerous career as an Underground Railroad conductor in the 1850s, Tubman depended on the money she earned from work as a domestic servant, help from other abolitionists, and her unshakable faith in God's guiding hand. She worked closely with the dedicated, self-sacrificing white Quaker, Thomas Garrett in Wilmington, Delaware, and counted on him to have the money or clothing she needed for her charges. Tubman's safety depended on maintaining secrecy about her activities, but she was well known to a circle of prominent abolitionists in New England who supported her efforts. In exchange for their support, she regaled them with stories of her adventures on the Underground Railroad.

Both fugitives from slavery and many northern freeborn blacks, such as William Still, had personal ties to people enslaved in the South. By the early

1860s, 90 percent of African Americans were enslaved, and with so many people in slavery, many of those who were free had friends or family members in slavery. Thus, nearly all black people had a personal interest in abolition. Free blacks were leaders in the Underground Railroad and in other aspects of the antislavery struggle. When militant white abolitionist William Lloyd Garrison began his newspaper, *The Liberator,* on January 1, 1831, just a few months prior to Nat Turner's revolt, he

Henry "Box" Brown emerges from the crate in which he shipped himself to Philadelphia from Richmond, Virginia, where he is greeted by William Still and other Philadelphia abolitionists. His brave and creative escape made him a celebrated figure.

entered an antislavery arena already organized by black abolitionists. With his newspaper, Garrison, probably the most radical white abolitionist of his time, became a lightning rod for southern antiabolitionist anger. The Georgia House of Representatives offered a reward of $5,000 for him, a fortune by mid-nineteenth-century standards, and South Carolina offered a $1,500 reward for the arrest of anyone distributing *The Liberator.* Many whites saw Garrison as a danger to both slavery and American racial traditions. He associated publicly with black friends, advocated racial equality, and was widely adored by African Americans for his commitment to freedom and racial justice. Garrison held his meeting to form the New England Anti-slavery Society in Boston in 1832 in the African Meeting House, the city's first black church. The society was integrated from the beginning, merging with the older Massachusetts General Colored Association, a black antislavery organization established in 1826.

Garrison's commitment was important to the gradual integration of the general abolition movement. His American Anti-slavery Society, a national umbrella organization formed in 1833, had prominent black members among its leadership. The talks by such articulate black abolitionists as Frederick Douglass, Sojourner Truth, and William Wells Brown, sponsored by the American Anti-slavery Society, were especially effective in winning northern

converts to the antislavery cause. Even black children became part of the movement. In several northern cities, African Americans founded youth associations,
where boys and girls debated questions of racial justice and antislavery and
raised money for antislavery activities. Boston's Juvenile Garrison Independent
Society, a singing group, performed at antislavery rallies and helped raise
money for local African American mutual aid societies. A New York City group
included a promise to work toward "the downfall of prejudice, slavery, and
oppression" in its constitution.[28] Students at New York's African Free School
took an oath that after graduation they would "go South, start an insurrection
and free our brethren in bondage." Indeed, several of those students became
influential abolitionists in later life.[29] Black students in Cincinnati were asked
to write an essay on the question, "What do you think most about?" One seven-
year-old wrote, "We get a man to get the poor slaves from bondage." A twelve-
year-old explained the students' dedication, writing, "what we are studying for
is to get the yoke of slavery broke and the chains parted asunder and slaveholding cease for ever [sic]."[30]

The commitment of northern free blacks to the struggle against slavery was
strengthened by communications that moved secretly from slaves to free people and
back throughout this period. Notes and letters were carried by African Americans,
or sometimes white allies, who traveled between the slave and free states.
Members of Richmond's First African Baptist Church kept in touch with friends
and relatives who had escaped to the North. "Several servants escaped to the North
from their masters," explained one church member, and "wrote back to Richmond
to their former comrades . . . detailing the manner of their escape and proposing
to them facilities and information for the same experiment." Eventually, local
authorities discovered their secret message system and closed it off, but another
opened to fill the void. Many underground communications networks depended
on black seamen and boatmen. African Americans had worked in water transport since colonial times, working on whaling crews and serving aboard ocean-
trade vessels and riverboats. In seaport and river port cities, such as Boston,
New Bedford, New York, and Cincinnati, large numbers of black men worked
on the docks. In the South, some slaves worked on the crews of riverboats or
coastal vessels or on the docks, and all of these men had access to information
and contacts with outsiders seldom available to plantation slaves.

Despite the efforts of southern authorities, many free black sailors from
the northern states, the West Indies, and England put ashore and spent time

between voyages in the black communities of southern ports. They passed along news from the outside and carried communications to specific people from common friends and acquaintances in the North. Boatmen who frequently traveled between northern ports and the South were particularly important as regular message carriers. One Cincinnati woman kept in touch with her enslaved mother for more than three decades through messages smuggled by black boatmen. During these years she consulted her mother about her choice of a husband and informed her of the birth of her children. Thus, in 1843 the news of her grandchild's enrollment at Oberlin Collegiate Institute found the proud grandmother in a Mississippi slave hut, bound in body, she reported, but free in spirit.[31]

Relationships across the boundary of slavery and freedom could be difficult and sometimes extremely complex. During the 1830s, Henry Williams escaped from slavery in Louisiana, and eventually he settled in Cincinnati. He found work and became a part of that city's free black community of more than two thousand people. Eventually, Henry met and married an Ohio woman, but he drew strong criticism from his fellow members at Cincinnati's Union Baptist Church, who objected to his marriage because they knew that he had had a wife in slavery in New Orleans. Despite Henry's difficult situation, the congregation charged him with bigamy for having "deserted" his wife in slavery and demanded that he obtain a signed release from her before his new marriage could be sanctioned. Henry's problem was obvious. How could a fugitive in Cincinnati safely contact a slave in New Orleans to secure a signed document? Henry found the answer in the underground communication network. He contacted his first wife through a boatman who regularly traveled to New Orleans. The boatman brought Henry a document signed with her X granting an end to the marriage, and the church recognized Henry's new relationship.[32]

The organization of black abolition, integrated antislavery organizations, and antislavery newspapers in the North put southern slavery under increasing attack. Facing calls for immediate and unconditional emancipation, southern supporters of slavery closed ranks and, by the 1830s, permitted less and less internal dissent. Earlier, opinion in the Upper South had been divided about slavery's desirability. Some supporters, like Thomas Jefferson, had considered it merely a necessary evil, essential for controlling the black population. Justifications for slavery in a democratic, freedom-loving society rested on arguments that it was an ancient institution that had existed in all great civilizations, that it was crucially important to the southern economy, and that blacks were naturally suited for slavery by genetic inferiority. Beginning in the 1820s, slavery's proponents developed new arguments, building on the old foundation but adding the power of theology and science to slavery's defense.

The debates sparked when western representatives to the Virginia legislature raised the issue of emancipation in the state after Nat Turner's rebellion gave new impetus to southern theorists' efforts to build a convincing case for the importance of maintaining slavery. Prominent southern politicians, clergymen, and academics presented a more positive view of slavery, as something not only necessary but also good for African Americans and for the entire society. Plantation dwellers, they said, were like an extended family, and the planter was the family's benevolent

This map from the 1850s sharply divides the United States into slave and free states, and compares the two regions through a range of statistics—not just population and congressional representation, but also size and value of farmland, number of newspapers and public libraries, and lengths of canals and railroads.

patriarch. South Carolina planter, congressman, governor, and then U. S. senator James Henry Hammond argued that the planter's fatherly protection of his workers assured the stable economy upon which the country's wealth depended. Ministers found support for the slave system in biblical references to slavery and in a racial interpretation of the story of Noah and the "curse" of Ham. Thomas R. Dew, the president of the College of William and Mary in Virginia, contended that without slavery, the revolts of degraded and desperate workers would create anarchy and destroy democratic government. Dew further argued that stability and orderly progress required the worldwide reintroduction of slavery. Scientists theorized that blacks and whites were separate species, an idea that physician and scientist Josiah C. Nott carried to its extreme by the 1850s with the declaration that blacks were created to be slaves.[33]

Southern apologists for slavery clung to their beliefs about the necessity and benevolence of slavery even though their arguments contradicted the principles of natural rights, individual freedom, and equality that underlay American democracy. Their contentions were also contradicted by the realities of slave life, the frequency of slave resistance, and occasionally by full-blown slave revolts. To fortify the theories in the face of such contradictions, southern thought came to emphasize authority over individualism, security over liberty, law over natural rights, and stability over free labor. Apologists for slavery decried Thomas Jefferson's championing of equality, according to James Henry Hammond, a foolish idea that had been taken up by the "ignorant, uneducated, semi-barbarous mass" in post-Revolutionary France.[34]

In an effort to keep southern slaves uncontaminated by antislavery ideas, southern politicians set out to restrict the movements of northern black sailors in southern ports, assemblages of southern free blacks, postal delivery of antislavery writings, and expressions of antislavery sentiment in the U.S. Congress. Responding to Congress's adoption of protective tariffs on manufactured goods in 1828 and 1832, and fearful of a strong federal government that could attack slavery, southern political forces led by South Carolinian John C. Calhoun expounded the doctrine that states could nullify federal law and threatened secession from the federal union. In 1835, northern abolitionists began their "great postal campaign," vowing to mail their pamphlets and newspapers to every village and town in the country. Southern postmasters reacted by intercepting antislavery literature, a mob in Charleston seized bags of mail containing abolitionist writings and set them on fire, and Georgia passed a law providing for the death penalty for anyone distributing material inciting slave rebellion. President Andrew Jackson urged Congress to ban abolitionist material from the mail. In the North, well-organized mobs led by "gentlemen of property and standing" physically attacked abolitionist gatherings and newspaper editors.[35] In October 1835, William Lloyd Garrison was dragged through the streets of Boston by such a mob, and in 1837 in Alton, Illinois, a small Mississippi River town near the slave state of Missouri, another newspaper editor, Elijah P. Lovejoy, was murdered by a proslavery mob. The abolitionist press recorded 160 instances of violence against antislavery forces between 1833 and 1838.[36]

Southern assaults on free speech gained attention for the antislavery cause, helping convince many northerners that the growing power of slavery's defenders was dangerous to civil liberties. A reinvigorated petition campaign took antislavery advocates door to door in rural areas and towns throughout the North, bringing the antislavery message to people's homes and asking them to commit to the abolition of slavery in the District of Columbia, an end to the internal slave trade, and a ban on the admission of any more slave states to the United States. Thousands of women engaged in this political action, and women numbered more than half of the petition signers. In 1836, abolitionists sent petitions with more than 30,000 signatures to Congress, and in response, the House of Representatives passed a gag rule providing for the tabling of antislavery petitions without discussion. In 1837, the American Anti-slavery Society announced a larger and more fervent petition effort, and after a brief hiatus, the House renewed the "gag rule." During the year following the announcement of the new petition campaign, abolitionists sent petitions with more than 400,000 signatures to federal legislators. They sent 400,000 the following year, and by 1840, more than two million people had signed antislavery petitions. The gag rule remained in effect until the end of 1844.[37]

Try as they might, southern planters could not keep news of the growing abolition movement from their slaves. As a twelve-year-old slave in Maryland, Frederick Bailey learned to read and write, first from his mistress and then by offering white children rewards for teaching him their lessons. Hearing slave owners condemn abolitionists for causing trouble with their slave property, he eagerly sought out a newspaper to find out more about abolitionism. Newspaper accounts of abolitionist petitions to Congress informed him that there were northerners committed to ridding the country of slavery, and they inspired him to seek his own freedom. He did finally escape from Baltimore in 1838,

This 1850 cartoon attacks a number of interests seen as dangerous for the Union, including abolitionism and the Free-Soil Party, which opposed the admission of any further slave states to the union. From left, Free-Soil advocate David Wilmot, abolitionist William Lloyd Garrison, Southern rights spokesman Senator John C. Calhoun, and anti-slavery journalist Horace Greeley are cooking up trouble like the witches in Macbeth, *throwing their dangerous beliefs into the simmering pot. The traitorous Benedict Arnold rises from under the pot, congratulating his servants.*

when he was about twenty years old, with the help of his fiancée, a free black woman named Anna Murray. After reaching the free states, he found shelter in New York City with David Ruggles, a free black man who was the head of the local vigilance committee, a man always ready to assist and encourage fugitive slaves. Bailey married Anna and moved to New Bedford, Massachusetts. To make it more difficult for his master to track him, and to celebrate his new freedom, Frederick Bailey changed his name to Frederick Douglass. In Massachusetts, William Lloyd Garrison heard Douglass tell of his experiences in slavery and invited him to speak at an antislavery convention in 1841. Douglass's eloquence and passion electrified his audience, and the American Anti-slavery Society hired him as a regular lecturer, beginning the antislavery career of one of America's best-known and most influential abolitionists.

By 1845, Douglass gained an even wider audience for the story of his enslavement and escape to freedom when he published the *Narrative of the Life of Frederick Douglass.* Douglass was an especially effective antislavery speaker because he could give a first-person account of the institution. As he said, "I can

Frederick Douglass, author of the most influential African American autobiography of his era, the Narrative of the Life of Frederick Douglass: Written by Himself, *first published in 1845. By 1850 around 30,000 copies of the* Narrative *had been sold in the United States and Great Britain.*

tell you what I have seen with my own eyes, felt on my own person, and know to have occurred in my own neighborhood." In a letter to his former master, he recounted the painful memories: "I remember the chain, the gag, the bloody whip, the death-like gloom overshadowing the broken spirit of the fettered bondman, the appalling liability of his being torn away from wife and children, and sold like a beast in the market."38 Women's rights advocate Elizabeth Cady Stanton described the forcefulness of Douglass's oratory during a Boston lecture:

> He stood there like an African prince, majestic in his wrath, as with wit, satire and indignation he graphically described the bitterness of slavery and the humiliation of subjection to those who... were inferior to himself. Thus it was that I first saw Frederick Douglass, and wondered that any mortal man should have ever tried to subjugate a being with such talents, intensified with the love of liberty.39

Frederick Douglass, tall, handsome, and strongly built, standing in front of an audience recounting his heart-rending tales of bondage and his longing for freedom, was indeed a powerful argument for abolition.

From the nation's beginning, there was contention over whether the institution of slavery would be extended as the country expanded. In the 1840s and 1850s the contest between proslavery and antislavery forces was also conducted in the arena of fugitive slave recovery or protection. For southern slaveholders, the major issue was their ability to recover runaway slaves. They also wanted to be able to travel freely with their slave property in northern free states, where they often spent the summer away from the South's unhealthy climate. Many northern states passed laws called personal liberty laws, generally beginning with attempts to protect free blacks from kidnapping. Such laws often included measures to keep slavery out of their state, and some protected fugitives and people who helped them escape. Many state personal liberty laws in the eighteenth and nineteenth centuries guaranteed African Americans accused of being runaways such legal rights as the right to a habeas corpus proceeding, the right to counsel, the right to a trial by jury, and the right to testify in their own defense. From 1788 to 1847 Pennsylvania passed various such laws, one of which was struck down by the U.S. Supreme Court in *Prigg v. Pennsylvania* (1842). In response to the *Prigg* ruling, Massachusetts in 1843 and Pennsylvania in 1847 refused to allow any state officials or facilities to be used in the capture and rendition of fugitive slaves. Pennsylvania's 1847 law also repealed the provision protecting slaveholders' right to keep slaves in the state so long as they stayed no longer than six months.[40]

African American sailors, free blacks who lived near the border of slave states, or black children were in particular danger of being kidnapped. Notorious gangs operated in Pennsylvania across the border from Maryland, for example, and cases of kidnapping reportedly increased as cotton prices rose or as the opening of new territory to slavery provided a new market for slaves. Solomon Northup, a free black man from New York State, was kidnapped in 1841. His father, Mintus, had been in slavery in Rhode Island, brought to New York State by the Northup family, and freed by his master's will in about 1800. Solomon Northup grew up on a farm, but at age thirty-two was a musician who played his violin at hotels in Saratoga Springs, New York, during the summer resort season. Two white men offered him a job as a musician during the winter of 1841, promising lucrative employment if he would accompany them first to New York City and then to Washington. Northup had little reason to be suspicious, as the men insisted that he obtain freedom papers from New York officials before he ventured into the South. Once in Washington, however, the men drugged his drink, robbed him of his money and identification, and sold him to a local slave dealer. Northup's protestations of his freedom brought him only whipping, and he soon learned to be careful with whom he shared his story.[41]

Solomon Northup was caught up in the internal slave trade; the slave dealers carried him to southern Virginia and then to a ship bound for the New Orleans slave market. On the ship there were two other men who had been kidnapped, one from Ohio and another from Virginia, and the three men plotted a revolt. They could not carry out their mutiny, however, because one of the plotters contracted smallpox and died. Northup did manage to confide in a sailor, a young Englishman from Boston, who found him a pen and paper and promised to deliver a letter to Henry B. Northup, a white member of the former slaveholding family, who could intercede with authorities and tell his wife and children what had happened to him. After receiving the letter sometime later,

Henry B. Northup took it to New York governor William H. Seward, but the two men decided they could not do anything then, since they did not know where Northup was to be enslaved. At the New Orleans slave market, Northup and his fellow slaves were paraded around for prospective buyers. He had to demonstrate his muscles and agility and show that he had strong healthy teeth. He discovered that he had been given the name of Platt to complete his transformation to a new identity, and undoubtedly to make him harder to trace. A Baptist preacher named Ford bought him, a man Northup described as a kindly master, but the following year he learned how precarious life was in slavery. Ford agreed to cover his brother's indebtedness, and in order to do so, sold eighteen slaves, Solomon Northup among them.[42]

Northup had a succession of cruel masters as he worked in Louisiana fields growing cotton and sugar and as a carpenter. His tragic situation was lightened only by his ability to play music, for which he was sometimes hired out, and by the friendship of fellow slaves. After nine years in slavery he was finally able to obtain a piece of paper and made some ink with which to write a note to his family, but he was betrayed by a white laborer and had to destroy it. It was two more years before Solomon Northup found someone he trusted. He was working on the plantation with a white carpenter from Canada named Samuel Bass, whose objections to slavery were tolerated by local whites as part of his eccentric personality. Northup told Bass his story, and they met secretly for short times at night to plan how to get word to New York authorities and Northup's family. Bass promised to write to Northup's family, and if necessary, to go to New York himself for the necessary papers to gain Northup's freedom. About five months later, Henry B. Northup, after considerable searching, arrived with the local sheriff to set Solomon Northup free. Northup was reunited with his family in January 1853, having endured the horrors of slavery in the Deep South for twelve years.

Conflict over kidnapping, fugitives, and slaveholder rights grew more heated with the passage of the federal Fugitive Slave Act of 1850. The law was one of five separate measures that constituted the Compromise of 1850, laws designed to reassure slaveholders that their rights were protected and to cool sectional tensions. Congress admitted California as a free state, provided popular sovereignty on slavery in the western territory, assumed Texas's debt, abolished the slave trade, though not slavery, in the District of Columbia, and established a stronger new fugitive slave law. With this fugitive slave law, recovering a fugitive became simply an administrative procedure in the hands of federal commissioners; much of the cost of recovery was borne by the federal government, and people accused as fugitives were denied the right to speak in their own defense. The enforcement provision that especially incensed northerners was the law's command to all citizens to actively assist in fugitive slave captures. People obstructing or failing to assist in such captures were subject to a fine of up to $1000 and a jail sentence of up to six months.

In the eyes of the abolitionists, the new fugitive slave law threatened to make every American a slavecatcher. Abolitionists, whites as well as blacks, were determined to prevent the return of fugitives to slavery. In protest meetings across the North, African Americans attacked the law, calling it "so wicked, so atrocious, so utterly at variance with the principles of the Constitution."[43] Many were reluctant to resort to violence, but they were so angry that they were willing to consider it. "If the American revolutionaries had excuse for shedding one drop of blood," declared a gathering of fugitives in New York State, "then have the American slaves for making blood to flow 'even unto the horsebridles.'"[44] Frederick Douglass drew hardy applause when he addressed a Boston audience and warned, should authorities attempt to enforce the fugitive slave law in that city, the streets "would be running with blood."[45] Chicago's Common Council denounced the law as unconstitutional and refused to require the city police to enforce it.[46]

The provisions of the Fugitive Slave Act of 1850 essentially overrode the personal liberty laws in the New England states, New York, New Jersey, and Pennsylvania, increasing the power of the federal government over the rights of the states in the interests of slaveholders. By the mid- to late 1850s northern states answered this exercise of federal power by defiantly passing new personal liberty laws. In 1852, Jonathan Lemmon and his wife stopped in New York City as they traveled by ship from Virginia to Texas, there being no ships that sailed directly from Virginia to the Gulf of Mexico. The captain warned them not to take their eight slaves off the ship in New York, but the couple repaired to a hotel with their slaves to wait for the three days before the ship sailed for Texas.

At the hotel the travelers came to the attention of a local black abolitionist, Louis Napoleon, who charged Lemmon with slave trading and petitioned the court for a writ of habeas corpus to make him deliver the slaves for a determination of their status. After hearing the arguments, the judge decided that since New York State law did not allow slavery, and since the slaves were not fugitives, they were

Abolitionists Protest the Fugitive Slave Law

This broadside protested the Fugitive Slave Act of 1850. Though an early law passed by Congress in 1793 allowed slaveholders to recover runaway slaves from other states, the stronger 1850 law made kidnapping free blacks more of a threat, since an accused fugitive had no right to a trial, and also threatened jail for anyone who refused to assist in the capture of an accused fugitive.

Read and Ponder the Fugitive Slave Law!

Which disregards all the ordinary securities of PERSONAL LIBERTY, which tramples on the Constitution, by its denial of the sacred rights of Trial by Jury, Habeas Corpus, and Appeal, and which enacts, that the Cardinal Virtues of Christianity shall be considered, in the eye of the law, as CRIMES, punishable with the severest penalties,—

Fines and Imprisonment.... Sec. 5 It shall be the duty of all marshals and deputy marshals to obey and execute all warrants and precepts issued under the provision of this act, when to them directed; and should any marshal or deputy marshal refuse to receive such warrant ... he shall ... be fined in the sum of $1,000 ... and ALL GOOD CITIZENS are hereby commanded to aid and assist in the prompt and efficient execution of this law whenever their services may be required.... Sec. 6. And be it further enacted. That when a person held to service or labor in any State or Territory of the United States has heretofore or shall hereafter escape into another State or Territory... the persons to whom such service or labor may be due ... may pursue and retain such fugitive persons, either by procuring a warrant from one of the courts, judges or commissioners ... or by seizing and arresting such fugitive, where the same can be done without process, and by taking ... such person ... before such court, judge or commissioner, whose duty it shall be to hear and determine the case of such claimant in a summary manner, and upon satisfactory proof being made, by disposition or affidavit in writing, to be taken and certified by such court ... a certification of such magistrate ... shall be SUFFICIENT TO ESTABLISH THE COMPETENCY OF THE PROOF, AND WITH PROOF, ALSO BY AFFIDAVIT, of the identity of the person whose service or labor is claimed to be due.... IN NO TRIAL OR HEARING UNDER THIS ACT SHALL THE TESTIMONY OF SUCH ALLEGED FUGITIVE BE ADMITTED IN EVIDENCE.... Sec. 7. And be it further enacted. That any person who shall knowingly and willingly obstruct, hinder or prevent such claimant, or agent, or attorney, or any person or persons lawfully assisting him ... or shall aid, abet, or assist such a person so owning service or labor ... directly or indirectly to escape ... or SHALL HARBOR or CONCEAL such fugitive ... shall, for either of said offences be subject to a fine not exceeding one thousand dollars, and imprisonment not exceeding six months.

entitled to their freedom. Local businessmen sympathetic to the Lemmons, including the judge who ruled in the case, contributed $5,000 to compensate them for their property loss. As a matter of principle, the State of Virginia appealed the case,

but the court upheld the original ruling and confirmed New York's ability to prohibit slavery in any form for any period of time within its boundaries. The Lemmons' former slaves had not waited for the outcome of the appeal but had made their way to freedom in Canada as soon as they were freed.[47]

Another case, in 1856, affirmed the freedom of a slave from Kentucky who had been allowed to hire himself out in Ohio. The judge declared that he had become free as soon as he arrived in the state, regardless of the fact that he had gone back and forth between Ohio and Kentucky. During the 1850s, all northern states except for New Jersey and Illinois concluded that slaves brought into their states were entitled to their freedom. Most excluded runaways from this guarantee, but in 1858 Vermont passed a law that seemed to promise freedom even to fugitives. The conflict between North and South was clear when Vermont declared, "Every person, who may be held as a slave, who shall come or be brought or be involuntarily, in any way, in this State, shall be free."[48]

During the 1850s the South continued to draw the federal government into the slavery controversy more

A broadside attacking 1850's Fugitive Slave Act. The law was bitterly controversial, since it permitted an escaped slave to be seized solely on an affidavit of anyone claiming to be his or her owner. The law stripped fugitive slaves of the right to a jury trial or to testify in their own defense.

directly in an effort to protect slaveholders' rights. Many people in the South and in the North had hoped that the Compromise of 1850 would settle the question of slavery, and some politicians had vowed to end the agitation on the subject. It soon became clear, however, that slavery remained a divisive issue, and the first test of antislavery resolve came soon after the passage of the new fugitive slave law. Fugitive James Hamlet was arrested in New York City in September 1850 and returned to bondage in Baltimore. Abolitionists, however, were not content to let the matter end there. Fifteen hundred people met at a black church in New York to protest Hamlet's capture. One black man pledged $100, and the meeting was able to raise $500 for a fund to buy his freedom. White businessmen and abolitionists added another $300 to meet the $800 demanded by his Maryland master.

Within the month Hamlet returned to New York, where he was met by his wife, his three children, and five thousand well-wishers. The ceremony held in a public park included speeches hailing his freedom and denouncing the fugitive slave law. New York's business community was deeply implicated in the system of slavery, having provided much of the capital that financed southern plantations. Yet some of the city's most prominent business leaders had been moved by the plight of the man who had lived in the city for three years before being taken from his family and returned to slavery, and many of the city's merchants were there to take part in the emotional reunion.

In Boston that fall, abolitionists were more successful in protecting William and Ellen Craft, fugitives from Georgia. Ellen, the daughter of a slave woman and her master, was light enough to pass for white, and taking advantage of her complexion, the couple formulated a clever and daring scheme of escape. Dressed in male clothing, with her face bandaged and her arm in a sling, Ellen pretended to be a young white man traveling north for medical attention. William played the role of the young man's servant. In this disguise, they traveled by boat and train to Philadelphia and then to Boston. They spent a year in Boston before sailing for Great Britain, where they spent six months lecturing in Scotland and England on behalf of the British antislavery movement. The couple returned to Boston in the fall of 1850 to take part in abolitionist meetings protesting the new fugitive slave law.

The Crafts became the first of Boston's fugitives directly threatened under the new law. The Crafts' owner, Dr. Robert Collins of Macon, Georgia, had been keeping track of their travels through the abolitionist press, and when they returned from Britain, he sent two agents to Boston to recapture them. Upon their arrival in the city, these slavehunters obtained warrants for the Crafts' arrest under the provisions of the fugitive slave law. News of the slavehunters' presence raced through the black community. Ministers in the city's black churches helped spread the word, and community activists kept the men under constant surveillance. Abolitionists sent Ellen to nearby Brookline, but William armed himself and took refuge at the well-fortified home of Lewis Hayden on Beacon Hill. Hayden was himself a fugitive from Kentucky who had lived in Boston for many years and was a black community leader active in the Underground Railroad. A number of armed black men, including Hayden's son, came to the house to join Craft and Hayden.

Ellen Craft, who took advantage of her light complexion to escape from slavery by posing as a chronically ill wealthy southern gentleman. Her husband, William, accompanied her as a slave valet. Their daring story captured the imagination of abolitionists and they became sought-after participants at abolition meetings.

When the slavehunters arrived, Hayden confronted them on the front steps, where he had placed two kegs of gunpowder. The slavehunters watched in horror and disbelief as Hayden lighted a torch and threatened to destroy the house and anyone attempting to enter it, rather than surrender the fugitive. Other armed black men soon appeared to offer assistance. When it became obvious that the fugitives could only be taken by a considerable force, the slavehunters withdrew from the city. Although the Crafts were safe for the moment, clearly Boston was not a secure place for them. The Boston Vigilance Committee arranged for their return to England, where they continued their antislavery work.[49]

As the Crafts' case demonstrated, many abolitionists, especially northern blacks, were determined to resist the Fugitive Slave Act of 1850 with force if necessary. They hoped that the law's assault on civil rights would convince the northern public that the federal government was championing slaveholders' rights at the expense of their own.

The writings of abolitionist Harriet Beecher Stowe in response to the new law did much to arouse sympathy for the slaves and to turn public opinion against the law. In 1851, she published a series of fictionalized stories about the plight of slaves in the *National Era*, an abolitionist newspaper. The series was so popular that it was released as a book even before the last episode appeared in the newspaper. Stowe's *Uncle Tom's Cabin* was published in March 1852 and was an overwhelming success. It sold ten thousand copies in the first seven days, one hundred thousand copies before midsummer, and three hundred thousand before the end of the year. Eventually, it sold more than three million copies and became the nineteenth century's most important book on American slavery. It was also one of the first novels written by a white American to portray a black central character compassionately. It was popular in the United States and in Europe, where it became important to Britain's foreign policy. Members of

The title page of Harriet Beecher Stowe's Uncle Tom's Cabin, which dramatically brought home the human cost of the draconian 1850 Fugitive Slave Act to thousands of white readers. The book had such a huge effect on attitudes toward slavery that Lincoln is said to have addressed Stowe as "the little lady who started this big war."

Britain's royal family read *Uncle Tom's Cabin* at a time when Britain was considering closing the Canadian border to the growing number of American fugitive slaves seeking sanctuary in Canada. Since Britain had outlawed slavery in its empire in the mid-1830s, Canada had refused to extradite fugitive slaves from the United States. The new fugitive slave law all but ensured the return of fugitives from the free states, and closing the Canadian border would have eliminated the only secure sanctuary for those who escaped to the North. Stowe's novel so impressed the crown that it kept Canada open as a haven for fugitive slaves.

Many blacks who made their way to Canada in the wake of the fugitive slave law were recent runaways, but some fugitives who were longtime residents of the free states also feared for their safety and left for Canada during the early 1850s. In 1851, Henry Bibb, who had escaped slavery in Kentucky a decade earlier, settled in Sandwich Township, Ontario, Canada, and established that country's first black newspaper, *The Voice of the Fugitive*. His editorials urged African Americans to come north to true freedom in Canada. In the spring of 1852, Bibb reported, "[Canada's] Underground Railroad is doing good business this spring."[50]

Communities in southern Pennsylvania, close to the South and thus most vulnerable to slavehunters, lost substantial proportions of their black populations during the 1850s. The African American population of Columbia, Pennsylvania, decreased by more than half in a matter of months. [51] *The Liberator* reported that in Pittsburgh "nearly all the waiters in the hotels [had] fled to Canada." Fugitives armed themselves with guns and knives, the newspaper explained, "determined to die rather than be captured."[52] Farther north, where fugitives had felt safe for years, many blacks also decided to leave the country. In Buffalo one black church lost 130 members of its congregation. Rochester's black Baptist church lost all but two of its 114 members, and Boston's Twelfth Baptist Church and the Hamilton Street Church in Albany, New York, each lost one-third of its members to Canadian migration.[53] Between the fall of 1850, when the law was passed, and 1860, an estimated 15,000 to 20,000 American blacks migrated to Canada.

In the face of this exodus, northern vigilance committees vowed to stand against the growing influence of slaveholders. There were some exciting fugitive slave rescues in the North, but the great majority of fugitives arrested under the new law were returned to slavery. One of the most famous cases was that of Anthony Burns, a fugitive from Virginia who was captured in Boston. In 1854 Burns was arrested and held in the federal courthouse. Quickly, an interracial abolitionist force gathered to storm the courthouse and attempt Burns's rescue. They smashed the windows of the building and forced open the front door, and, during a pitched battle in the lobby, killed a U.S. marshal. The appearance of federal troops prevented the abolitionists from securing Burns's freedom. The trial of Anthony Burns attracted thousands of supporters from Boston and the surrounding communities, but public opinion could not prevent Burns from being taken back to slavery in Virginia. The troops marched the captive down Boston streets where the buildings were draped in black. Along the route, American flags were hung upside down, and a huge coffin labeled "Liberty" was suspended across State Street. For many northerners, the sight of a fugitive slave guarded by federal troops being marched to the wharf in Boston, the stronghold of abolition, was proof that the federal government was in the hands of an increasingly aggressive "slave power," as the abolitionists called slaveholders who threatened to assault the rights of all Americans opposed to slavery.[54]

The South's recovery of Anthony Burns and other fugitives from northern cities raised the awareness of many northern whites to the evils of slavery. Congress had tried to limit the spread of slavery with the Missouri Compromise of 1820, and a new political party formed in 1848, called the Free Soil Party, was committed to reserving the Western Territories for free labor, but by the mid-1850s, it seemed clear that slavery was determined to extend its grasp. A plan to annex Cuba, one of the few regions in the Western Hemisphere besides the United States that still tolerated slavery, in the 1850s received wide support in the American South. The incorporation of another slave territory into the nation would increase slavery's political strength and make additional slaves available for the plantation South. In the United States, the designs of slaveholders were also apparent when the Kansas–Nebraska Act of 1854 effectively rescinded the Missouri Compromise and opened the Kansas territory to slavery, should its people so choose.

In angry response, abolitionists vowed to prevent the incursion of slavery into what had been free territory and sponsored the migration of free-soil advocates from New England and New York State to Kansas. Meanwhile, proslavery forces were determined to make Kansas a slaveholding state. The southerners who migrated from Missouri and other states farther south and east brought their slaves with them. These opposing forces clashed in violent conflict, and the territory soon took on the name "Bleeding Kansas." By 1855, a kind of civil war was being conducted in the Kansas territory. New England staunchly supported a free Kansas, and abolitionist ministers such as Henry Ward Beecher urged their parishioners to donate funds to supply free-soil settlements and to equip them with weapons. Shipments of repeating rifles were packed in crates marked "bibles," and the guns were nicknamed "Beecher's Bibles."

Into this volatile atmosphere, a stern-faced man from Connecticut named John Brown brought his five sons and his iron will to destroy slavery. Brown had studied for the Congregational ministry and soon established a nationwide reputation as an antislavery soldier. He and his sons settled at Osawatomie in Miami County, Kansas, and took up arms in the struggle against proslavery raiders. Before Brown left the territory he had led armed abolitionists into combat against proslavery forces, freed a number of slaves, and lost a son in battle. He emerged from "Bleeding Kansas" with the nickname "Old Osawatomie" and a reputation stained by his role in the execution of five proslavery men. John Brown was a hero to abolitionists, free blacks, and slaves, but to southern slaveholders he was a murderer and a symbol of abolitionist aggression. His war on slavery, and the violence in the Kansas territory generally, made many Americans believe that a wider sectional confrontation was inevitable.

This belief grew even stronger as the violence surrounding the issue of slavery in Kansas moved from the dusty plains to the halls of Congress itself on May 22, 1856. On that day, Preston Brooks, a U.S. Representative from South Carolina, walked onto the floor of the U.S. Senate, found Charles Sumner, the abolitionist senator from Massachusetts, seated at his desk, and proceeded to beat him with a walking cane until Sumner lay unconscious on the floor. Brooks was reacting to a speech Sumner had given attacking South Carolina Senator Andrew P. Butler, Brooks's cousin, for supporting the spread of slavery into the Kansas Territory. Sumner was severely injured, and his constituents in Massachusetts were furious. Shortly after the attack, a protest meeting in Boston passed a resolution declaring, "we regard every blow inflicted upon our Senator as a blow aimed at us." Five thousand gathered in the New York City Tabernacle to express their outrage at what most considered an act of southern violence. This perception seemed to be confirmed when southern supporters celebrated Brooks's attack. The *Richmond Whig* called it an "elegant and effectual canning," and southern groups, including students at the University of Virginia, presented Brooks with a number of ornately carved canes.[55]

Blacks and white abolitionists who were already furious at the federal government for having implemented the harsh fugitive slave law were further alienated by southern reaction to Brooks's attack on Sumner. For them, the final blow came in 1857 with the U.S. Supreme Court decision in the case of *Dred Scott v. Sandford*, a decision that assaulted the basic rights of African Americans. Dred Scott was a slave in Missouri before his master, a military officer, took him to live in the free territories of Wisconsin and Illinois for a number of years. When his master returned him to slavery in Missouri, Scott sued for his freedom on the grounds that living in a free territory had made him free. Scott initially won his case on the basis of earlier cases that affirmed state personal liberty laws and provided precedent for his claim. His owner appealed, however, won the appeal, and the case moved to the U.S. Supreme Court. In 1857, in nine sep-

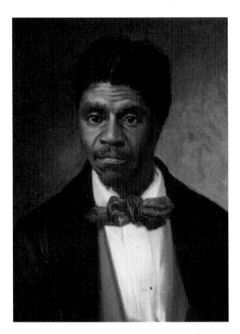

Dred Scott, a Virginia slave, was the plaintiff in the landmark U.S. Supreme Court case Scott v. Sandford. *The court decided 7–2 against Scott, and each of the Supreme Court justices rendered a separate opinion, revealing the huge gap between the proslavery and antislavery views prevalent in the country at that time*

arate opinions, the Supreme Court ruled against Dred Scott. Eighty-year-old southern-born slaveholder Chief Justice Roger B. Taney read the court's opinion aloud. The opinion went far beyond a simple decision, as Taney declared that Scott's claim to freedom was not valid because Congress had no authority to exclude slavery from the territories. This ruling contradicted the position of the newly formed Republican Party, which sought to stop the expansion of slavery into the western territories. Then Taney attacked all African Americans, declaring that they were not, had never been, and could never be American citizens, and thus had no rights guaranteed under the U. S. Constitution. According to Taney, Scott had no right to sue in the court, since he "had no rights which the white man was bound to respect."[56]

There was intense reaction to the Dred Scott decision in many quarters of the North, but none was stronger than from African Americans themselves. Just a month after the Court's decision, abolitionist speaker Charles Lenox Remond gave voice to the rage so many of his fellow African Americans were feeling. At a Philadelphia meeting he told an excited crowd, "We owe no allegiance to a country which grinds us under its iron heel and treats us like dogs. The time has gone by for colored people to talk of patriotism."[57] He and other blacks vigorously supported the formation of black military associations across the North to encourage military preparedness in African American communities.

By the mid-1850s many blacks had grown convinced that the only hope of ending slavery was through military action. In 1855 Boston blacks petitioned the Massachusetts legislature to charter a black military company. When legislators refused, they formed the Massasoit Guard without state sanction. In November 1857, after the Dred Scott decision was announced, the Guard paraded through the streets of Boston, armed and in full uniform. Elsewhere in the North, African Americans formed similar military companies. In New York, Ohio, and Pennsylvania blacks formed military units all waiting for the anticipated moment. The time would soon come, predicted J. J. Simmons, an officer in the New York contingent, when northern black military troops would be called to strike a blow for freedom, marching through the South with "a bible in one hand and a gun in the other."[58]

Yet, by the late 1850s, the South seemed stronger than ever. Its economic power had become so great that it could not be ignored. Cotton had become America's most valuable export, more valuable, in fact, than everything else the nation exported to the world combined. The worth of slaves increased correspondingly, so that on the eve of the Civil War it was greater than the total dollar value of all the nation's banks, railroads, and manufacturing. The South was able to translate its economic power into political power. By 1860, slaveholders and their sympathizers controlled the Supreme Court and the major committees of Congress and had a strong supporter in the president, Pennsylvania-born James Buchanan. Still, the slaveholding South feared that its ability to protect slavery was in danger. Convinced that the influence of the abolition movement was growing, many southerners began to call for secession from the United States. If slavery and the southern way of life that it made possible were to be protected, they argued, the South must become an independent nation.

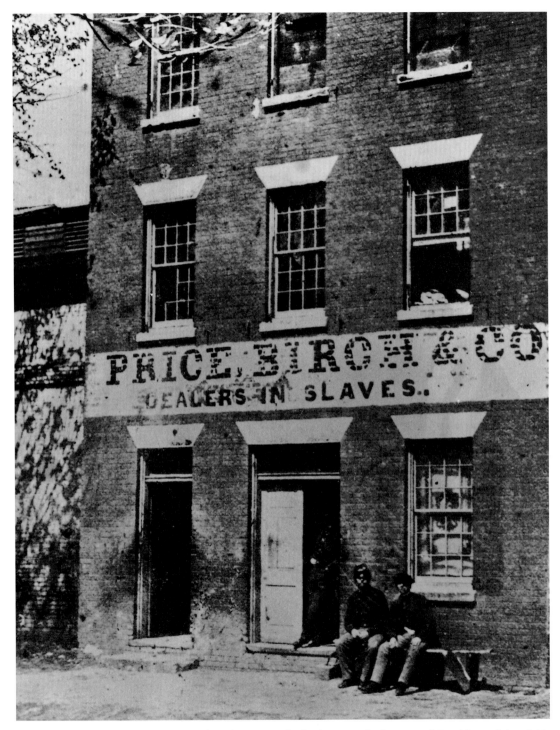

By the time of the Civil War, Price, Birch and Company had taken over the business of Franklin and Armfield in Alexandria, Virginia. Located near the nation's capital, this was the largest slave-trading company in the nation. The building was used in 1864 as a military prison.

A Hard-Won Freedom: From Civil War Contraband to Emancipation

At 7:05 in the morning on October 17, 1859, an emergency message flashed over the telegraph lines. The passenger train traveling east out of Virginia toward Baltimore had made an unscheduled stop at Monocacy, Maryland, across the river from Harpers Ferry. The conductor sent an alarm: "My train eastbound was stopped at Harpers Ferry this morning about 1:30 by armed abolitionists—They say they have come to free the slaves." John Brown's raid on Harpers Ferry, Virginia, was under way. Harpers Ferry, a village of three thousand people situated at the confluence of the Potomac and Shenandoah rivers, had been home to one of two national armories since George Washington's presidency. Brown and his raiders had come for the guns and ammunition produced and stored in this arsenal. They planned to free slaves in the area, arm them with pikes and guns, then march their gathered army toward the mountains, liberating slaves as they went. This action, Brown believed, would spearhead a general slave uprising.

John Brown, a gray-bearded man almost sixty years old, established his headquarters in a farmhouse two hours' walk from the river. On Sunday evening, October 16, the men loaded a horse-drawn wagon with one thousand pikes specially manufactured in Connecticut. Brown left three men at the farmhouse to guard their equipment and led his raiding party, including three of his own sons, stealthily toward the slumbering town. Each of the thirteen whites and five blacks was armed with a rifle and two pistols. They crossed the Baltimore and Ohio Railroad bridge sometime after 10 p.m. and moved to the federal armory at the eastern end of town. The sound of their approach alerted the armory's night watchman, who emerged from his office expecting to see his supervisor. The raiders took him prisoner, forced him to open the armory gate, cut the telegraph wires to the town, and took cover inside the armory. Brown announced that he had come from Kansas to free the slaves of Virginia.

Ironically, the first person the antislavery raiders killed was not a slave-holder, but a black railroad worker, Hayward Shepherd, the station baggageman who had come in search of the watchman. It is likely that in the darkness Brown's men did not recognize him as African American. Shepherd was one of 150 free blacks in the town's population, which was 12 percent black, half free and half slave. Most of the free black men worked as laborers or wagon drivers, but a few were skilled craftsmen who worked as masons, plasterers, butchers, and blacksmiths supporting the town's major armament manufacturing enterprise. Raiders also killed three white men, the mayor of the town, a prominent citizen, and a U.S. marine.

John Brown had spent years planning this action, raising the necessary financial resources, and recruiting followers. In the summer of 1859, he posed as Isaac Smith, a cattle buyer from New York, and rented a two-story Maryland farmhouse across the Potomac River and about seven miles from Harpers Ferry from a family named Kennedy. The Kennedy farm became the headquarters where he stockpiled weapons and assembled his army. Brown quartered his men in the attic for three months while he finalized his plans. There were a few tense moments, as when a neighbor spied one of the African Americans and raised questions about what they were doing there, but few neighbors seemed suspicious.

Many abolitionists, blacks as well as whites, found the drama and complexity of Brown's scheme intriguing, and he found considerable support among free blacks, particularly fugitives from slavery, in the communities of the northern United States and southern Canada. In April of 1858 Brown traveled to Saint Catharines, Ontario, a town just north of Buffalo, New York, with at least a thousand fugitive slaves. There, he met the famed fugitive slave and Underground Railroad worker Harriet Tubman, whose name, some people contended, was more familiar to slaves than the Bible.[1] Brown was mightily impressed by this small woman with an enormous presence. He called her General Tubman and asked her to join and to recruit for his revolutionary army. She agreed, drummed up support for the venture, and assisted in its planning. At the time of the raid, however, she was ill and did not take part.

Brown also visited Chatham, Ontario, Canada, northeast of Detroit. Chatham's considerable fugitive slave population, about one third of the town's almost five thousand people, provided fertile ground for recruiting. African Americans in Canada and the northern United States greatly admired Brown, and most supported his plan, even though many thought it foolhardy and doomed to failure.

In the end only five blacks actually joined his band. Two of these were residents of Oberlin, Ohio, the home of abolitionist Oberlin College, the first integrated college in the nation. John Anthony Copeland, Jr., born free in Raleigh, North Carolina, a student in the preparatory department of Oberlin College, enlisted with Brown in September 1859. He joined at the urging of his uncle, Lewis Sheridan Leary, a saddler and harness-maker also from North Carolina and the other black Oberliner. Osborn Perry Anderson was also free-born, a thirty-year-old Pennsylvanian, who lived and worked as a painter in Canada. Shields Green, a young fugitive slave in his early twenties from Charleston, South Carolina, was also part of the group. Green traveled to Chambersburg, Pennsylvania, with Frederick Douglass to meet and talk with Brown about his planned raid. Douglass believed it was a futile venture and would not go, but Green signed on with Brown.

Dangerfield Newby, a former slave from Fauquier County, Virginia, was forty-four years old when he joined the raiders. He had been freed by his Scottish father, but his wife, Harriet, and their six children remained in slavery. His family was held by a Virginia planter who lived near Harpers Ferry. Just before the raid Newby received a letter from his wife, telling him that she feared they were about to be sold south. "If I thought I should never see you," she told him, "this earth would have no charms for me." And then she begged, "Do all you can for me, which I have no doubt you will. I want to see you so much . . . [come] this fall without fail." Newby carried this letter with him on the raid.[2]

By morning, the townspeople discovered the invaders, and church bells rang out the alarm. Officials sent messengers to alert the Virginia militia in nearby Shepherdstown and Charlestown. Some of Brown's men argued that they should take what arms they could and escape to the mountains, but Brown refused. Instead, he waited, fortifying his forces inside the armory. He knew that the western Virginia area around Harpers Ferry held many whites who opposed slavery and blacks willing to rise up against it, and he assumed that his presence would attract new recruits. "When I strike the bees will swarm," he had told Frederick Douglass during their recent meeting in Pennsylvania. But before such an army could be attracted, townspeople and local militia, and then federal troops, besieged the raiders. Although it is tempting to see Brown's hope for a massive reaction from local Virginians as folly, it was not inconceivable. Opinion in western Virginia had long been divided on slavery, and many people thought the news believable when word reached the White House in Washington that an interracial force of seven hundred revolutionaries had taken control of Harpers Ferry and had begun a civil war. President James Buchanan immediately ordered three companies of artillery and a detachment of marines to the scene. The federal forces were commanded by Colonel Robert E. Lee of the U.S. Second Cavalry, assisted by Lieutenant J.E.B. Stuart of the First U.S. Calvary.[3]

When Lee and his forces arrived on Monday night they found Brown and his men cut off and under attack and the town in disorder. Many local townsmen had been drinking most of the day, and inebriated men were keeping the raiders under siege. Lee first ordered the taverns closed, then he turned his attention to the engine house where the raiders were trapped. The federal troops assaulted the engine house on Tuesday morning and smashed their way inside before Brown could finish negotiating a surrender that would give his men a chance to escape. By the end of the morning ten of Brown's men had been killed or mortally wounded, including two of Brown's sons. Five men were taken prisoner immediately, two were captured soon after, and five escaped.

Of the blacks, Leary was wounded and lived only for eight hours afterward. Copeland and Green were captured and later executed. Dangerfield Newby had been the first of the raiders killed. The letter from his wife urging him to come to her rescue was found in his pocket. Anderson escaped to Canada, where he lived until the Civil War broke out. Two years after the raid he wrote an eyewitness account, *A Voice From Harper's Ferry, 1859,* and in 1864 he enlisted in the U.S. Army, again to serve the antislavery cause. Anderson survived the war and finally died of consumption in Washington, D.C., in 1872.

John Brown was wounded in the assault but survived to face trial on the charge of treason against the State of Virginia. Brown rejected his

After his execution, the fiery abolitionist John Brown became a celebrated martyr for the antislavery cause. His address to the Virginia court that executed him was widely published; it included the chilling words "I, John Brown, am now quite certain that the crimes of this guilty land will never be purged away but with blood."

They Fought with John Brown

Dangerfield Newby and John Anthony Copeland, Jr., were two of the five black men who attacked the arsenal at Harpers Ferry, Virginia, with John Brown. The letters below show both the personal and the political reasons for their joining Brown's crusade.

Newby was the first of Brown's men to be killed. This letter from his wife, dated August 16, 1859, was found in his pocket. After it was found, Harriet Newby was sold to a Louisiana slave dealer.

———————————————

Dear Husband - It is said Master is in want of money. If so, I know not what time he may sell me, and then all my bright hopes of the future are blasted, for there has been one bright hope to cheer me in all my troubles, that is to be with you. If I thought I should never see you this earth would have no charms for me. Come this fall without fail money or no money. Do all you can for me, which I have no doubt you will. The children are all well. The baby cannot walk yet. You must write soon and say when you think you can come.

    Your affectionate wife, Harriet Newby

———————————————

Copeland was captured after the raid, tried, found guilty of treason against the state of Virginia, and executed at Charlestown on December 16, 1859. From his cell, he wrote the following letter to his parents in Oberlin, Ohio.

———————————————

DEAR PARENTS, - my fate as far as man can seal it is sealed but let this not occasion you any misery for remember the cause in which I was engaged, remember that it was a 'Holy Cause,' one in which men who in every point of vew better than I am have suffered and died, remember that if I must die I die in trying to liberate a few of my poor and oppress people from my condition of servitude which God in his Holy Writ has hurled his most bitter denunciations against and in which men who were by the color of their faces re-moved from the direct injurious affect, have already lost their lives and still more remain to meet the same fate which has been by man decided that I must meet.

    John Anthony Copeland, Jr., December, 1859.

attorney's attempt to mount an insanity defense. "I reject, so far as I am capable, any attempt to interfere in my behalf on that score." He defended his actions on the grounds that it was part of the "holy war" against slavery:

> Now, if it is deemed necessary that I should forfeit my life for the furtherance of the ends of justice, and mingle my blood further with the blood of my children and with the blood of millions in this slave country whose rights are disregarded by wicked, cruel, and unjust enactments—I submit; so let it be done!

John Brown was executed on December 2, 1859.

Brown's attempt to raise slaves in open rebellion horrified white southerners. They were especially dismayed by several letters left at the Kennedy farm that connected six prominent white northerners—businessmen, ministers, educators, and financiers—to the plot. This seemed to confirm suspicions that John Brown had been acting as an agent for powerful northern abolitionists. African Americans saw Brown as a hero and a martyr in the cause of freedom. On the day of his execution, blacks in cities across the North mourned his passing. Three thousand gathered in Boston to condemn slavery and to thank Brown for his efforts. In Detroit a subdued crowd listened to antislavery speeches, and the Brown Liberty Singers offered a musical selection entitled "Ode to Old Capt. John Brown."[4] Within months of Brown's execution, Canadian blacks met to consider ways to honor his memory, calling him and his men "martyrs to the cause of Liberty." The editor of *The Weekly Anglo-African* compared Brown's raid with Nat Turner's slave rebellion, touting it as one of the country's most effective attacks on slavery. A group of black women wrote to Brown's widow, Mary, praising him for his efforts and calling him "our honored and dearly-loved brother."[5]

In the aftermath of John Brown's raid, the northern black military companies formed a few years before redoubled their training, certain that the anticipated fight for abolition was imminent. John Rock, a black abolitionist from Boston, called for preparedness. "Sooner or later, the clashing of arms will be heard in this country," he contended, and "the black man's service will be needed...to strike a genuine blow for freedom." Defiantly echoing the Supreme Court's language in the Dred Scott case, he predicted that when black men raised their hands to strike against slavery, they would do so with a "power which white men 'will be bound to respect.'"[6] Tensions ran high on the eve of the presidential election of 1860. Delegates from the Deep South walked out of the Democratic convention in Charleston and formed the Southern Democratic Party, while the remaining delegates moved the convention to Baltimore. Democrats nominated Illinois senator Stephen A. Douglas for president. Douglas was the author of the Kansas–Nebraska Act and was called the "little giant" for his diminutive stature, barely five foot in height, and his powerful rhetoric and towering will. The Southern Democrats nominated Vice President John C. Breckinridge of Kentucky. Some Democrats committed to maintaining national unity formed yet another party called the Union Party and chose John Bell of Tennessee as their candidate.

The Republican Party settled on Abraham Lincoln, a tall well-spoken, likable, loyal party man from Illinois with an effective sense of humor, as their presidential candidate. Lincoln had been born in the slave state of Kentucky, but his family moved to Indiana when he was seven. The Lincolns left Kentucky partly because they had trouble gaining title to land there, but Abraham later recalled that his father moved the family "partly on account of slavery." As a Baptist, Lincoln's father, Thomas, classed slavery with profanity, intoxication, horse racing and other human vices. As a struggling small farmer, he saw slavery as the means by which slaveholding "nabobs" with vast plantations monopolized the best, most fertile soil. At age nineteen Lincoln took a trip to New Orleans, where he saw a young mixed-race woman being auctioned in a public market. Revolted, he told his cousin Dennis Hanks, "By God, boys, if I ever get a chance to hit [slavery], I'll hit it and hit it hard."[7] While serving in the Illinois state legislature in the 1830s, Lincoln denounced slavery as unjust and bad governmental policy. In 1854, speaking in Peoria, Illinois, he quoted the Declaration of Independence and argued that slavery was "a total violation of this principle" because the slaveholder "not only governs the slave without his consent; but he governs him by a set of rules altogether different from those which he prescribes for himself."[8]

In 1858, when Illinois Republican candidate Lincoln challenged Democratic incumbent Stephen A. Douglas for the U.S. Senate, slavery was a central issue. The candidates debated its place in the nation, and in the western territories in particular, in a series of seven confrontations, one in each of the seven congressional districts in the state. Douglas argued that the question of slavery should be left to local communities as the nation expanded, repeating his belief that "the signers of the Declaration had no reference to the [N]egro whatever,

During the senatorial election in 1858, Republican Abraham Lincoln and his opponent, Democrat Stephen A. Douglas, toured Illinois, debating the questions of the day. Slavery and its extension into the western territories were central issues that divided them.

when they declared all men to be created equal."[9] He scoffed at Lincoln's notion that African Americans were included in the Declaration and pandered to the white supremacist Illinois crowd, as he argued that America "was made by white men for the benefit of white men and their posterity forever." While Lincoln did not argue for political or social equality between the races, he did declare, "I believe that the right of property in a slave is not distinctly and expressly affirmed in the Constitution." Lincoln believed that slavery was a moral wrong, and he wanted to contain its expansion, keeping it out of the western territories. Although personally opposed to slavery, as president, he said, he would tolerate it in the states where it was sanctioned by law.[10]

Thus, in the presidential election of 1860, only the Republicans opposed slavery, and they only opposed its expansion. Breckinridge and the Southern Democrats took the radical southern position, threatening secession unless slavery was protected. John Bell and the Union Party represented a more moderate position, promoting regional compromise, and Douglas and the northern Democrats were also willing to compromise with the South to protect slavery. Southerners attempted to portray Lincoln as an abolitionist, but he was a northern moderate who said again and again that he had no intention of taking action against slavery in the South.

Most of the nation's half million free blacks, especially those in the northern states supported the Republicans, though not wholeheartedly. They knew from Lincoln's public statements that he was not an abolitionist nor a believer in racial equality. Blacks had been skeptical of the Republican Party, its platform, and its program to contain slavery from the party's inception in 1854, since Republicans seemed only interested in preserving the western territories for free white labor. From the standpoint of African Americans, Republicans were far preferable to the openly proslavery Democrats, but they were by no means an ideal party. "We do not pledge ourselves to go further with the Republicans," one black leader declared, "than the Republicans will go with us."[11]

In New York African Americans had another reason to go to the polls. Since 1822, the state had imposed property requirements only on black voters, and a constitutional amendment striking down this provision was on the ballot in 1860. State Republicans unanimously supported the removal of the property requirements, while Democrats solidly favored their retention. During the campaign, however, Republicans were afraid that Democrats might use this issue as a weapon against Lincoln, and they rarely mentioned the amendment. Although Lincoln and the Republicans carried New York State, the black suffrage amendment was soundly defeated. Frederick Douglass, living in Rochester, New York, at the time, felt betrayed by Republicans' weak support for the suffrage measure. Shortly after the election he wrote in his newspaper, "The blow is a heavy and damaging one. Every intelligent colored man must feel it keenly."[12]

More than 81 percent of eligible voters cast ballots in the presidential election. Lincoln won, carrying all of the free states except New Jersey, where he split the vote with Douglass. Douglass carried only Missouri, Bell took the three Upper South states of Tennessee, Kentucky, and Virginia, and Breckinridge won eleven slave states. Thus, Abraham Lincoln became president of the United

States after garnering less than 40 percent of the popular vote and carrying none of the southern states.[13] African Americans knew that Lincoln's election was not necessarily an abolitionist victory, but they consoled themselves that the election had brought, as Frederick Douglass put it, "at least an antislavery reputation to the Presidency." Black leaders had reacted forcefully to southern threats to secede from the United States. "If the Union can only be maintained by new concessions to the slaveholders," Douglass declared, "let the Union perish."[14] Within days of Lincoln's election, H. Ford Douglass, a former Virginia slave, stood before a crowd of Chicago blacks and addressed South Carolina: "Stand not upon the order of your going, but go at once . . . there is no union of ideas and interests in the country, and there can be no union between freedom and slavery."[15]

Fearful and defiant white southern slaveholders saw Lincoln's election as a triumph for abolitionism. Despite Lincoln's statements to the contrary, they insisted that he intended to move against slavery in the South and argued that the South must take immediate action to defend the very foundation of its way of life. One New Orleans newspaper argued that the election was "incontrovertible proof of a diseased and dangerous public opinion all over the North, and a certain forerunner of further and more atrocious aggression."[16] Long before the election, Joseph E. Brown, "the ploughboy" governor from northern Georgia, had warned about northern "fanatical abolitionist sentiment." Now that a Republican was about to take the White House he was sure, as he said in the pages of Milledgeville's weekly *Federal Union*, that Lincoln was "the mere instrument of a great triumphant party, the principles of which are deadly hostile to the institution of slavery."[17] Most white southerners were certain that any hostility toward slavery endangered the South. As one Georgia editor later confirmed, "[N]egro slavery is the South, and the South is [N]egro slavery."[18]

South Carolinians convened a state convention in Columbia in mid-December to consider their political future. On December 20, after three days of discussion, the convention issued an Ordinance of Secession, concluding, "the union now subsisting between South Carolina and other States, under the name of the 'United States of America,' is hereby dissolved."[19] Southern newspapers urged quick action, warning that the South remained in grave danger so long as it remained under the control of the federal government. "They [northerners in the U.S. government] know that they can plunder and pillage the South, as long as they are in the same Union with us," asserted one New Orleans editor. They can "steal Southern property in slaves, without risking civil war," he insisted, "[a war] which would be certain to occur if [they stole] from [an] independent South."[20]

Mississippi, Florida, Alabama, Georgia, Louisiana, and Texas promptly joined South Carolina in withdrawing from the United States, and on February 4, 1861, representatives from all the seceding states except Texas met as a constitutional convention in Montgomery, Alabama, to establish the Confederate States of America. The Texas delegates had to wait for a referendum in their state and came later. The Confederate Constitution adopted in March 1861 followed the pattern of the U.S. Constitution, except that it emphasized state power over federal power, including in the power of taxation and regulating internal commerce, and it explicitly protected the rights of slaveholders. The Confederate Constitution required that "the institution of [N]egro slavery, as it now exists in the Confederate States, shall be recognized and protected by Congress and by the Territorial government" in any territory the Confederacy might acquire. It further protected slaveholders' right to move their human property to any area under Confederate control, saying that "the inhabitants of the several Confederate States and Territories shall have the right to take to such Territory any slaves lawfully held by them in any of the States or Territories of the Confederate States." Clearly, the new southern nation dominated by slaveholders required the protection for slave property it felt was denied under the U.S. Constitution.[21]

Anna Kingsley was among the free black people in the South concerned for their own freedom and the safety of their families when the Confederate states seceded in 1861. In the 1830s Anna had lived in a plantation settlement built and operated by her son George on the Spanish side of the island of Hispaniola. During her time on that island, shares of the profit from this estate and the rental of her Florida land and slaves provided her income. Zephaniah had gone back to sea after leaving Florida, but he visited Haiti frequently to see his growing family. When Zephaniah died in 1843, at age 78, his will directed that some land and personal items be given to his three nephews, and the rest of his vast holdings be divided into twelve shares and distributed to Anna and other family members. As he had feared, however, Kingsley's white relatives contested the will on the grounds that Florida law prohibited people of African descent from inheriting a white man's property. Eventually, the Florida Supreme Court upheld the black heirs' rights, ruling that they were full citizens under the treaty with Spain by which the United States had acquired East Florida. That didn't end the contention, however, and George sailed for Florida in 1846, planning to defend his inheritance right to some of the land about to be sold at auction. On the trip he was drowned in a storm at sea.[22]

The loss of her son, uncertainty over the disposition of the estate, and political unrest in Haiti prompted Anna to return to Florida the following year. She bought a farm midway between her daughters' plantations, just north of Jacksonville, and returned to active management of her own properties and slaves. Florida law required that she have a guardian, and having her white son-in-law, John Sammis, appointed to oversee her affairs must have rankled the wealthy, independent Anna Kingsley. Nevertheless, Anna lived through the tumultuous years of the 1850s surrounded by family and protected by her sons-in-law. By 1860, Anna, sixty-seven years old, was no longer able to manage her properties and had moved to a house on her daughter Martha's plantation. For help and companionship, she had her young granddaughter, Isabella, the daughter of John Maxwell Kingsley, who had taken over the properties on Hispaniola. Anna might have lived out her life peacefully in Florida in the midst of her family, their slaves, and a small community of almost forty free blacks who had once been Kingsley slaves, but the war threatened her security. The family's known loyalty to the federal government placed them in particular jeopardy. Confederate forces occupied the region, burning and looting plantation buildings, and confiscating much of the Kingsley property.

Abraham Lincoln was inaugurated as president of the United States on March 4, 1861. By then, the Confederate States of America was almost a month old, and former U.S. secretary of war Jefferson Davis of Mississippi had been sworn in as its president. Reporters barraged Lincoln with questions during the twelve-day train trip from his home in Springfield, Illinois, to Washington, D.C., but Lincoln remained silent on his intentions. The breakup of the country posed such a danger to the new president that security guards took unusual precautions and brought him into the national capital, he said, "like a thief in the night." The military presence at his inaugural address emphasized the danger of Confederate attack. His words were exalted, offering an olive branch to the South. He explained that they were friends not enemies and appealing to the "better angels of our nature." African Americans were not encouraged when he promised the southern leadership that he had "no purpose, directly or indirectly, to interfere with the institution of slavery in the States where it exists. I believe I have no lawful right to do so," he declared, "and I have no inclination to do so."[23]

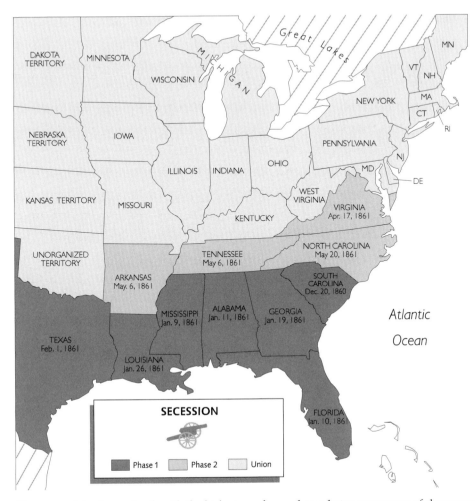

The states of the Lower South with the highest number and population percentage of slaves were the first to secede from the United States. The Upper South followed their example and joined the Confederacy after the firing on Fort Sumter in April 1861.

Northern abolitionists were concerned by Lincoln's conciliatory words, but southerners largely discounted his message. They labeled him a "Black Republican," a denunciatory term reserved for Republicans committed to anti-slavery and black rights, and the nation remained at an impasse for the next month. Finally, on April 12, 1861, Confederate batteries in Charleston Harbor opened fire on the federal Fort Sumter. In response Lincoln issued a call for 75,000 volunteers to put down the rebellion in South Carolina. As the war began, those southern states that had not formally declared their loyalty to either the United States or the Confederacy could no longer postpone acting. The slave states of Virginia, Arkansas, Tennessee, and North Carolina withdrew from the United States. Maryland, Delaware, Kentucky, and Missouri, also slave states, remained loyal to the U.S. government.

The United States seemed to have every advantage in population and resources with which to fight the war. Twenty-two million Americans faced a Confederate population of approximately five million free people and four million slaves. More than 90 percent of the facilities manufacturing arms and producing railroad equipment remained within the United States. But the Confederacy had important military advantages. Almost one-third of the U.S. army officer corps, including important West Point–trained men, resigned to join the rebellion against the United States. There was a great need for trained officers during the first year of the war, as the U.S. Army expanded from 16,000 men to more than 714,000.[24]

African Americans volunteered to serve the U.S. cause immediately after the firing on Fort Sumter. Jacob Dodson, a free black man employed by the U.S. Senate in Washington, wrote directly to Secretary of War Simon Cameron. "Sir I desire to inform you that I know of some three hundred . . . reliable colored free citizens of this City who desire to enter the service for the defence [sic] of the City." In Pennsylvania, Massachusetts, Ohio, and New York, African Americans eager for the opportunity to defend their country and fight against slavery petitioned state legislatures and the federal government, but everywhere the answer was the same. As the office of the secretary of war wrote to Dodson, "this Department has no intention at present to call into service of the Government any colored soldiers."[25]

Cincinnati blacks were concerned about the short distance across the Ohio River to Kentucky, where Confederate sentiment ran high, and readied their military company for service as a Home Guard to protect the city. They called a series of meetings to plan the defense, but the police forbade such activity and confiscated the keys to their meeting place. Tempers flared when local police forced blacks to remove the American flag from the local shop they were using as a recruiting office. A policeman insulted them, saying, "We want you d____d niggers to keep out of this; this is a white man's war." Threats of violence reinforced the message that white Cincinnatians would not accept African American military service.[26]

African Americans' historical record of military service notwithstanding, most whites, including Lincoln and other government officials, refused to believe that they would make good soldiers. Whites believed that ex-slaves in particular, by nature and training, were too submissive and cowardly to fight, especially when the enemy was their former masters. Such sentiments drew black outrage and indignation. African American troops had served with distinction in the American Revolution and in the War of 1812. Frederick Douglass caustically observed, "Colored men were good enough . . . to help win American independence, but they are not good enough to help preserve that independence against treason and rebellion." Why, he asked, would the American government attempt to fight "rebels with only one hand?"[27] Not enlisting blacks handicapped the Northern war effort: The United States suffered more than two hundred thousand casualties during the first year of the war.

While white U.S. causalties mounted and the government rejected black volunteers, Confederates used slaves in work to support their cause. An article in the *Montgomery Advertiser* reminded southerners of the advantages slave labor gave them in the war. The presence of slaves working the plantations under the direction of those unable to bear arms allowed a greater proportion of southern white men to fight. "The institution is a tower of strength to the South," the editors argued, and northern abolitionists who call it a "moral cancer," will find it "one of the most effective weapons employed against the Union by the South."[28] Pointing to such statements, African American leaders and white abolitionists argued that to achieve victory the United States would have to put an end to slavery. Frederick Douglass referred to the war as the slaveholders' rebellion and argued that if U.S. troops did not liberate slaves as they advanced into Confederate territory, they would "strike at the effect [of the war] and leave the cause unharmed."[29]

Far from freeing slaves, U.S. military commanders were following Lincoln's policies and returning runaway slaves to their southern masters. In April 1861, just days after the fall of Fort Sumter, General Benjamin Butler offered his Massachusetts troops to put down a rumored slave rebellion in Maryland, and other commanders continued to do so throughout the border states. Just a month later, however, Butler took a subtle but significant step in the opposite direction and refused to return three fugitive slaves who sought sanctuary behind U.S. lines at Fortress Monroe, Virginia. He labeled them contraband of war and, instead of returning them to their Confederate masters, put them to work laboring for the U.S. forces. Within three months there were some nine hundred contrabands under Butler's control. They were not exactly free, but he had not returned them to slavery.[30]

During the Civil War, people who escaped slavery in the rebellious southern states and made their way to the federal troops were considered contrabands of war. They were housed in makeshift refugee camps and they provided labor and intelligence for the U.S. forces. This camp was established in Richmond, Virginia, after the fall of the Confederate capital in 1865.

The status of the mounting number of contrabands in U.S. military camps was further obscured when, in a Fourth of July message, Lincoln restated his intention not to interfere with slavery where it existed. In August General John C. Frémont, military commander of the U.S. Army's Western Department, took another step toward black freedom. He declared martial law in Missouri and issued orders freeing all the slaves claimed by the state's Confederates, thrilling northern abolitionists but prompting President Lincoln's objection. Fearful of alienating slaveholders in the loyal border states, Lincoln revoked Fremont's order and freed only those slaves performing direct service for the Confederacy.

Many U.S. commanders were unwilling to distinguish between fugitives who had been supporting Confederate military operations and fugitives simply fleeing slavery. A congressional investigation of the contraband situation found that some northern-born military men who had not been antislavery advocates before the war changed their opinions when they confronted the brutality of slavery. Officially the southern masters who occasionally entered U.S. lines to inquire about their runaways were entitled to recover their "property," and sometimes troops returned the fugitives to them. One officer explained, however, that fugitives were not always left with their masters. In some cases

"Maryland owners had obtained possession of their slaves, and immediately set to work flogging them in view of the troops." Soldiers incensed by the slave-holders' actions "would go out and rescue the Negro, and in some instances would thrash the masters." According to the officer, his men were "excellent soldiers, but [after one such incident] they were resolute . . . they would not per-mit any [slaveholder] to come into our lines upon a similar mission."[31]

Abolitionists had refrained from criticizing Lincoln during the five months after his election, but they were enraged by his policy of returning fugi-tives to their owners and labeled it "timid, depressing, [and] suicidal." Douglass called slaveholders in the border states "the mill-stone about the neck of the Government" and thought Lincoln's effort to please them was foolish. One abo-litionist from Cincinnati wrote, "I cannot convey to you the burning sense of wrong which is filling the breasts of our people here, as they gradually come to see that there is no President of the United States—only a President of Kentucky."[32] A new antislavery organization calling itself the Emancipation League dedicated itself to making emancipation a central aim of the war. Members praised Frémont's freedom proclamation and argued that ending slav-ery would hasten the war's end. Their one concession to maintaining the loyal-ty of the border states was their endorsement of the idea of compensating loyal slaveholders for the loss of their slaves. By the fall of 1861, the Emancipation League also called for the enlistment of black troops as a necessity of war.

In November 1861, the federal naval fleet attacked the Sea Islands off the coast of South Carolina southwest of Charleston, a hotbed of southern seces-sion. They quickly overwhelmed the defending fortifications, and when troops landed after the bombardment the following day, the white population hastily abandoned the islands. They took only a few house servants and whatever they could carry, set fire to bales of harvested cotton, and left the area to the occu-pying forces and to ten thousand slaves. President Lincoln's policies made the future of these enslaved people uncertain, but they were confident that the flight of their masters and protection by federal troops marked the beginning of their freedom.[33]

The landing army found the black population in great need of food, cloth-ing, and medical care. Federal officials hoped to harvest the rest of the cotton on the nearly two hundred plantations and sell it to northern mills for money to help finance the war and to support these people. Northern philanthropists believed that the liberated slaves needed churches and schools to fit them for the future. Militant antislavery advocates saw the contrabands as potential soldiers in a fight against slavery. Northern abolitionists and missionaries quickly took up the challenge. Just four months after the federal occupation began, a group of fifty-three antislavery missionaries from the Boston area and New York City arrived to begin their work among the former slaves. Before the end of the war, several hundred people came to supervise, teach, recruit and care for the people of the Sea Islands. The government, private philanthropists, and freedmen gained experience there and set precedents for dealing with the problems that later would be associated with freeing millions of southern slaves.

The war brought new popularity to antislavery sentiment in the northern states. After the U.S. forces suffered almost three thousand casualties at the Battle of Bull Run in Virginia in July 1861, and suffered another three thousand casualties during the fall, even such mainstream newspapers as Horace Greeley's *New York Tribune* began to suggest emancipation as a means to military victory.

Black life on the Sea Islands off the coast of South Carolina and Georgia changed dramatically before the Civil War ended. The islands were captured by the U.S. early in the conflict, and freedmen's aid societies sent teachers and other aid workers to start schools, provide health care, and help former slaves begin their lives in freedom.

In December 1861 abolitionist editor William Goodell declared, "Never has there been a time when Abolitionists were as much respected as at the present. Announce the presence of a competent abolition lecturer and the house is crammed."[34] Lincoln responded to popular feeling by proposing a plan of compensated emancipation that would encourage states to end slavery. Congress adopted the plan, but pressure continued to mount for more definitive action against slavery.

Congress acted in April 1862, abolishing slavery in the District of Columbia and providing former masters with compensation for the loss of their slaves. A congressional commission, consulting with a Baltimore slave dealer, set the amount to be paid for each slave at an average of $300. Under this arrangement, the federal government paid a total of almost one million dollars in compensation for the slightly more than three thousand slaves in the District. Congress also provided $100,000 to finance the voluntary migration of African Americans to Haiti or to Liberia, the colony that had become an independent nation in 1847. Although Lincoln later said that many free blacks were enthusiastic about the prospect of emigration, the vast majority rejected the idea, especially since American freedom seemed a realistic possibility.[35]

For African Americans and their white allies, April 16, 1862, the day of emancipation in the District of Columbia, signaled the beginning of the federal government's commitment to black freedom. A slave woman in Baltimore, whose status was legally unaffected by abolition in Washington, "clapped her hands and shouted . . . let me go tell my husband that Jesus has done all things well." On learning the news, Frederick Douglass wrote to Massachusetts Senator Charles Sumner, "I trust I am not dreaming, but the events taking place seem like a dream." The editor of *The Anglo-African* expressed the feelings of many blacks, "[W]e rejoice less as black men than as part and parcel of the American people. . . . We can point to our Capital and say to all nations, 'IT IS FREE'." Washington blacks celebrated Emancipation Day with parades and festivals for many years after the war.[36]

Emancipation in Washington encouraged even greater numbers of slaves to attempt escapes to the protection of the federal government in the District of Columbia, to advancing federal troops, and to federal encampments. Deciding to flee to U.S. troops was risky because the chances were good that slaves would be returned to bondage, or worse. As one southern newspaper correspondent wrote from Tennessee, "All 'contrabands' captured by the rebels on the Federal wagon-trains are immediately shot." Emphasizing the seriousness of the threat, he added, "Twenty thus killed are lying on Murfreesboro pike."[37] Despite the dangers, U.S. troops moving through the South often attracted hundreds of runaway slaves.

Charlotte Forten was the first black teacher to go to Port Royal in the Sea Islands to work with the contrabands. Forten was an accomplished and well-educated member of a wealthy black abolitionist Philadelphia family. Her grandfather, James Forten, Sr., had fought in the American Revolution as a boy, had made his money as a sailmaker, and was both a supporter of Paul Cuffe's dreams of a black settlement in West Africa and an early mainstay of William Lloyd Garrison's *Liberator*. Charlotte's parents, Robert and Mary, were active in antislavery organizations, and Robert Forten and her uncle, Robert Purvis, were members of Philadelphia's Underground Railroad vigilance committee. Charlotte had been educated in Salem, Massachusetts, where her family sent her to live with a prominent black abolitionist family. She became part of the circle of famous antislavery activists in the Boston area and was celebrated for her refinement and her talent as a poet and a pianist. With teaching experience in Salem in the 1850s, it was logical for Forten to become a teacher of former slaves on the Sea Islands.

Forten applied to the government for a teaching position soon after the U.S. army restored peace to the islands. She arrived at Port Royal in the fall of 1862 and worked for two years with two white teachers, also from Philadelphia, at a school on St. Helena Island. Landing at Hilton Head Island, she observed the "dismal" condition of the black population and took a steamboat to the town of Beaufort, picturesque with its planters' mansions. Black boatmen rowed Forten and her party across the channel to St. Helena as the sun was setting. She was entranced by the beauty of the setting and the boatmen's "sweet and strange and solemn" renditions of "Roll, Jordan, Roll" and "No Man Can Hinder Me." Traversing the southern countryside by carriage after dark, Forten and her companions quelled their fears and expressed the excitement of their mission by singing "John Brown," the anthem of antislavery soldiers.[38]

Teachers who went South faced a daunting task. Their pupils flooded the areas occupied by federal troops. Many contrabands came from the local area, others had followed the army as it moved South, and many had made their way from territory still controlled by the Confederacy. Children and adults were eager to learn to read and write, and teachers conducted crowded day and night schools. Laura Towne ran the school on St. Helena, taught, and worked doctoring the sick. The Sea Island plantations had been among the most isolated in the South, with a population that was about 80 percent black. African Americans there had preserved much of their African cultures and spoke a language called Gullah, a patois of English and African dialects, that made the teachers' work even more challenging.

Harriet Tubman was one anti-slavery activist who didn't wait for the government to organize aid to contrabands. Convinced that the outbreak of war meant the end of slavery was at hand, Tubman left the safety of Canada and headed for the South. In May 1861 she accompanied General Benjamin Butler's Massachusetts regiment into Maryland, where she had once been enslaved. When Butler's troops were stationed at Fortress Monroe in Virginia, Tubman helped care for the growing number of refugees,

Two former slave women with their white teacher, Kate Foote of the New England Freedman's Aid Society, posing with a grammar, in South Carolina.

nursing the sick, feeding the hungry, and finding the clothing they needed. By late that summer, more than a thousand contrabands were living and working at Fortress Monroe. The escaped slaves deprived the Confederacy of their labor, and they also became a valuable resource for the U.S. army, doing heavy labor, building fortifications, working in the camps, cooking, and doing laundry.[39]

That fall, when Port Royal fell to the U.S. troops, Harriet Tubman was in New England, describing the condition of the refugees and soliciting funds and material for their relief from her network of antislavery patrons and friends. At the behest of abolitionist Massachusetts governor John Andrew she took a military transport for the Sea Islands. In Beaufort, she was a volunteer attached to the command of General David Hunter, commander of the

Department of the South and a strong abolitionist who believed the South's runaway slaves should be enlisted to fight in the U.S. Army. Tubman did whatever she could to help the contrabands, spending much of her time working in the hospital. She was already renowned among the troops and teachers as the Moses of her people for her exploits on the Underground Railroad. An inveterate storyteller, she was never shy about entertaining people with stories of escapes to freedom, and on a visit to Beaufort Charlotte Forten was inspired by Tubman's tales. In South Carolina, Tubman also became known for her competence as a root doctor, as she treated contrabands and soldiers for dysentery, smallpox, and other fevers.

One of the fugitives from slavery, Robert Smalls, came into the U.S. lines bringing the navy an extraordinarily valuable gift. Smalls, enslaved in South Carolina, had been hired out by his master at the age of twelve to work in the Charleston shipyard. By the time Confederates fired on Fort Sumter, he was a twenty-three-year-old boat pilot navigating the waters of Charleston Harbor and adjacent waterways. The Confederates used him and eight other slaves on the crew of a steam-powered side-wheeler vessel refitted as a gunboat named *Planter*. Each night, while the white crewmen retired to their homes, Smalls and the other blacks worked to clean and ready the ship for the next day's duty.

Smalls devised a plan to escape, and when he explained it to his brother John and the other black crew members, they signed on enthusiastically. They informed their families, who planned to escape with them, and waited for their best opportunity. Well aware of the risk they were taking and of the consequences for failure, the entire party resolved not to be taken alive. If discovered, they would use the *Planter*'s guns to fight the Confederates and go down with the ship rather than be captured.

On the evening of May 12, 1862, the white officers and sailors left as usual, but this night the *Planter* was loaded down with a special shipment, valuable supplies to be delivered the following day to two Confederate forts. The black men moved normally about the boat that night. The arrival of family members sometime after eight didn't arouse the suspicions of the dock patrol, since they sometimes brought supper to the crew. Nor was the patrol alarmed when a black man from another crew came aboard. Very early the next morning, Smalls ordered the boilers fired and the *Planter*, flying the Confederate flag, moved slowly out of port and into the harbor. They saluted the harbor forts with the customary blasts on the whistle and passed under the forts' heavy guns manned by Confederate guards. When the vessel was safely past the Confederate outposts, Smalls and his tense but jubilant crew brought down the Confederate flag and replaced it with a white flag. The vessel they delivered to the U.S. forces was, according to Smalls, "a gunboat which cost nearly thirty thousand dollars," fitted with "six large guns, from a 24-pounder howitzer to a 100-pound Parrott rifle."[40] They also brought invaluable knowledge of Confederate defenses and local waterways. As he turned over the prize to the U.S. commander, Smalls was reported to have said, "I thought the *Planter* might be of some use to Uncle Abe."[41]

The northern press hailed Smalls and his crewmen as heroes, and Congress ruled that they should receive half the value of the prize they presented to the U.S. cause. Smalls joined the fight against slavery, enlisting in the U.S. Navy. He was commissioned as second Lieutenant with the thirty-third Regiment, United States Colored Troops, and was assigned as the pilot on the *Planter*. In November 1863 the *Planter* engaged in fierce combat with Confederate forces, and the ship's captain contemplated surrender. Fearlessly, Smalls rallied the crew and urged the gunners to continue firing, saving the ship and the crew from being captured. When word of his actions reached the military hierarchy, navy officials dismissed the captain and promoted Smalls to his position. Former slave Robert Smalls, captain of the *Planter*, became an African American hero of the Civil War.

Smalls's position of authority in the U.S. Navy was unusual but not unique. African Americans had been seafarers before the Revolution, and the federal government had been willing to accept black sailors in military ranks from the beginning of the Civil War. Just a few weeks after the war started, U.S. naval commanders began gathering intelligence about southern coastal and inland waterways from fugitive slaves and used their labor on shipboard. Many southern slaves had worked as boatmen before the war, and Confederate forces were making good use of slaves on their wartime vessels. As one officer wrote to Secretary of the Navy Gideon Welles in the summer of 1861, "If [N]egroes are to be used in this contest, I have no hesitation they should be used to preserve the government not to destroy it."[42] The recognition of the importance of slaves to the Confederate navy and the growing need for hands on U.S. naval ships forced the Navy to act. By the early fall of 1861 the secretary authorized the use of contrabands on U.S. ships.

Blacks continued to volunteer as the war rolled into the early months of 1862, but Lincoln and the military establishment remained reluctant to enlist them in the land forces. Frustrated by official reluctance and greatly in need of manpower, in March 1862 General Hunter declared marshal law and issued a proclamation freeing all the slaves in the Department of the South. Using special emergency authority, Congress had given his predecessor, General Thomas W. Sherman, the power to arm the slaves on the Sea Islands, so Hunter recruited the former slaves for military action. President Lincoln, however, modified Hunter's emancipation order, as he had General Frémont's in the Western Department nearly a year before. "[Neither] General Hunter nor any other commander or person has been authorized by the Government of the United States to make proclamations declaring the slaves of any State free," Lincoln declared. He pronounced Hunter's directive "void" but again urged loyal slaveholders in the border states to take advantage of his offer of compensated emancipation.[43]

Hunter had already started to form a black military company when Lincoln revoked his orders. Not waiting for blacks to volunteer, he had rounded up hundreds of former slaves and forced them into service, only to have to disband the unit within a few weeks. Lincoln had refused the black troops offered to federal forces by General Hunter and by commanders in Louisiana and Kansas, even though the federal government was under intense pressure. By the summer of 1861 General George McClellan and his troops were mired in the Virginia campaign against Confederate general Robert E. Lee, and the need for troops was growing. The United States lost 16,000 dead, wounded or missing during the Seven Days' Battle in Virginia, and more than 14,000 at the Second Battle of Bull Run. There were rumors that support for the Confederacy was building in Britain and western Europe, assistance that would surely turn the war towards the South. Lincoln called for 300,000 volunteers in July 1862, but few white men enlisted. Finally, on July 17, Congress authorized the president to "employ as many persons of African descent as he may think necessary and proper for the suppression of this rebellion." It then authorized the recruitment of blacks into the army.[44]

At first, Lincoln, still fearful of losing the border states, resisted the call for black troops and refused to accept an offer of two regiments of black soldiers from Kansas. "To arm the [N]egroes," he argued, "would turn 50,000 bayonets from the loyal Border States against us that were for us."[45] The abolitionists' answered that many more than 50,000 African Americans were ready to fight for the U.S. cause. The army's need was compelling, however, and in a matter of weeks the War Department instructed General Rufus Saxton, military governor of the Sea

Islands, to raise five regiments of black soldiers. Building on the remnants of General Hunter's force, Saxton organized the First South Carolina Volunteers, the first officially authorized black regiment of the Civil War. Saxton invited Massachusetts abolitionist Thomas Wentworth Higginson to take charge of the unit. Higginson, readily agreed, resigned his position with a Massachusetts regiment, and went south to Port Royal.

Charlotte Forten saw Higginson as the best white man imaginable to recruit and lead a troop of black soldiers. He was a Harvard graduate, a Unitarian minister, an adventurer, and a dedicated radical abolitionist. He had worked closely with free blacks in Boston and had been arrested for his part in storming the courthouse where the fugitive slave Anthony Burns had been held captive in 1854. He had visited Kansas in 1856, was an agent for the Kansas National Commission, aimed at making Kansas a free state, and had solicited funds for John Brown and for Brown's widow. Convinced in the 1850s that a war to end

A black United States soldier, from an 1864 illustration in Harper's Weekly. The image is a section of a larger picture, which also shows the same soldier in his former degraded state as a contraband slave.

slavery was coming, he began to study military theory and to train. When the war began he had planned to find what was left of John Brown's followers and carry out raids in Virginia but instead worked recruiting troops and joined the army himself in late summer 1862.[46]

Higginson understood what a bold and dangerous venture he was undertaking. Most whites, including governmental officials and Lincoln himself, questioned blacks' bravery. One white corporal from a New York regiment bluntly summed up the general feeling among white recruits. "We don't want to fight side and side with the nigger. We think that we are too superior race for that."[47] Many believed that ex-slaves in particular would be too submissive and too cowardly to be good soldiers. Higginson's First South Carolina Regiment was composed entirely of former slaves from the heart of the Confederacy. Should Higginson's black troops fail to prove themselves in battle, it would confirm the racial inferiority that many northerners assumed. Despite the dangers, Higginson was thrilled at the opportunity, later recalling that it "fulfilled the dream of a lifetime."[48]

African Americans surely understood the importance of this experiment, but most also saw the irony that, after the military service and sacrifice of their ancestors in America's previous wars, their ability and patriotism should be questioned. Outraged black leaders scoffed at the notion that "Colored men . . . good enough . . . to help win American independence," were now being forced to prove that they were good enough to defend it. Yet from the beginning they resigned themselves to proving again their ability and their valor to white America. Higginson had great respect for the courage, ability, and motivation of the men he recruited, and he was determined that they would prove themselves. He set out to make the First South Carolina a well-trained and disciplined fighting force. Higginson had other talents besides military aptitude that suited him for leading the regiment. He was a poet and a writer, well connected to the abolitionist press, and would be in a good position to report on the accomplishments of the black soldiers and their capabilities for a life in freedom.[49] In its first year, the First South Carolina regiment engaged the Confederate enemy many times in combat along the Georgia–Florida border, and the battlefield performance of his men impressed Higginson. He wrote, "Nobody knows anything about these men who has not seen them in battle. . . . No officer in this regiment now doubts that the key to the successful prosecution of this war lies in the unlimited employment of black troops."[50]

The war situation and the enlistment of black soldiers prompted Lincoln to rethink his position on slavery. He was under increasing abolitionist pressure and needed to energize northern support for the war. Additionally, he wanted to refocus the war's aims, partly as a means to draw support from British and European abolitionists and block Confederate attempts to gain recognition and material aid from abroad. On September 22, 1862, Lincoln found an occasion to announce his decision, seizing on the marginal military success of the Antietam campaign in Maryland that, five days before, had forced troops under Confederate general Robert E. Lee into retreat. He declared that on January 1, 1863, he would issue a proclamation freeing all slaves under the control of people still in rebellion against the United States. His proclamation would not apply to those slaves controlled by masters loyal to the United States. This was a qualified step toward freedom, but its impact was significant.

This engraving celebrates the emancipation of the slaves in Washington, D.C., in 1862.
Emancipation was greeted with great jubilation by the District's African American community,
and for many years afterward, black Washingtonians celebrated Emancipation Day on
April 16 with parades and festivals.

Lincoln's announcement met mixed reactions. Generally, northern whites were uncomfortable with the president's changing the aim of the war from simply saving the Union to including emancipation. Only abolitionists would have been willing to go to war to free southern slaves at the outset. African Americans were skeptical about the qualified nature of the announcement but were hopeful that if the president issued the proclamation it might ultimately lead to complete emancipation. Lincoln did indeed issue his proclamation on January 1, 1863, a joyous event on a day that slaveholders had traditionally held slave sales that fractured black families. In cities and towns throughout the North, crowds had gathered to await the official announcement of the proclamation. In Washington Henry M. Turner, a free African American born in South Carolina and minister of the Israel Bethel African Methodist Episcopal Church, was one of the first to get the word from a local newspaper. He raced to the church to spread the word. "Down Pennsylvania Ave. I ran as for my life," he recalled, "and when the people saw me coming with the paper in my hand they raised a shouting cheer that was almost deafening." As one celebrant reported, "men squealed, women fainted, dogs barked, white and colored people shook

Slaves often learned of the Emancipation Proclamation from U.S. troops advancing through the South. In this painting, African American soldiers inform slaves of their freedom.

hands, songs were sung, and by this time cannons began to fire at the navy-yard." The president came to the window of the White House and bowed to the swelling crowd, and "thousands told him that if he would come out of that palace, they would hug him to death."[51]

At Fort Scott in Kansas the men of the First Kansas Colored Volunteer Infantry gathered to hear speeches and celebrate the proclamation. The officers reviewed a dress parade, and then the men stacked their arms and took places at tables set up for the ceremony. The entire party sang the "Star-Spangled Banner" and listened as their officers explained the meaning of the proclamation. African Americans were engaged in "no mere struggle for conquest, but a struggle for their own freedom," the unit commander told his troops. Theirs was a fight for all those who had "long suffered oppression and wrong at the hands of our enemies." The men then gave three cheers for President Lincoln, sang hymns and read aloud from the proclamation. Finally, in one of the best-remembered speeches of the day, an officer pointed to the American flag and said, "Now boys, do you understand that? It means that you may hunt, shoot and destroy every rebel slaveholder in the land and that flag . . . and all under it shall not hinder but aid you in such righteous retribution." In response, the entire gathering broke into "tumultuous cheering."[52]

The soldiers, teachers, missionaries, labor superintendents, and local residents of the Sea Islands held an enormous celebration in Beaufort, complete with prayers, speeches, hymns, poems, songs, and feasting. The highlight of the event came when a white resident, who had freed his slaves some time before, read the Emancipation Proclamation. At the end of the reading, a chaplain from New York stepped up to the commander of the First South Carolina regiment to present a flag made by the women of his church. As Higginson began to wave the flag, an elderly man below the speakers' platform broke into spontaneous song. Immediately two women joined their voices to his, and soon all of the African Americans were singing:

> My Country, 'tis of thee,
> Sweet land of liberty,
> Of thee I sing!

As they went through many verses, Colonel Thomas Wentworth Higginson was moved by the thought that it was the "first day they had ever had a country, [and] the first flag they had ever seen which promised anything to their people."[53]

The camp of the Tennessee Colored Battery in Johnsonville, Tennessee. The soldiers quartered here, among the first African Americans to join the Union Army, fought bravely at the battles of Nashville and Fort Pillow.

Creating Freedom During and After the War

In the Sea Islands, having a regiment composed of local fugitives from slavery imparted one great advantage: they were able to provide intelligence about the countryside. The U.S. army was running low on lumber, and the white troops who had been sent out to find supplies had returned empty-handed. In January 1863, the First South Carolina had a chance to prove their worth on a foraging expedition. They went to the area from which their sergeant had escaped, up the St. Mary's River on the border between Florida and Georgia. More than four hundred sixty men boarded three gunboats and made their way to St. Simon's Island off the coast of Georgia. There, naval officers warned them about Confederate soldiers who were entrenched on the banks of the St. Mary's River. While waiting for their third boat to arrive at the island, the men busied themselves by salvaging massive iron bars from abandoned Confederate forts. Some of the men had built these forts as conscripted slave labor, and Thomas Wentworth Higginson noted that they dismantled the bunkers and magazines with great enthusiasm. A raiding party suffered its first casualties in a confrontation with Confederate cavalry a short way up the river, but the men acquitted themselves well.

On the expedition the men who had come from the area provided invaluable information. The corporal who led them up the road through the woods to the Confederate cavalry camp knew the road well, as he had helped build it. He also piloted their boat through the treacherous waters of the river, up to his former plantation and the mill, where they found a store of lumber. They discovered that local slaves, at first reluctant to help them, were of great assistance after being informed of the Emancipation Proclamation. Higginson carried copies of the proclamation, which he dispensed to the slaves. Although mainly illiterate, they seemed comforted to have the promise of their freedom in writing. On the way back down the river their boat, loaded with bricks and plundered

President Abraham Lincoln issued the Emancipation Proclamation on September 22, 1862.
The proclamation declared freedom for all blacks enslaved in areas still in rebellion against the
United States as of January 1, 1863.

provisions, came under heavy fire, and the boat captain was killed. But the bravery of the men on this expedition and their knowledge of the area encouraged General Hunter to consider sending the black troops on other forays into enemy territory.

The following month, when the government formed the Second South Carolina Volunteers, another black regiment, under the leadership of Colonel James Montgomery, Harriet Tubman found a chance to use the skills she had developed on the Underground Railroad. Montgomery, born in Ohio, was a teacher and a minister for a time in Kentucky and settled in Kansas after the passage of the Kansas–Nebraska Act. In Kansas he helped organize the free state militia to keep proslavery forces from driving him and other antislavery advocates off their land. A comrade and supporter of John Brown, Montgomery and his militia conducted guerrilla raids into Missouri to free slaves, burning and plundering along the way. In 1858 they engaged in a gun battle with federal troops, but a general amnesty in Ohio saved them from criminal prosecution. Shortly after the Civil War started, Montgomery and his men joined the Kansas infantry.

James Montgomery put his militia experience into the service of the federal cause in the Sea Islands. Whereas Higginson and his men, as a point of honor, had carefully avoided wholesale plunder in their raids, Montgomery had no such scruples. Montgomery was familiar with Harriet Tubman's adventures rescuing people from southern slavery, and he engaged her to support his operations along the southeastern coast. Tubman gathered a group of nine men from localities stretching from Charleston to Jacksonville, Florida, to operate as scouts and river pilots under her command.

One raid in early June up the Combahee River into the South Carolina interior from Charleston Harbor was reported in the northern press and brought Harriet Tubman public renown after many years in the shadows. After a thorough scouting mission and after collecting intelligence from refugees on the islands, Montgomery's force steamed up the river on three gunboats. They moved under cover of darkness into a lightly guarded rice plantation area, avoiding underwater mines and destroying bridges and railroad tracks to cut off Confederate supplies. At first, as the soldiers raided and torched the plantations, slaves ran off into the woods. When they learned that the gunboats had come to set them free, they picked up their children and their pigs and chickens, put baskets holding their meager supplies on their heads, and headed for the boat landing. Overseers reportedly were powerless to drive them back to the fields. Harriet Tubman stood on the deck of a gunboat and sang to encourage the people to escape:

> Of all the whole creation in the East or in the West,
> The glorious Yankee nation is the greatest and the best.
> Come along! Come along! Don't be alarmed,
> Uncle Sam is rich enough to give you all a farm.[1]

So many people clung to the landing boats that the boats could only leave the shore when, after each verse of Tubman's song, the excited slaves threw up their hands and shouted "Glory!" By midday the following day, more than seven hundred fifty slaves had boarded the boats bound for the federal encampment at Beaufort.

The new abolitionist direction of the war set by the Emancipation Proclamation gave the United States cause a holy, dramatically crusading quality. For African Americans it also opened wider the doors to military service. Immediately, Governor John A. Andrew of Massachusetts was authorized to form the Fifty-fourth Massachusetts Volunteers, the first black military regiment recruited from the North. Although the governor organized a substantial recruiting effort in cooperation with many of the state's most prominent black leaders, African Americans did not hurry to enlist. Having had their initial offers of service rejected and having endured almost two years of insults from a government that asserted time and again its belief in white supremacy, many blacks hesitated. Throughout the North, African Americans convened public meetings to demand a guarantee of fair treatment. They would serve only if they could serve with dignity and equality. Black recruiters worked diligently, calling upon black men to meet their responsibility to the race. Most did recognize the importance of being part of the fight against slavery, and by the spring of 1863 thirty or forty men a day were enlisting in the Massachusetts Fifty-fourth.

The black troops being recruited in New England, the Middle Atlantic states, and the Midwest faced special disabilities. Initially, only white men could be commissioned officers, and black soldiers were paid less than white soldiers, even when they ranked higher or performed the same duties. A white private was paid $13 per month plus a uniform allowance, and a white regimental sergeant received $21 per month plus allowances; blacks at all noncommissioned ranks earned only $10 per month, from which $3 was subtracted for uniforms. At this substandard rate of pay, soldiers could not provide for their families, and some wives and children were forced into poorhouses while their husbands and fathers served on active duty.[2] Frederick Douglass gained an interview with Lincoln to discuss this situation. The president told him that because the white public was greatly offended by blacks in military service and because blacks were fighting for a larger cause, they should be willing to be soldiers under any circumstances. It was impossible to push public opinion any further, he said, and this lower pay rate was a necessary compromise that would eventually be rectified.[3]

Many of the men of the Massachusetts Fifty-fourth were not willing to accept this inequality. Some refused to serve without full pay and requested discharges so they could support their families. Others refused to take anything for their service, rather than accepting inferior wages. Their pay boycott became a widely publicized

In this broadside, the Philadelphia committee in charge of recruiting black soldiers for the United States army in the Civil War stressed the crucial importance of the war for freeing the slaves. Overall, 186,000 black soldiers served in the U.S. army, and another 29,000 in the U.S. navy.

and effective but very costly form of protest. More than twenty men of the Fourteenth Colored Rhode Island Heavy Artillery were jailed for refusing their wages. Sergeant William Walker led his men in refusing to serve for inferior payment, for which he and the entire company were charged with mutiny, and Walker was executed. Massachusetts Governor Andrew wrote to Lincoln to ask why "the Government which found no law to pay him except as a nondescript or a contraband, nevertheless found law enough to shoot him as a soldier."[4]

In addition to the injustices imposed by their own government, black troops faced mistreatment at the hands of the enemy. The Confederate government refused to regard captured black soldiers as prisoners of war, threatening them with enslavement or execution. Even the few relatively fortunate black soldiers who were spared and held as Confederate prisoners were ill treated and ill fed compared with their white fellow soldiers. Yet despite such dangers and disparities, tens of thousands of black men enrolled in the U.S. military.

As the number of black soldiers grew, white northerners continued to ask the question that betrayed both their racist assumptions and their ignorance of history: will the Negro fight? Robert Gould Shaw, son of a white abolitionist family and the commander of the Massachusetts Fifty-fourth, was anxious to show the valor of his men. He wrote letters to Governor Andrew asking that his regiment be transferred to a place where they would have the opportunity to join in the heaviest fighting. In the summer of 1863 the Fifty-fourth was sent to James Island, South Carolina, where they saw their first hard combat. Almost immediately the unit engaged and defeated an enemy force, saving the white soldiers of the Tenth Connecticut Infantry regiment from a massive Confederate attack. They then marched to Morris Island and, not having eaten or slept for two days, were ordered into battle. They were to storm the ramparts of Fort Wagner, a heavily fortified Confederate stronghold perched atop the high ground overlooking the beach.

An 1863 recruiting poster for black troops in the Civil War, showing a black unit with its white officer. Black troops typically fought in units commanded by white officers and black noncommissioned officers. The discrimination black troops suffered extended to pay: black soldiers were initially paid a net $7 per month, against $13 for white soldiers.

The attack on the all-but-impenetrable citadel was costly—at least 272 of the 600 soldiers who assaulted Fort Wagner were killed, wounded, or captured. Yet, these black men fought with a courage and skill that impressed even the most racist skeptics. Colonel Shaw was killed in the battle, and, in a gesture of contempt, the Confederates cast his body into a mass grave with the black soldiers who had fallen in the battle. Later, when the site was in U.S. hands, Shaw's family refused to have his body moved, saying that he surely considered it an honor to be buried with his men. One of the African Americans in this battle was Sergeant William H. Carney, who, though painfully wounded, had planted the American flag on the Confederate parapet. Carney was carried to the U.S. lines bleeding and exhausted but raised his head to say, "Boys, the old flag never touched the ground." For his actions, Carney was the first black man to be awarded the Congressional Medal of Honor.[5]

Sergeant William H. Carney received the Medal of Honor for his service in the Civil War. He was the first African American to receive this prestigious award. Another fourteen black soldiers were also honored with this medal for their heroism during the war.

Harriet Tubman was at Fort Wagner at the time of the battle. She had served Colonel Shaw his last meal, and after the charge, helped nurse the injured and bury the dead. She captured the glory and pathos of the fighting sometime later when she described a battle, probably Fort Wagner: "And then we saw the lightning, and that was the guns; and then we heard the thunder, and that was the big guns; and then we heard the rain falling, and that was the drops of blood falling; and when we came to get in the crops, it was dead men that we reaped."[6] Northern newspapers were effusive in their praise for the Massachusetts Fifty-fourth. The editor of the *New York Tribune* compared the men's bravery under fire to the courage of white troops at the battle of Bunker Hill, apparently unaware of the black soldiers honored for their role in that famous Revolutionary War battle. Abraham Lincoln urged General Ulysses S. Grant to increase black enlistments, saying, "I believe [they are] a resource which, if vigorously applied now, will soon close the contest."[7]

Black troops also had an opportunity to prove their worth in the Mississippi region in the summer of 1863. This was in an area whose French

Soldiers from Company E, Fourth U.S. Colored Infantry. In the Civil War black soldiers fought in segregated units commanded by white officers. Although the War Department at first rejected their services, eventually 186,000 fought in the U.S. Army.

and Spanish background still influenced racial identity and custom. Black soldiers, even slaves, had served with the French and the Spanish when Louisiana was a territory of those nations, fighting the Choctaw Indians and defending against English forces during the late eighteenth century. Blacks continued to serve in the militia even after Louisiana became a part of the United States, forming a black military unit commanded by black officers called the Louisiana Native Guard. As one New Orleans newspaper reminded its readers, many of those who volunteered to serve in the Native Guard in the 1860s were the descendants of those who had served with Andrew Jackson and defended the city at the Battle of New Orleans during the War of 1812.[8]

When Louisiana seceded from the United States in January 1861, hundreds of free black men joined the Native Guard and offered their services. The reasons they were willing to serve in the Louisiana militia were varied and complex. Most of the men were prosperous, well-educated New Orleans men of mixed European and African heritage. In New Orleans, 80 percent of free people of color were of mixed ancestry, compared with only 10 percent in the rest of the state. Their light complexion elevated their status over darker blacks, particularly in the eyes of Louisiana whites, and gave them a unique opportunity to prosper. This created a mulatto class in New Orleans connected to many white slaveholding families by kinship. A few of these wealthy mulattoes even held slaves. Although there were a number of African American slaveholders throughout the South by 1860, almost all held friends, spouses, and relatives in nominal bondage because state laws either prohibited emancipation, made it difficult, or required freed blacks to leave the state. By contrast, some of the African American slaveholders in Louisiana, and particularly in New Orleans, employed slave labor on large flourishing plantations or in fine city homes. As one free man of color, a wealthy New Orleans wine merchant, explained his willingness to fight for Louisiana, he feared reprisal and loss of his property should he not show loyalty to the state's defense.[9] The Native Guard received an ambivalent reception from white Louisianans. In early 1862, the Louisiana legislature declared the militia open only to white men and officially disbanded the Native Guard.

In the spring, U.S. troops under the command of General Benjamin Butler entered New Orleans, forcing Confederate troops to evacuate the city. Slaves flocked to the federal forces and labored for the army at such tasks as building fortifications, washing clothes, and repairing and maintaining buildings and equipment. At one point the Twelfth Connecticut Infantry had forty black women doing laundry and other domestic work. Butler, who had vowed never to recruit black soldiers, found himself in need of fighters, as the Confederates attacked Baton Rouge just to the north and threatened New Orleans. When the Confederate forces had withdrawn, the African American militia had refused to leave the city. Instead they had offered their services to the U.S. army, and by the late summer of 1862, Butler accepted their offer. "I shall…have within ten days," Butler wrote in late August, "a regiment of 1,000 strong, of Native Guards (colored)." The general seemed pleased that his African American troops were composed of free black men, "the darkest of whom is about the complexion of the late Mr. [Daniel] Webster," former U.S. Senator from Massachusetts.[10]

General Butler's description of the Native Guard was only partly correct. Almost all of those who had served in the old Native Guard had been free before the U.S. occupation. As newly constituted, however, the Native Guard consisted of two regiments. There was the First Corps d'Afrique, which became the Seventy-third United States Colored Troops in 1864, and the Third Louisiana Native Guards, which was composed of former slaves, most of a much darker hue than the members of the original Native Guard. African American officers remained in command of the First Corps d'Afrique, but white officers led the

Third Louisiana Native Guard. By the fall of 1862 the Native Guard paraded through Canal Street in the heart of New Orleans waving the U.S. flag, marching to the beat of "Yankee Doodle," and wearing the blue uniform of the U.S. Army. By the next spring this Native Guard had grown to three regiments commanded by twenty-one black officers, mainly lieutenants and captains, the elite of New Orleans's free black society.[11]

In late May 1863, General Nathaniel P. Banks and federal troops settled in for a protracted siege at Port Hudson, over 100 miles northwest of New Orleans. Before long the Confederate forces ran out of food and were reduced to eating their draft animals. One Confederate soldier described the food supply after the first few weeks of the siege. "The last quarter ration of beef had been given out to the troops on the 29th of June. On the 1st of July, at the request of many officers, a wounded mule was killed and cut up for experimental eating. All those who partook of it spoke highly of the dish." Shortly, the search for food became more desperate. "Some horses were also slaughtered," the soldier reported, "their flesh was found to be very good eating, but not equal to mule." Finally, "Rats, of which there were plenty about the deserted camps, were also caught

African American troops played a crucial role in the successful siege of Vicksburg, Mississippi, a key point in the western theater of the war. The victories of black soldiers at Port Hudson in May 1863 and Milliken's Bend the following month paved the way for the fall of Vicksburg in July and quieted some of the harshest critics of African American recruitment.

by many officers and men, and were found to be quite a luxury—superior, in the opinion of those who eat them, to spring chicken."[12] Confederate morale, already low, was finally crushed when on July 4 word came that the U.S. Army had captured Vicksburg. Five days later, on July 9, 1863, Confederate forces surrendered at Port Hudson.

As black men in the federal force took charge of what one colonel from the Sixth Michigan Infantry referred to as "proud old Southerners and their fiery sons," he felt sure that some of the prisoners "recognized their own waiters and field hands among the sentinels...clad in federal blue and carrying Springfield muskets."[13] A few southern reports downplayed the role of the Native Guard. A report in the *Charleston Mercury* claimed that black troops were forced against their will to charge the Confederate lines, but even accounts from Confederate soldiers discredit such stories. African Americans' bravery in battle contradicted the basic philosophy of the Confederacy.[14]

The valor of black troops at Port Hudson, as at Fort Wagner, helped change northern minds about the worth of black soldiers. The letters of white U.S. soldiers, official reports released to the public, and major newspapers all commented on the bravery of black troops. Some even exaggerated their accomplishments, making them larger-than-life heroes. Drawings of black soldiers planting the American flag atop the Confederate defenses at Port Hudson in *Frank Leslie's Illustrated Newspaper* gave the false impression that the Native Guard actually had penetrated Confederate lines. The *New York Times* lavished praise on the African American troops. No matter how impressive the accounts of black valor, many white Americans continued to accept black inferiority as an irrefutable fact. The *Times* tempered its accolades by the suggestion that much of the credit for the extraordinary actions of the black troops should go to their white officers. "It is no longer possible," one editor wrote, "to doubt the bravery and steadiness of the colored race when rightly led."[15] U.S. soldiers' eyewitness accounts were more straightforward. The quartermaster's clerk of the Forty-ninth Massachusetts recorded, "All agree that none fought more boldly than the native guard...six times did they go over the ground (toward the Confederate line) heaping it with their slain."[16]

Black people throughout the nation fervently hoped that the soldiers' display of courage and commitment to country would open a wedge in the national wall of racial prejudice. Lincoln seemed genuinely impressed with the black troops, but the War Department still refused them equal treatment or equal pay.

The First Mississippi Cavalry escorts captured Confederate soldiers into Vicksburg.

After the victory in Louisiana, Port Hudson became a recruiting center for African American troops, and General Banks moved to create a larger corps of black troops to help white units drive out the last Confederate holdouts. White and black soldiers sometimes worked well together, but white troops resented the black officers, and Butler's refusal to support the black officers in confrontations with lower-ranking white soldiers eventually led the black officers to resign. White officers immediately replaced them, and the Native Guard was brought in line with the army's other black units.

The protests of blacks and their allies, combined with the rising stature of black soldiers, led Congress finally to provide equal pay, arms, equipment, and medical services for black soldiers in June 1864. Confederates, however, still refused to treat captured black troops as prisoners of war. In the spring of 1864, southern units under the command of General Nathan Bedford Forrest had attacked the U.S. garrison at Fort Pillow, Tennessee. The Confederates had a more than two-to-one advantage, but the U.S. troops stubbornly refused to surrender. Forrest, a former slave trader, was incensed that about half the soldiers fighting against him were African American, seemingly mocking him and his cause. Forrest, known for his bad temper, raged at his men and ordered them to "kill the last damned one of them," even the captured soldiers.

His men were at first reluctant to comply, but finally followed his orders and conducted one of the bloodiest massacres of the war, killing at least three hundred men, according to a later Congressional inquiry. They clubbed the wounded to death, burned some alive, and nailed others to walls. When some federal soldiers attempted to escape by running into the river, Forrest's men shot them, as one said, the soldiers' "heads presenting 'beautiful' targets." The killing went on until even Forrest could stand no more, and he finally halted his frenzied men. "If General Forrest had not run between our men and the Yanks with his pistol and sabre drawn," one southern soldier later wrote, "not

CREATING FREEDOM DURING AND AFTER THE WAR   203

a man would have been spared." As Forrest later recalled the extent of the car-
nage, "the river was dyed with the blood of the slaughtered for 200 yards."[17]

In his dispatches, African American war correspondent Thomas Morris
Chester called such Confederate atrocities "evidence of Southern barbarism and
inhumanity," and northern newspapers carried outraged headlines about the
"Fort Pillow Massacre." The *New York Tribune's* headline referred to Forrest as
"BUTCHER FORREST." Black soldiers, incensed by the slaughter of their comrades, vowed never to forget the inhumane acts. Less than a week after the massacre, 1,200 black troops in Memphis fell on their knees to take a solemn oath
of revenge. "Remember Fort Pillow!" became their rallying cry.[18]

Major U.S. victories in Georgia, Tennessee, and Virginia during the fall
and winter of 1864 pushed the Confederacy to the point of desperation. As U.S.
forces destroyed or occupied large areas of the South and southern armies suffered mounting battlefield losses, desertion became an increasing problem for
the Confederacy. The South seemed to be running out of everything, including
weapons, war equipment, food, and even uniforms and shoes for its troops.[19]
By early 1865 Confederate commander Robert E. Lee wondered what would
have been unthinkable at the war's onset: "whether slavery shall be extin-
guished by our enemies and the slaves be used against us, or use them ourselves
at the risk of the effects which must be produced upon our social institutions."
He and others, including Confederate president Jefferson Davis, urged that slaves
be armed as Confederate soldiers.

There was sharp debate in the Confederate Congress on the subject.
Journalist Chester, who interviewed "deserters and refugees, of both colors,"
reported in his correspondence from Richmond in February 1865 that there
was "no subject which (was) engrossing so much attention in Richmond as the
proposition to arm a corps of [N]egroes."[20] Having argued for the inferiority of
African Americans, many southerners could not conceive of enlisting blacks. As
Confederate General Howell Cobb observed, "The day you make soldiers of
[blacks] is the beginning of the end of the revolution. If slaves will make good
soldiers our whole theory of slavery is wrong." Indeed, Lee had recommended
to the Confederate Congress that immediate freedom be provided for slaves
willing to serve in the military and that "a well-digested plan of gradual and
general emancipation" be established at the end of the war.[21]

Lee's proposal was not popular with most white southerners, particularly
those serving in the Confederate army. Chester's sources told him, "The rank

Led by their white commander, Robert Gould Shaw, the Fifty-fourth Massachusetts Colored Regiment attacks the Confederate Fort Wagner in South Carolina in 1863.

and file, most of whom have been thrust into the army against their inclination," would use the arming of blacks as an excuse "for laying down their arms and returning home in disgust."[22] As one Confederate soldier wrote to tell his mother after hearing the news of the plan, "I did not volunteer my services to fight for a free Negroe[']s country but to fight for a free white man[']s country & I do not think I love my country well enough to fight with black soldiers."[23]

Nor were the consequences of enlisting black soldiers in the Confederacy clear. The information that Chester received from slaves must have been alarming to Confederates. If armed and placed in southern ranks, they said, some slaves were determined to escape to U.S. lines as soon as they could, while others planned a more deadly strategy. According to Chester, "The more thoughtful of the [N]egroes in Richmond rather liked the idea, and, hoping that it would be put into execution, began to prepare the minds of their people for an important chapter in the struggle, in which they were praying to be permitted to take part."[24] The *New Orleans Tribune*, America's first daily black newspaper, picked up Chester's reports, contending that secret associations were organized in Virginia and plans circulated to slaves in many parts of the South. A meeting of African Americans in Richmond concluded that "black men should promptly respond to the call of the rebel chiefs, whenever it should be made, for them to take up arms." Then, once armed they should be prepared to act decisively. "[A]s soon as the battle began the Negroes [at the head of Confederate units] were to rise a shout about Abraham Lincoln and the Union, and, satisfied there would be plenty of supports from the Federal force, they were to turn like uncaged tigers upon the rebel hordes." According to this plan, armed slaves in the rear ranks would open fire on white Confederate troops, catching them in a cross fire. The truth of this story and the effectiveness of this plan were never tested. The Confederacy passed a bill authorizing the recruitment of slaves on March 13, 1865, but by then, it was too late for them to see action. Three weeks later the war was over. [25]

When the Confederate capital fell 5,000 black infantrymen and 1,800 black cavalry troops were in Richmond. In fact, the African American troops were there ahead of the white U.S. units but were held back so that white troops, not conquering blacks, could enter the city first. "History will show," wrote the editor of Philadelphia's *Christian Recorder*, "that [the black troops] were in the suburbs of Richmond long before the white soldiers, and but for the untimely and unfair order to halt, would have triumphantly planted their banner first upon the battlements of the capital of 'ye greate confederacie.'"[26] Black soldiers understood the symbolism of being first to "tear down Jeff Davis' nest" and deeply resented being denied the opportunity to lead the triumphant forces.[27]

Some of these soldiers had been slaves in Virginia before the war and were coming home to liberate friends and family. They took great pride in being part of the occupying force, and the black population of Richmond greeted them as conquering heroes. Garland White, once a Virginia fugitive, returned as a chaplain with the Twenty-eighth U.S. Colored Troops. He remembered the welcoming crowd he addressed as "one huge sea [of] black faces filling the street."[28]

Thomas Morris Chester noted the enthusiasm and pride of the city's blacks as they watched African American soldiers march through the streets. Old and young men laughed aloud, shook hands, and slapped one another on the backs. Women threw their arms around the black soldiers, and they all sang out boldly, "Richmond town is burning down, High diddle diddle inctum inctum ah." It was a day like none Richmond had ever seen, but it was soon surpassed by the arrival of President Lincoln. Blacks welcomed him as the great emancipator, and the president, master of symbolic expression, walked the streets of the city greeting black soldiers and civilians. He then entered the

Alexander H. Johnson, who at the age of fifteen served as the drummer boy of the Fifty-fourth Massachusetts Regiment.

Confederate White House and sat in Jefferson Davis's chair. At Boston's Faneuil Hall Frederick Douglass expressed the hopes of the crowd when he told the packed room that the surrender of Richmond marked "the fall of the rebellion" and the start of "the upbuilding of liberty though the Southern States."[29]

Confederate commander Robert E. Lee's surrender to General U. S. Grant at Appomattox Court House, Virginia, brought an end to the costliest war in American history. A quarter of a million Confederate men died in combat, from accidents, or from disease. U.S. forces had lost 360,000 men, 37,000 of them African Americans. In all, 620,000 Americans had died in four brutal years of fighting. The southern economy was all but destroyed, its money was worthless, and its slave property, the South's most valuable investment, was free. The wealth of the former Confederacy had declined by as much 43 percent. Cotton production had plummeted by half, not recovering until 1879, and the emancipation of almost four million slaves represented a property loss to slaveowners of two billion dollars.[30]

Two days after Lee's surrender, Abraham Lincoln addressed the nation, outlining pressing postwar and postemancipation problems that faced the government and the people. He spoke of shaping a new government in the South from the "disorganized and discordant elements" of "Jefferson Davis's fugitive government" and of providing the vote to literate blacks and black veterans. Among those in Lincoln's audience was John Wilkes Booth, an actor, a southerner, and an ardent supporter of the Confederate cause. Booth was furious at the Confederacy's defeat and especially angered by Lincoln's seeming embrace of the Radical Republican stand on race. "That means nigger citizenship," Booth told a friend. "That is the last speech [Lincoln] will ever make."[31]

Booth's statement was no idle threat. He led a group of southern conspirators who laid plans to kidnap the president and turn him over to the South. When this plan failed, Booth vowed to kill Lincoln. On the evening of April 14 the president and the first lady were watching a play at Ford's Theater in

Washington when Booth suddenly appeared at the rear of the presidential box, aimed his pistol, and shot the president. "Now the South is avenged—be it so to all tyrants," screamed Booth as he leapt from the box to the stage and escaped from the theater. Almost simultaneously another man attacked and seriously wounded Secretary of State William H. Seward at his home. Seward survived, but Lincoln did not. He died of his wound at 7:22 the next morning, becoming the first sitting American president to be assassinated. This calamitous end to the tragic war stunned the nation. A New Orleans Republican newspaper asked a painful and frightening question, "Who next?"[32]

Lincoln had not always enjoyed great popularity among black Americans, but after the Emancipation Proclamation, with its great symbolic significance, most considered him their friend and ally. Their affection for him was confirmed by his second inaugural address in 1864. In that startling speech Lincoln had detailed his belief about the connection between the war and slavery. "Fondly do we hope—fervently do we pray—that this mighty scourge of war may speedily pass away," he had said. He contended that God might use the war to deprive Americans of the wealth they had unjustly amassed from slave labor and that war might continue "until every drop of blood drawn with the lash, shall be paid by another drawn with the sword." He seemed to confirm what African American hymns and stories had asserted for generations, that God's judgment would not sleep forever, and, in the words of the Bible, "the judgments of the Lord, are true and righteous altogether."[33]

The war seemed to have emboldened the president and perhaps changed his mind on the question of slavery. Black Americans felt his death as a deeply personal loss. One member of the Forty-first U.S. Colored Troops described the mood of the men on learning of the president's death. "This cast a gloom over our camp," he said, "one could see and hear the grief of those poor colored men over his tragic end." Another soldier called him the "oppressed Americans' friend, who cherish his name as a household word." As the president's funeral procession moved down Pennsylvania Avenue from the White House to the Capitol, members of the Twenty-second U.S. Colored Regiment took their stations along the route. Shortly after the funeral, the unit joined the search for Booth. Thousands of African Americans lined the railroad tracks to view the funeral train returning Lincoln's body to Springfield, Illinois.[34]

At the end of the war it was not clear how the reuniting America would define black freedom, although it was clear that slavery was dead. In January

Searching for Lost Family

After the Civil War, black people who had been separated from their loved ones by slavery tried to find their lost family members. These advertisements from a black newspaper, the Black Republican, *in New Orleans were typical of their efforts.*

INFORMATION WANTED Mrs. Susan Patterson wishes to find her daughter LOUISA PATTERSON. She was born on Mr. Jos. Moss' plantation, Attakapas, La. Any information respecting her please address this office.

INFORMATION WANTED Mrs. Ritty Green wishes to find her son DUDLEY GREEN. Both are from Scotts County Kentucky, near Georgetown. Any information respecting him may be addressed to this paper.

INFORMATION WANTED Evans Green desires to find his mother, Mrs. Phillis Green, whom he left in Virginia some years ago. She belonged to old Squire Cook of Winchester, whose son was an attorney at law. Any information respecting her will be thankfully received. Address this paper. Winchester paper please copy.

INFORMATION WANTED Robert F. West seeks to find the whereabouts of his two sisters, Mrs. Sarah Carter and Mrs. Emily Thompson, who belonged to a Mr. Grubbs near Waterford, Virginia. Also his two brothers, George West and John Williams, who lived in Lovettsville, Louden County Virginia. Please address this paper.

INFORMATION WANTED Mrs. Louisa Stewart seeks to find her son Joseph Nelson who belonged to Mr. McManus, Cypress Creek near Florence, Ala. Any information please address this paper.

1865, by a vote of 121 to 24, Congress passed the Thirteenth Amendment to the U.S. Constitution, providing for the total abolition of American slavery. Ratified before the year was out, it seemed to many whites and blacks to be the fulfillment of the American Revolution. At last all Americans would have the promise of liberty and justice found in the Declaration of Independence. First, however, the country faced the task of ensuring the survival of people made destitute by slavery and the war. The immediate needs of the freed people were great, greater than could be met by the efforts of the private philanthropies that had been active during the war. In March 1865, before the fall of Richmond, the government had established the Bureau of Refugees, Freedmen, and Abandoned Lands, placing it in the War Department. The Freedmen's Bureau established operations in every department of the occupied South and provided aid to impoverished whites as well as freed slaves. Bureau agents established schools for the freed people and registered legal marriages for former slaves. Attempting to restore order to the war-ravaged southern plantation economy, and to bring in tax money to support federal assistance, agents negotiated millions of labor contracts, many between freed people and their former owners. As state governments were reestablished, the Bureau also oversaw voter registration.

Freed people had definite ideas about the meaning of freedom. Some took new names to denote their new status, as some black people had done after they escaped from slavery before the war, calling themselves Freeman or Freedman, for example. Some dropped slave names given to them by their masters in favor of the names they had been known by in the slave quarters. Others who had been known by a succession of names as they were sold from owner to owner, settled on the name of the fairest or kindest master. Some took the names of masters they had when they were parted from family members. In this way, they hoped, it would be easier for husbands, wives, mothers, fathers, or children to find them.

Freedom meant keeping families together and finding lost family members. In slavery many people had tried to keep track of family members who were sold away. Slaves and free blacks whose occupations let them travel through the South had provided important links, carrying information and messages between people separated by slavery. Many men, like Maryland's Charles Ball who had run away twice from farther south, had endured the hardships of escaping in order to return to wives and children whom they had been forced to leave behind. Even in the same area, husbands and wives owned by different planters had sometimes gone without sleep and risked harsh punishment in order to see

There was great celebration in the U.S. House of Representatives when the Thirteenth Amend-ment to the U.S. Constitution, outlawing slavery in the United States was passed by Congress on January 31, 1865. The amendment became law almost a year later, on December 6, 1865, when it was ratified by the states.

their mates. Tamar Grandy and her husband were both slaves in eastern North Carolina in the early 1800s. She was sold to a Georgia trader but escaped and traveled a hundred miles to return to her husband and her mother. Her husband lived twenty-five miles away from where she was in hiding. For years he came to visit her, leaving home as soon as he finished his work, spending part of the night with his wife, and walking the long distance back in order to arrive home before sunrise, when he would be called to the fields.[35]

With freedom came relief from the slaves' greatest fear—having family members sold away. Touching reunions occurred during and after the war. Ben and Betty Dodson found each other in a refugee camp. They had been sold to separate masters twenty years before, and he had spent all that time searching for her. One Virginia mother found her eighteen-year-old daughter in a refugee camp. The girl had been sold away when she was just an infant. Finding children who had been sold away when they were young or finding the parents who had been sold away when the children were young was exceedingly difficult. With each succeeding sale, a child may have been given a different name, and intervening years made it difficult to recognize the adult who was once some-one's child. For such children to be able to find their families required a slave community that kept the children's family histories alive during long periods of separation. Even with the community's help, however, reuniting families was often impossible. Slave mortality was high, especially in the lower South, and it was likely that people sold down the river many years before had not survived until freedom came.[36]

The seemingly insurmountable odds notwithstanding, freed people traveled great distances, tracking down every lead, in efforts to find their families. They questioned every person they met from the area where their relative was last heard of. Freedmen's Bureau teachers and missionaries wrote thousands of letters for the illiterate freed people, following every rumor that someone had seen or heard of their relatives. People placed advertisements in newspapers, giving information about the missing person's former life, personal characteristics, injuries, and scars. Nearly a generation after the Civil War, newspapers still carried such ads:

> Information Wanted, of Caroline Dodson, who was sold from Nashville, Nov. 1st, 1862, by James Lumsden to Warwick, (a trader then in human beings), who carried her to Atlanta, Georgia, and she was last heard of in the slave pen of Robert Clarke, (human trader in that place), from which she was sold. Any information of her whereabouts will be thankfully received and rewarded by her mother. Lucinda Lowery, Nashville.[37]

Land ownership was also important to the freed people. For many ex-slaves, the promise of self-sufficiency, independence, and opportunity that freedom represented rested on the ownership of land. Various military commanders had allowed former slaves to work land abandoned by fleeing Confederates, and rumors persisted that the federal government would eventually grant land to the freed people. On January 16, 1865, just months before the South's surrender, U.S. General William T. Sherman took time from his devastating Georgia campaign to meet with twenty black community leaders in Savannah and discuss the issue of confiscated Confederate land in Georgia, South Carolina, and northern Florida. Secretary of War Edwin M. Stanton joined the discussions and approved Sherman's Special Field Order 15, declaring that "the islands from Charleston south, the abandoned rice-fields along the rivers for thirty miles back from the sea, and the country bordering the St. Johns River, Florida, are reserved and set apart for the settlement of the [N]egroes now made free by the acts of war and the [Emancipation] proclamation of the President of the United States." Each family was to be issued forty acres and an army mule to

Freedman's Village, a settlement of newly freed former slaves was established during the Civil War on the Robert E. Lee plantation in Arlington, Virginia, near Washington, D.C.

use in its cultivation. A few months later, the plan seemed confirmed by the government's placement of responsibility for refugees, freedmen, and abandoned lands in the same department.[38]

In the spring of 1865, as the war came to an end, Vice President Andrew Johnson from Tennessee replaced the slain president in the oval office. Johnson had been Lincoln's wartime political choice, another strategy to hold the slave-holding border states, and was a political conservative. The new president spent the early days of his administration granting amnesty to former Confederate military leaders and handing out pardons wholesale to Confederates. White southerners needed simply to swear loyalty to the United States and agree to support the abolitionist provisions of the Thirteenth Amendment to have their property and general citizenship rights restored. Members of the southern aristocracy who had led the Confederacy in its war on the United States quickly applied for and received pardons. Thus, most of the land was returned to its prewar owners, and the former slaves who had been living on and cultivating the land during the last year of the war were expelled. Former abolitionists in Congress were never successful in their attempts to pass legislation granting former slaves land from the thousands of acres of confiscated Confederate land still under federal control. Ultimately, left without this foundation for independence, the freed people were forced to depend on former slaveholders to employ them or rent them land to farm.

Once pardoned and returned to political power, men from the planter class passed new laws reinstating much of their control over black people. In an attempt to re-create the southern racial etiquette of slave days, they punished black farm laborers for questioning white landlords, attacked black businessmen and their establishments for being too successful or competitive, attacked black students for displaying too much intelligence, confronted blacks who dressed too well or too neatly, and assaulted white people for encouraging black aspirations. Angered and distressed by the growing independence of their former slaves, planters complained that freed people were unwilling to work for what the planters considered reasonable wages. According to one Texas planter, the exorbitant wages offered by white employers with no sense of the "proper racial hierarchy" had spoiled the former slaves and led them to have outrageous expectations. Planters believed this had encouraged an inappropriate feeling of equality among the newly freed blacks.

After emancipation many African Americans did try to withdraw from the workforce. As a mark of their freedom, some men wanted their wives to be able to leave the fields and keep house for their families. Virtually all blacks wanted their children to be able to attend school, and some black people did demand respect from southern whites. As one former Georgia slave explained, many blacks vowed to take "no more foolishness off white folks." Long-standing customs and laws governing interracial contact in the South were designed to reinforce white supremacy. Whites addressed a black man as "boy" and a black woman as "girl" no matter how old they were, and either might be addressed as "nigger." The title of Uncle or Aunty that whites used for elderly blacks was the closest thing to respect an African American could expect. In Helena, Arkansas, after the war, when an elderly former slave addressed a white man on the street as "Mr." the white man followed the prewar convention and replied "Howdy uncle." The black man was insulted, made it clear they were not related, and demanded, "Call me Mister."[39]

From the standpoint of former slaves, such confrontations were part of an effort to make freedom a reality of daily life in the South, a reality that white southerners were anxious to avoid. What ensued was a determined struggle between African Americans seeking dignity and respect and southern whites attempting to maintain the principle of white supremacy. White leaders argued that only strong restrictive measures would restore the black workforce to its prewar level of usefulness. Many southern states enacted black codes, limiting the freedom of former slaves and returning them to near slavery. Vagrancy pro-

After the Civil War ended most African Americans remained in the South and most southern blacks continued as agricultural workers. Northern textile mill owners were anxious for southern plantations to restore cotton production, and Freedmen's Bureau officials negotiated contracts for the workers.

visions imposed fines and jail time on unemployed African Americans, forcing former slaves into low-paying agricultural jobs and ensuring white planters a steady supply of cheap plantation labor. Without land, the ability to bargain for jobs, or the right to vote or hold office, southern blacks stood only marginally above their former slave position.

Almost all southern blacks were agricultural workers, and without land of their own, they had to depend on white land-owners for work. After the war cash was in short supply in the South, so landowners offered shares of the crop instead of wages in return for black labor. Share-cropping, as this system was called, seemed an equitable solution to the problem. Sharecroppers lived on the land, worked it as if it were their own, brought in the crop, and were entitled to a portion of the harvest at the end of the season. For landowners this ensured an agricultural labor force without the need for cash, and for share-croppers it offered an approximation of the independent family farm. Unequal resources and power, however, led to white landholders' binding black share-croppers to the land through real or contrived indebtedness.

Essentially, the bonds of debt peonage replaced the chains of slavery, and planters could control their labor force almost as completely as slaveholders had controlled theirs. To purchase seed, tools, teams of mules or horses, and other supplies, impoverished sharecroppers were forced to rely on credit advanced against the following year's crop. They also purchased food, clothing, and other necessities on credit, either at stores operated by the landowner or at independently owned stores in the vicinity. Interest rates were generally high and sharecroppers found themselves falling further and further into debt each season. "[Landowners] didn't pay everything they promised," recalled one Arkansas sharecropper. When he attempted to appeal to local authorities, he found that a white man's accounting superseded any argument an African American could offer. "They said figures didn't lie," he reported. He understood that this could be a very dangerous situation, for any black man who questioned a white man's word was putting his life at risk. "You know how that was," he explained, "You dassent dispute a [white] man's word then."[40]

Henry Blacke sharecropped for much of his adult life. He later explained, "[N]o matter how good accounts you kept, you had to go by [the white landowners'] account, and—now brother, I'm telling you the truth about this—it has been that way a long time."[41] White southerners seemed to operate with a different set of ethics when dealing with blacks. As one Freedmen's Bureau official put it, white "men who are honorable in their dealings with their white neighbors will cheat a Negro without feeling a single twinge of their honor." Whites argued that the survival of southern civilization demanded completely controlling blacks, and, as in slavery, any black person who showed signs of contesting their control must be brought into line immediately. A Freedman's Bureau official described white attitudes toward blacks in the Reconstruction South saying, "Wherever I go . . . I hear the people talk in such a way as to indicate that they are yet unable to conceive of the Negro as possessing any right at all." Even among "honorable" white men, he noted, "to kill a Negro [white southerners] do not deem murder; to debauch a Negro woman they do not think fornication; to take the property away from a Negro they do not consider robbery."[42]

The Republican-controlled Congress attempted to protect African American rights, but President Johnson fought efforts to strengthen and broaden the powers of the Freedman's Bureau and to pass a Civil Rights Act nullifying the black codes and providing citizenship rights to black people. Johnson campaigned widely for Democratic candidates in the Congressional election of 1866. He spoke against Republican candidates, attacked programs to aid the former slaves, and referred to some of the strongest supporters of the U.S. war effort against the Confederacy as traitors to the nation. Even the most moderate Republicans were outraged, and, after Republicans made substantial gains in the election, they joined with their more radical colleagues in solid opposition to the president. The Republican Congress passed the Civil Rights Act of 1866 and the Fourteenth Amendment, which wrote its provisions guaranteeing black citizenship into the Constitution. They took control of reconstructing southern state governments, passing measures limiting the power of the old southern elites and calling for new state constitutions.

Congress also passed several measures to limit Johnson's power, including the Tenure of Office Act. According to that law, the president could not dismiss any cabinet member appointed with the advice and consent of the Senate until the Senate had approved a successor. In early 1868, Johnson violated this law, and the Republican-dominated House of Representatives voted to impeach him. Although Johnson was saved from being removed from office by one vote in the Senate, his presidency was so weakened that he ceased to be a significant obstruction to Congressional plans for reconstructing the South. Under Congressional Reconstruction, African Americans were allowed to participate in the state conventions that drew up the new constitutions, constitutions that gave blacks the right to vote. In South Carolina, Mississippi, Louisiana, and other southern states where blacks formed either a majority or a substantial proportion of the population, African Americans attained political power.

In 1866, pressured by abolitionists in Congress, the federal government passed the Southern Homestead Act, giving former slaves and whites who had remained loyal to the United States preferential access to 44 million acres of public land in five southern states for one year. The land, however, was poor—rocky, infertile, marshy, or otherwise unsuitable for farming. Penniless former slaves found it impossible to support themselves while waiting for the first crop, and few could take advantage of the program. A few blacks pooled their meager resources and bought some decent farmland. In Charleston two hundred freed people formed a land investment group called The Freemen's Land and Home Society and collectively purchased a 600-acre plantation on Remley's Point near the city, paying about ten dollars an acre.[43] Many soldiers pooled their military pay and bought small plots, but the vast majority remained landless.

The ratification of the Fifteenth Amendment to the U.S. Constitution in 1870, outlawing the use of race to disenfranchise voters, brought more black men to the polls. Black women, too, were active in southern politics, even though, like white women, they could not vote. They attended political meetings and rallies and were a strong arm of the Republican Party, especially in the South where African American political power was most significant during Reconstruction. According to one historian, in South Carolina, "Freewomen as well as children left the rice fields when it was time to register, attended political meetings and rallies where their influence over the lowcountry vote was recognized and manipulated, and were found at the polls on election days."[44] The presence of so many black women at political events apparently made some white Republicans uneasy. In Charleston, white Republicans attempted to convince black men to "leave their wives at their firesides, or, better still, to 'cut grass.'" The effort was apparently unsuccessful, for black women continued to be active advisers to their male representatives and participated in almost every phase of the voting process, except actually casting a ballot. Black leaders generally encouraged black women's participation in politics and recognized important, sometimes nontraditional, roles for them. During the mid 1870s black women armed with clubs patrolled polling places in South Carolina to keep order and protect Republicans who came to vote.[45]

With large numbers of freed African Americans in the South and 10 percent to 20 percent of southern white males still disqualified from voting because of their rebellion against the United States, blacks were a majority of the electorate in five southern states. Their votes provided the foundation for the Republican Party in the South, a party that had not existed there before the war. Blacks found allies among white Republicans from the North who came to the South during and after the war. Southern Democrats called these whites carpetbaggers after the bags in which many carried their possessions, denoting their newcomer status. Although generally characterized as political opportunists, most were teachers and nurses who came to aid and educate former slaves.

The southern Democrats' most venomous charges were leveled at those people called scalawags, white southerners who became Republicans or supported the Republican Party. Such southern whites who allied themselves with blacks were the targets of public ridicule and violence. This was especially true with the rise of such vigilante political terrorist groups as the Knights of the White Camilla, The Pale Face Brotherhood, and others organized in the mid- to late-1860s in an effort to frustrate Republican rule and force black people back to a place of servitude in southern society. The longest lasting and most notorious of these groups was a social club formed in Tennessee in 1866 that became the Ku Klux Klan. It was led by the former slave trader, Confederate general, and notorious commander of the Fort Pillow massacre, Nathan Bedford Forrest.

These groups used intimidation and violence to discourage blacks and white Republicans from voting. In the spring of 1866, whites invaded the black community in Memphis, Tennessee. When newly discharged black soldiers and

In this 1874 cartoon, an African American family are terrorized by the White League and the Ku Klux Klan. These groups' political terrorism became a new form of racial control that lasted well into the twentieth century.

local freedmen defended themselves against the marauding whites and city police, forty-six blacks and two whites died. The political motivation was clear when a local newspaper called the riot proof that "the southern men will not be ruled by the [N]egro."[46]

A few months later in New Orleans a white mob, also assisted by the police, attacked the meeting of the state constitutional convention called to establish the new state government and enfranchise African Americans. As a procession of some two hundred blacks, including drummers, a flag bearer, and many war veterans demanding the right to vote, marched toward the Mechanics Institute where the convention was to be held, angry whites confronted them, denouncing black participation in politics. In an inauspicious beginning, a white man pushed one of the black soldiers, who then punched the man. Someone fired a shot, and the marchers assembled in defensive military formation to protect the people moving into the convention hall. Others rallied outside and continued the confrontation that became a two-and-one-half-hour battle with bricks, rocks, and finally guns. The police and hundreds of white young men and boys attacked and killed blacks, many of whom had nothing to do with the march.[47]

The police and a mob of whites invaded the hall, which was filled with delegates and Republican supporters. Many of the invading whites wore white handkerchiefs around their necks, the badge of the secret white society called The Southern Cross. Unarmed delegates and spectators attempted to appeal to the police who were shooting all who stood in their path. "Gentleman, I beseech you to stop firing," pleaded the Reverend Dr. Horton, one of the convention's black supporters. Waving a white handkerchief, he declared, "we are noncombatants. If you want to arrest us, make any arrest you please, but we are not prepared to defend ourselves." His plea was answered by a policeman who replied, "We don't want any prisoners; you have all got to die."[48]

Ex-soldiers led the defense, beating back the police with chairs and, after several attempts, barring the door to the hall. The police again fired into the hall, killing Horton and several others. Blacks returned their fire, attempting to divert the attackers' attention so that others might escape through windows on the other side of the building. The mob shot some blacks as they emerged from the hall, and tracked others down and shot them on the street. They shot at least one other on the road, miles away from the hall. In all, the mob killed forty-eight blacks associated with the constitutional convention.[49] Later, reviewing the events of the day, General Philip H. Sheridan wrote to General Ulysses S. Grant, summing up what was obvious to African Americans. "The more information I obtain of the affair of the 30th in this city the more revolting it becomes," he said. "It was no riot; it was an absolute massacre."[50]

In 1868 Republican and former general Grant replaced Andrew Johnson as president. Congress reacted to the continuing southern violence in the early 1870s by enacting a number of anti-Klan measures, which the president signed into law. In 1871 Grant suspended the writ of habeas corpus in nine South Carolina counties where the Klan was particularly active, making it easier to arrest people suspected of terrorist activity, and sent in federal troops to augment the government's efforts to quell the violence. Congress launched an extensive investigation of the Klan and political terrorism in the South, and the federal officials arrested and indicted hundreds of whites in Mississippi, South Carolina, and North Carolina for their participation in terrorist activity. Some observers were surprised that, in addition to poor whites, many of those arrested for such crimes were professional men, doctors, lawyers, ministers, and college professors.[51]

Seeing African Americans hold political office especially incensed white southern Democrats. They accused blacks of being ignorant, incompetent people attempting to rise above their naturally subservient place in society. The vast majority of southern blacks were illiterate at the end of the war, but most black political leaders were educated. Oscar J. Dunn, who became lieutenant governor of Louisiana, for example, was born a slave but had been able to educate himself. Many, like Dunn, were self-educated, but many others had been formally educated. Hiram Rhodes Revels, a freeborn North Carolina barber and an ordained African Methodist Episcopal minister, became America's first black U.S. senator in 1870. He was a Republican who represented Mississippi for one year, completing the term of Jefferson Davis, who had given up his Senate seat in 1861 to become president of the Confederacy. Revels was well educated, having attended a Quaker seminary in Indiana and Knox College in Illinois. After his term in the Senate, Revels served as president of Mississippi's Alcorn Agricultural College (now Alcorn University), the first land-grant college for black students. Blanche K. Bruce, the first African American to serve a full term as a U.S. senator, was also educated in the North. Bruce, a Republican elected in Louisiana in 1874, was born a slave in Prince Edward County, Virginia, in 1841, but he had escaped and lived in the North before the war. There he operated a school for black children and studied at Oberlin College in Ohio.[52]

Many black officeholders had educational credentials equal to any politician of the day. Jonathan Gibbs, the son of a Philadelphia minister, graduated from Dartmouth College and Princeton Theological Seminary before serving as Florida's secretary of state from 1868 to 1872. Later he served as Florida's state superintendent of education. In Florida in 1884, Anna and Zephaniah Kingsley's grandson, Egbert Sammis, was elected to the Florida State Senate.[53] Anna and her family had escaped from Florida in April 1862, when U.S. troops briefly occupied the area. They had fled on a military transport ship, first to federally occupied Hilton Head, South Carolina, and then lived in New York during the war. After the war, they returned to Florida to reclaim their property. Anna died in Florida in 1870, surrounded by her family.[54]

Francis Louis Cardozo was another black Reconstruction politician from a successful family. Cardozo was born free in Charleston, the son of a prominent Jewish businessman and economist and a free black woman. He was educated in Europe at the University of Glasgow and the London School of Theology. Cardozo was a delegate to South Carolina's state constitutional convention in 1868 and served as South Carolina's secretary of state until 1872. He was state treasurer for five years until 1878, when he received an appointment to the Treasury Department in Washington, D.C.[55] In Louisiana, Pinckney Benton Stewart Pinchback, also of mixed race, became the nation's first African American governor. Pinchback was born in Macon, Georgia, to a slave woman and her master, a wealthy white planter. He had been educated in the North before the war and earned a law degree from Straight University in New Orleans after he completed his time in office.[56]

Hundreds of African Americans, former soldiers, abolitionists, businessmen, ministers, lawyers, and teachers, helped guide southern governments for a brief time in the turbulent years of Reconstruction. Many had been born in the South, had left to work and live in the North, in Canada, or in Europe, and returned to take advantage of the unprecedented opportunities for community service and black political leadership. Facing incredible economic and political problems, they worked with white Republicans and even some white Democrats to rebuild the South. In the years between the end of the Civil War and the first decade of the twentieth century, more than six hundred African Americans served in state legislatures, twenty were elected to the U.S. House of Representatives, and two were elected to the U.S. Senate.

During Reconstruction, federal and state government efforts held the promise of improving many people's lives in the South. The majority of the delegates to the South Carolina constitutional convention were black, and 57 out of the 124 blacks had been slaves. This convention passed a number of progressive measures in 1868: abolishing racial discrimination in voting, schools, and the militia; protecting married women's property rights; establishing the state's first divorce law and the first free public school system; providing for elected rather than appointed judges; and abolishing dueling, imprisonment for debt, and property requirements for voting and holding office. The Freedmen's Bureau established and ran more than four thousand schools in the South, open to whites as well as blacks. Many of these schools served areas where there had previously been no public education. The bureau ended most of its aid programs in 1868 but continued to operate schools that educated students from kindergarten to college until 1872. For the freed people, education was an important mark of their freedom and represented their hope for a better future. Since many slaves had been legally prohibited from learning to read and write, education was doubly important to them. About 95 percent of slaves were illiterate in 1863, but by 1877 more than six hundred thousand black children were in elementary schools.[57]

Black people had flocked to Freedmen's Bureau schools during and immediately after the war, they demanded good schools and strong educational programs from the new state governments during Reconstruction, and black politicians responded to the people's desire. When Robert Smalls returned to his native South Carolina, he became a member of the Beaufort County School District Board. His adventures as deliverer and captain of the *Planter* during the war made him a war hero and a strong candidate for political office. He was especially interested in developing the educational system in a state that offered little education to its citizens, either black or white. He sat as a delegate to the 1868 state constitutional convention, where he sponsored a resolution calling

Former slave Robert Smalls became a Civil War hero for delivering a Confederate gunboat, the Planter, *to U.S. forces. After the war, he became a prominent politician in South Carolina.*

for public schools. Smalls went on to serve in the South Carolina House of Representatives and in the South Carolina State Senate, and public education remained one of his central concerns.[58]

Southern Democrats were determined to reinstate the racial control of the prewar South and to further this aim tried to ensure black economic dependence and discourage black education. They used many methods in their postwar campaign, but violence became their signature. Outbreaks of racial violence, generally called riots but often seeming more like open rebellion, continued during the 1870s. Throughout the South, violence was the common political tool of those bent on returning to absolute and unquestioned white domination. Leading southern Democrats routinely rationalized the most heinous crimes if they helped "save southern civilization." Wade Hampton of South Carolina, who served as governor and U.S. senator, rallied his political colleagues by arguing that almost any illegal action, even murder, was completely acceptable if done in the name of white supremacy. He urged Democrats to do all in their power to "control the vote of at least one Negro, by intimidation, purchase, keeping him away or as each individual may determine, how may best accomplish it." Then he moved to the deadly specifics. "Never threaten a man individually. If he deserves to be threatened, the necessities of the times require that he should be killed." [59]

African Americans did not meekly submit, however. They used whatever power they had to enforce the law and protect themselves and their communities. Black judges issued arrest warrants, and black sheriffs jailed white terrorists.[60] Armed African Americans, especially war veterans, confronted white vigilante groups. Many black veterans had retained their military weapons, and some formed militia units to protect their communities. In Wilmington, North Carolina, black troops arrested the white chief of police when he refused to surrender his weapon as ordered, and in Victoria, Texas, blacks lynched the white killer of an African American townsman. In South Carolina, when a Confederate veteran stabbed a black Army sergeant for refusing to leave a railroad car in which white women were seated, black soldiers decided the veteran was guilty and shot him.[61]

Southern whites quickly realized that racial intimidation could not be effective so long as these black militia units existed, and they tried to legally disarm and disband them. White Republican officials in the South were sometimes willing to accede to white petitions in order to gain the cooperation of prominent local citizens. As black militia units were disbanded, African American communities were left open to attack from the growing number of terrorist groups. Blacks were forced to depend on the law for protection, an increasingly unlikely possibility as conservative whites returned to power, or to defend themselves. In 1868, for example, black Mississippi politician Charles Caldwell was wounded by a white man. He shot and killed his assailant but was then charged with murder. Such confrontations were common, but Caldwell's acquittal by an all-white jury on the grounds of self-defense was unusual.[62]

One armed force, calling itself the White League, marched on the State House in New Orleans in September 1874 to intimidate blacks and white Republicans. They were determined to overthrow the Republican Louisiana state government and openly declared their willingness to use any means necessary, including assassination, to accomplish their aim. The official platform of the state's Democratic Party made their commitment to white supremacy clear. It began, "We, the white people of Louisiana."[63] In Vicksburg, Mississippi, white terrorists slaughtered three hundred blacks as part of a campaign to undermine their support of the Republicans and install Democrats in power. In South Carolina groups calling themselves Rifle Clubs and Red Shirts combined political violence with racially motivated attacks on black leaders and prominent black citizens in an effort to reestablish white conservative control. To intimidate voters, armed Red Shirts paraded through such towns as Spartanburg, Edgefield, and Sumter during the election of 1876. South Carolina Democrats forced blacks to form Democratic clubs and then argued that gubernatorial candidate Wade Hampton had broad African American political support.[64]

Black voters in South Carolina constituted a majority, but white Democrats were determined to keep African Americans away from the polls. Blacks in some communities demanded their rights, and some whites chafed at what they considered African American arrogance. Such insults, the white southerners contended, "no white people upon earth had ever to put up with before."[65] Whites in the small town of Hamburg on the Savannah River in South Carolina complained that they were forced to give way to black parades and were treated with disrespect and even arrested "on the slightest provocation" by the local

Depiction of southern blacks voting during Reconstruction from Frank Leslie's Illustrated Newspaper. *New state constitutions in the post-war South provided the franchise to African American men. White supremacist organizations such as the Ku Klux Klan made voting dangerous for African Americans and white Republicans in the South.*

black police. Tensions exploded during the country's centennial celebration on July 4, 1876, when a parading black militia company forced a local white farmer's son and son-in-law to halt their carriage. Although Dock Adams, the militia commander, opened the ranks to let them through after some contention, the next day the farmer brought charges against Adams for impeding his travel. The black militia confronted armed white men in the town, and a well-known Democratic politician demanded that Adams disarm his militia company. He refused, the men began fighting, and the black militiamen retreated to the armory. Hundreds of whites from Augusta, Georgia, just across the river, invaded Hamburg to answer the challenge, bringing a cannon to aid in avenging the insult to their racial honor. The whites killed the town's black marshal and killed at least five other blacks after they had been captured. Blacks killed one young white man. The white mob also looted and vandalized African American homes and businesses. A grand jury indicted seven whites for murder and dozens more as accessories, but all were acquitted.

As the violence increased and it became clear that African Americans were not safe anywhere in the South, growing numbers of blacks began to reconsider colonization. African Americans from several southern states met in New Orleans in December 1875 to discuss migrating to the independent West African nation of Liberia. The racial troubles in America created substantial interest in Liberia, and not only among southern blacks. Northern blacks faced less continual violence but confronted discouraging racial discrimination in public places, in the job market, and in housing.[66] In 1878, one colonization group in Pennsylvania received almost fifty thousand inquiries from African Americans considering migration possibilities.

Although many were interested in West Africa, many more African Americans looked to lands in the American West as a place of opportunity and a safe haven. A few people made their way to New Mexico, Arizona, Colorado, and Oklahoma. Groups of North Carolina and Mississippi blacks migrated to Nebraska, and others looked to the frontier state of Kansas. Exodusters, as migrants to the American frontier were called, led by such men as former slave Benjamin "Pap" Singleton from Tennessee, moved their families from the Deep South westward into Kansas during the 1870s. Kansas had a special appeal: it had plenty of unoccupied land and was associated in the minds of African Americans with the Underground Railroad and John Brown. For them, it was an abolitionist territory that had battled proslavery forces and finally entered the Union as a free state. By the mid-1870s many southern blacks were taken with "Kansas Fever" fueled by rumors of free land, free transportation, and free supplies. The reports were largely exaggerated, but they did draw thousands from the violent South to the promise of a new life. By 1878 the town of Nicodemus, Kansas, boasted a population of seven hundred African Americans, all recent migrants from the Deep South. In April of the next year, hundreds more Exodusters traveled up the Missouri River by steamboat to the eastern Kansas settlement of Wyandotte.[67]

Most African Americans did not leave the South. They did not have the resources, debts bound them to the land on which they sharecropped, or family ties held them in place. The proportion of blacks living in the South had dropped from 94 percent at the start of the Civil War to 84 percent by 1880, but the vast majority were still southerners.[68] For this vast majority of black people in America, their brief political influence was rapidly fading. In the presidential election of 1876, pitting Democrat Samuel J. Tilden against Republican

During the Civil War thousands of slaves escaped from the South, hoping for a better life in the North. Most traveled by land, but a few fortunate ones were able to find transportation by ship to northern ports.

Rutherford B. Hayes, both parties claimed victory in Louisiana, South Carolina, and Florida, and thus the presidency. When an electoral commission sustained Hayes's claim, Democrats in Congress refused to certify the election. After the chaos of civil war and the disruption of the Reconstruction, the nation was in no mood for such political uncertainty. From every quarter—business interests, state and local governments, churches, and universities—came the demand that the election be settled quickly. A series of meetings led to a compromise whereby the Republican, Hayes, would take the presidency. Democrats would not contest economic policies benefiting Republican business interests, and in return the Hayes administration would remove the last U.S. troops from the South, leaving southerners to handle civil stability and civil rights in their states. The compromise that saved the nation from uncertainty and placed the Republican in the White House had been struck at African Americans' expense.

In the following years Southern Democrats, assisted by rulings of the U.S. Supreme Court, removed federal protections for black rights in the South. The court weakened or struck down much of the preceding decades' civil rights legislation and placed the responsibility for enforcing the Fourteenth and Fifteenth amendments on the states. Southern blacks denied the right to vote or lacking legal protection found their only recourse was to state authority. As conservative Democrats moved into positions of power at all levels of southern state governments, there was little recourse at all. Starting in 1890 in Mississippi, and then spreading across the South, a constellation of laws restricted the franchise to whites only. Poll taxes generally put the vote financially out of reach for sharecroppers and other poor blacks. Literacy testing was often devised and administered so that no black person, no matter how educated, could qualify to vote. Meanwhile, a clause in state regulations safeguarded the voting rights of illiterate whites by waiving the literacy requirement for voters deemed people of good conduct or whose grandfathers had voted before 1860, a time when almost all southern blacks were slaves.

Other laws provided for racial segregation in public accommodations, transportation, and almost every phase of life. The Mississippi Plan, and the host of laws that followed in every southern state and many border states, were the foundation for the extensive southern system of racial segregation often called the Jim Crow system. The Jim Crow segregation system was named after a character played by white actor, Thomas Dartmouth "Daddy" Rice. In the 1840 and 1850s, Rice blackened his face and danced, playing Jim Crow, a racial stereotype born of the white imagination. By the mid-1890s it was clear that Reconstruction's promise of real freedom was coming to an end, and there seemed little blacks could do about it. In 1895 Booker T. Washington, president and founder of Tuskegee Institute, a black college in Alabama, and the most influential black leader in the South, gave a speech at the Cotton States Exposition in Atlanta, Georgia. He seemed to accept racial segregation and second-class citizenship for

The original Jim Crow was a stereotypical character played by white entertainer Thomas "Daddy" Rice on the minstrel stage. The term Jim Crow came to identify the southern system of legal racial segregation.

Exodusters Migrate West

After the Civil War, thousands of newly freed African Americans left the South to seek greater opportunity in the West. Many migrated to Kansas, where they could own land and become independent farmers. Life was hard on the Kansas plains but less dangerous than in the South, where they faced the Ku Klux Klan and other white terrorist groups. This broadside urged African Americans in Lexington, Kentucky, to strike out for a new and better life in Kansas.

All colored people that want to go to Kansas, On September 5th, 1877, can do so for $5.00.

IMMIGRATION.

WHEREAS, We, the colored people of Lexington, Ky., knowing that there is an abundance of choice lands now belonging to the Government, have assembled ourselves together for the purpose of locating on said lands. Therefore,

BE IT RESOLVED, That we do now organize ourselves into a Colony, as follows:— Any person wishing to become a member of this Colony can do so by paying the sum of one dollar ($1.00), and this money is to be paid by the first of September, 1877, in instalments of twenty-five cents at a time, or otherwise as may be desired.

RESOLVED. That this Colony has agreed to consolidate itself with the Nicodemus Towns, Solomon Valley, Graham County, Kansas, and can only do so by entering the vacant lands now in their midst, which costs $5.00.

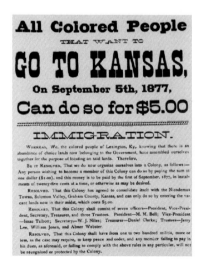

RESOLVED, That this Colony shall consist of seven officers...and three Trustees....

RESOLVED, That this Colony shall have from one to two hundred militia, more or less, as the case may require, to keep peace and order, and any member failing to pay in his dues, as aforesaid, or failing to comply with the above rules in any particular, will not be recognized or protected by the Colony.

blacks in the South as inevitable. Southern whites in the audience were elated, many blacks, however, refused to accept Washington's Atlanta Compromise, as it came to be called. In the South, as well as the North, thousands of African Americans became even more determined to fight for full citizenship rights. In less than a year, however, in 1896, the Supreme Court endorsed this Jim Crow system. In the case of *Plessy v. Ferguson*, the court declared that separating races of people was constitutional, so long as each race was provided facilities of equal quality. This ruling established the "separate but equal" doctrine, which, combined with the economic dependency of southern black sharecroppers and the denial of black voting rights, circumscribed black opportunities and rights and defined southern race relations throughout the first half of the twentieth century. The South could not reinstate slavery, but it did re-create many of the mechanisms for racial control that the slave system had provided in the old South.

Portrait of Booker T. Washington, former slave and founder of Tuskeegee Institute in Alabama. Washington attempted to placate southern whites by encouraging African Americans to remain in the South and forego demands for political equality in exchange for restricted economic opportunity in agricultural and manual labor.

Some southern black politicians continued in office until the first few years of the twentieth century, but it was clear in the late nineteenth century that southern blacks had been deprived of political power. Yet Reconstruction was not a total failure. Slavery was ended, and black people no longer faced the awful prospect of having their children and other family members sold away from them. African Americans made great gains in literacy and education, and a few even managed to acquire land. The Constitution was changed: the Thirteenth Amendment abolished slavery, the Fourteenth Amendment guaranteed African Americans citizenship rights, and the Fifteenth Amendment forbade the denial of voting rights on account of race. Constitutional guarantees may not have been honored, but they established legal principles to which plaintiffs could appeal. African Americans had struggled before the Civil War to end slavery and during Reconstruction to attain citizenship rights, and they continued their struggle for full freedom through the twentieth century.

Leaders of the Niagara Movement, founded in 1905, the forerunner of the National Association for the Advancement of Colored People. W. E. B. Du Bois is second from the right in the second row.

In 1905 black activists, including W. E. B. Du Bois, and white progressives, including descendants of abolitionists, created the Niagara Movement to carry on the struggle against racial injustice. Its successor organization, the National Association for the Advancement of Colored People (NAACP), was founded four years later and carried on a long legal campaign using the constitutional victories of Reconstruction to demand African American civil rights. It brought suit against racially restrictive laws in the South that had all but eliminated blacks from southern politics. The NAACP's first major victory came in 1915 when the U.S. Supreme Court struck down the grandfather clause as a violation of the Fifteenth Amendment. It also led a massive protest movement against D.W. Griffith's *Birth of a Nation,* a 1915 movie with racially distorted depictions of Reconstruction, glorification of the Ku Klux Klan, and a sympathetic treatment of the racial and political terrorism that had prompted the lynching of thousands of blacks in the South during the late nineteenth and early twentieth centuries.

Civil rights groups, using the Reconstruction amendments as the foundation for their attacks, scored a string of court victories against the system of legal discrimination in the 1930s and 1940s. World War II and the horrors of the Holocaust made racial discrimination more difficult for Americans to justify, and the postwar civil rights struggle received a major boost in 1947 when President Harry Truman issued an executive order integrating the U.S. armed forces. Under the direction of Charles Houston as chief counsel, the NAACP marshaled the resources of Howard University's Law School to bring before the courts a number of cases attacking racial segregation in education. In 1939 Thurgood Marshall, one of Houston's former students, had established the

NAACP Legal Defense and Educational Fund to carry on this work. Finally, in 1954 in the case of *Brown v. the Board of Education of Topeka, Kansas,* the U.S. Supreme Court struck down the concept of separate but equal that had been established in *Plessy v. Ferguson.* In its effect, the earlier ruling had sanctioned the imposition of separate and unequal racial conditions in American society. Encouraged by the *Brown* decision, civil rights groups engaged in a multitude of civil rights actions during the 1950s and 1960s. Under pressure from massive protests, including a historic March on Washington in 1963, and in response to intense lobbying by President Lyndon Johnson, Congress passed the Civil Rights Act of 1964, which outlawed racial discrimination in public accommodations and employment. The following year, the Voting Rights Act of 1965 eliminated all qualifying tests for voter registration. These acts were the most important civil rights legislation of the twentieth century, and they signaled a new national commitment to the enforcement of the Reconstruction amendments.

Despite the progress made against racial injustice, slavery still has an impact on Americans more than a century after its abolition. Its legacy remains in the history and heritage of the South that it shaped, in the culture of the North where its memory was long denied, in the national economy for which it provided much of the foundation, and in the political and social system it profoundly influenced. Slavery and its effects are embedded in the national culture and in the assumptions and contradictory ideals of American society. The central issues under debate today—issues involving race, class, region, religion, and national identity—are all imperfectly understood without the historical context of American slavery and without an understanding of the means by which a freedom-loving people rationalized their tolerance of slavery's development. Although it is troubling to consider, it is nonetheless true that slavery was, and continues to be, a critical factor in shaping the United States and all of its people. As Americans, we must understand slavery's history if we are ever to be emancipated from its consequences.

Notes

Introduction

1. John Dickinson, *Letters from a Farmer in Pennsylvania to the Inhabitants of the British Colonies* (Philadelphia, 1768), 38, quoted in F. Nwabueze Okoye, "Chattel Slavery as the Nightmare of the American Revolutionaries," *The William and Mary Quarterly* 3rd ser., 37, 1 (Jan. 1980): 3–28, 3.

2. John E. O'Connor and Martin A. Jackson, eds., *American History/American Film: Interpreting the Hollywood Image* (New York: Continuum, 1988), xix.

3. *See* Ulrich Bonnell Phillips, *American Negro Slavery* (New York: D. Appleton, 1918) and *Life and Labor in the Old South* (Boston: Little, Brown, and Co., 1929).

4. Kenneth M Stampp, *The Peculiar Institution: Slavery in the Ante-Bellum South* (New York: Vintage Books, 1956); Stanley Elkins, *Slavery: A Problem in American Institutional and Intellectual Life* (Chicago: University of Chicago Press, 1959).

5. John W. Blassingame, *The Slave Community: Plantation Life in the Antebellum South* (New York: Oxford University Press, 1972); Eugene D. Genovese, *Roll, Jordan, Roll: The World the Slaves Made* (New York: Pantheon Books, 1974); Leslie Howard Owens, *This Species of Property: Slave Life and Culture in the Old South* (New York: Oxford University Press, 1976); Herbert G. Gutman, *The Black Family in Slavery and Freedom, 1750–1925* (New York: Pantheon Books, 1976); Robert William Fogel and Stanley L. Engerman, *Time on the Cross: The Economics of American Negro Slavery* (Boston: Little, Brown, 1974); Alex Haley, *Roots: The Saga of an American Family* (Garden City, N.Y.: Doubleday, 1976).

6. Debra Gray White, *Ar'n't I a Woman?: Female Slaves in the Plantation South* (New York: W.W. Norton, 1987); Jacqueline Jones, *Labor of Love, Labor of Sorrow: Black Women, Work, and the Family from Slavery to the Present* (New York: Basic Books, 1985); Peter Kolchin, *Unfree Labor: American Slavery and Russian Serfdom* (Cambridge, Mass.: Harvard University. Press, 1987); Phillip D. Morgan, *Slave Counterpoint: Black Culture in the Eighteenth-Century Chesapeake and Lowcountry* (Chapel Hill: University of North Carolina Press, 1998); Brenda E. Stevenson, *Life in Black and White: Family and Community in the Slave South* (New York: Oxford University Press, 1996); Wilma King, *Stolen Childhood: Slave Youth in 19th Century America* (Bloomington: University of Indiana Press, 1998); Ira Berlin, *Many Thousands Gone: The First Two Centuries of Slavery in North America* (Cambridge, Mass.: Harvard University Press, 1998) and *Generations of Captivity: A History of African American Slaves* (Cambridge, Mass.: Harvard University Press, 2003).

Chapter 1

1. John Thornton, *Africa and Africans in the Making of the Atlantic World, 1400–1680* (Cambridge: Cambridge University Press, 1992), 51–53.

2. Colin Palmer, "African Slave Trade: The Cruelest Commerce," *National Geographic* (September 1992): 67–68.

3. Ira Berlin, *Many Thousands Gone: The First Two Centuries of Slavery in North America* (Cambridge, Mass.: Harvard University Press, 1998), 17–28; Johannes Menne Postma, *The Dutch in the Atlantic Slave Trade, 1600–1815* (Cambridge: Cambridge University Press, 1990), 68–69.

4. Peter C. W. Gutkind, "Trade and Labor in Early Precolonial African History: The Canoemen of Southern Ghana" in *The Workers of African Trade*, Catherine Coquery-Vidrovitch and Paul E. Lovejoy, editors (Beverly Hills, Calif.: Sage Publications, 1985), 25–50.

5. John Thornton, *Africa and Africans*, 46.

6. K. G. Davies, "The Living and the Dead: White Mortality in West Africa, 1684–1732," in Stanley Engerman and Eugene Genovese, eds., *Race and Slavery in the Western Hemisphere* (Princeton, N.J.: Princeton University Press, 1975), 94–98.

7. Daniel L. Schafer, *Anna Kingsley* (revised and expanded edition) (St. Augustine, Fla.: St. Augustine Historical Society, 1997).

8. Venture Smith, *A Narrative of the Life and Adventures of Venture, A Native of Africa, But Resident Above Sixty Years in the United States of America. Related by Himself* (Middletown, Conn.: J. S. Stewart, Printer and Bookbinder, 1897 [1798]), 4.

9. Olaudah Equiano, *The Life of Olaudah Equiano, or Gustavus Vassa, the African, Written by Himself* (1789), reprinted in *Great Slave Narratives*, Arna

Bontemps, ed. (Boston: Beacon Press, 1969), 27. Some scholars have recently questioned whether Equiano's description of West Africa was based on personal experience or oral history. *See* Vincent Carratta, "Olaudah Equiano or Gustavas Vasa? New Light on an Eighteenth-Century Question of Identity," *Slavery and Abolition*, 20, 3 (1999): 96–105.

10. William D. Piersen, "White Cannibals, Black Martyrs: Fear, Depression, and Religious Faith as Causes of Suicide Among New Slaves," *Journal of Negro History* 62 (1977): 147–159, 148.

11. Piersen, "White Cannibals," 149.

12. Equiano, *The Interesting Life*, Bontemps, ed., *Great Slave Narratives,* 28–29.

13. J. D. Fage, "Slavery and the Slave Trade in the Context of West African History," in Paul Finkleman, ed. *Slave Trade and Migration: Domestic and Foreign* (New York: Garland, 1989), 121–132.

14. Ray A. Kea, *Settlements, Trade, and Politics in the Seventeenth-Century Gold Coast* (Baltimore: Johns Hopkins University Press, 1982), 1, 104–107.

15. Basil Davidson, *The Search for Africa: History, Culture, Politics* (New York: Random House, 1994), 73; Colin A. Palmer, *Passageways: An Interpretive History of Black America, 1619–1863* vol. 1 (Fort Worth, Tex.: Harcourt Brace College Publishers, 1998), 5.

16. John Thornton, *Africa and Africans.*

17. Equiano, *The Interesting Life*, Bontemps, ed., *Great Slave Narratives,* 29.

18. Equiano, *The Interesting Life*, Bontemps, ed., *Great Slave Narratives,* 30.

19. Antonio T. Bly, "Crossing the Lake of Fire: Slave Resistance during the Middle Passage, 1720–1842," *The Journal of Negro History*, 83, 3 (Summer, 1998): 178–186.

20. Alexander Falconbridge, *An Account of the Slave Trade on the Coast of Africa* (London, 1788), 16–22.

21. William Loren Katz, *Eyewitness: the Negro in American History* (Belmont, Calif.: Fearon Pitman Publishers, 1974), 6.

22. Bly, "Crossing the Lake of Fire," 184. In another more famous slave revolt aboard the *Amistad* in 1839, the slaves led by Joseph Cinqué killed the captain and the cook and ordered the crew to sail to Africa. Already in the Caribbean, crew members tricked the rebels, and the fifty-two slaves were landed in the United States. After three years in jail, the court determined that the rebellious slaves had been illegally captured and ordered the return of the surviving thirty-five Africans to their homeland.

23. James Oliver Horton and Lois E. Horton, *Hard Road to Freedom: The Story of African America* (New Brunswick, N.J.: Rutgers University Press, 2001), 29.

24. Martha Hodes, *White Women, Black Men: Illicit Sex in the Nineteenth Century South* (New Haven, Conn.: Yale University Press, 1997).

25. Hodes, *White Women, Black Men.*

26. Winthrop Jordan, *White Over Black* (Chapel Hill: University of North Carolina Press, 1968); Lorenzo J. Greene, *The Negro in Colonial New England 1620–1766* (1942; reprint, New York: Atheneum Press, 1968); Debra L. Newman, "Black Women in the Era of the American Revolution in Pennsylvania," *Journal of Negro History* 61, 3 (July 1976): 276–289.

27. Edmund Morgan, *American Slavery, American Freedom: The Ordeal of Colonial Virginia* (New York: W.W. Norton, 1975).

28. William M. Wiecek, "The Statutory Law of Slavery and Race in the Thirteen Colonies of British America," *William and Mary Quarterly*, 3rd Series, 34 (1977): 258–280; Peter Wood, *Strange New Land: Africans in Colonial America* (New York: Oxford University Press, 2003), 39.

29. Alan Kulikoff, *Tobacco and Slaves: The Development of Southern Cultures in the Chesapeake, 1680–1800* (Chapel Hill: University of North Carolina Press, 1986).

30. Simon Hart, *The Prehistory of the New Netherland Company* (Amsterdam: City of Amsterdam Press, 1959), "1614, July 23. Declarations of Crew Members of the Ship the 'Fortuyn', Master Hendrick Christiaensen," 80–83.

31. A. Leon Higginbotham, *In the Matter of Color: Race and the American Legal Process* (New York: Oxford University Press, 1978); Joyce D. Goodfriend, *Before the Melting Pot: Society and Culture in Colonial New York City, 1664–1730* (Princeton, N.J.: Princeton University Press, 1992). See also Shane White, *Somewhat More Independent: The End of Slavery in New York City, 1770–1810* (Athens: University of Georgia Press, 1991) and Edgar J. McManus, *Black Bondage in the North* (Syracuse, N.Y.: Syracuse University Press, 1973).

32. Equiano, *An Interesting Life*, Bontemps, ed., *Great Slave Narratives.*

33. Ira Berlin, *Generations of Captivity: A History of African-American Slaves* (Cambridge, Mass., Harvard University Press, 2003), 44.

34. Robert Olwell, *Masters, Slaves and Subjects: The Culture of Power in the South Carolina Low Country, 1740–1790* (Ithaca, N.Y.: Cornell University Press, 1998), 22; John K. Thornton, "African Dimensions

of the Stono Rebellion," *American Historical Review* 96, 4 (October 1991): 1101–1114, 1111.

35. Olwell, *Masters, Slaves and Subjects*, 26–29, 62–63.

36. Bernard Bailyn and Barbara DeWolfe, *Voyagers to the West: A Passage in the Peopling of America on the Eve of the Revolution* (New York: Alfred A. Knopf, 1986), 324.

37. Robert Cottrol, *The Afro-Yankee* (Westport, Conn.: Greenwood Press, 1982), 19; *New York Weekly Journal*, August 9, 1742, quotation in Edgar J. McManus, *A History of Negro Slavery in New York* (Syracuse, N.Y.: Syracuse University Press, 1966), 87; Kenneth Scott, "The Slave Insurrection in New York in 1712," *New-York Historical Society Quarterly* 45 (1961): 43–74.

38. Daniel Horsmanden, *The New York Conspiracy*, Thomas J. Davis, ed. (Boston: Beacon Press, 1971).

39. Thomas J. Davis, *Rumor of Revolt: The Great Negro Plot in Colonial New York* (New York: Free Press, 1985).

40. *Ibid.*

41. Howard Zinn, *A People's History of the United States, 1492–Present*, (New York: HarperCollins, [1980], 1995), 51; Gary Nash, *The Urban Crucible: Social Change, Political Consciousness, and the Origins of the American Revolution* (Cambridge, Mass.: Harvard University Press, 1979), 134–136; Benjamin Colman to Mr. Samuel Holden, Boston, May 8, 1737, Colman Papers, unpublished papers, v. 2, Massachusetts Historical Society; James Oliver Horton and Lois E. Horton, *In Hope of Liberty: Culture, Community and Protest Among Northern Free Blacks, 1700–1860* (New York: Oxford University Press, 1997), 46.

42. Jesse Lemisch, "Jack Tar in the Streets: Merchant Seamen in the Politics of Revolutionary America," *William and Mary Quarterly* 25 (1968): 371–407; Zinn, *People's History*, 51; Nash, *Urban Crucible*, 221–223.

43. Lemisch, "Jack Tar in the Streets," 379.

44. Ira Berlin, *Generations of Captivity: A History of African-American Slaves* (Cambridge, Mass.: Harvard University Press, 2003); John Michael Vlach, *By the Work of Their Hands: Studies in Afro-American Folklife* (Ann Arbor, Mich.: UMI Research Press, 1991).

45. Horton and Horton, *In Hope of Liberty*, 16.

46. Berlin, *Generations*; Sylvia R. Frey, *Water from the Rock: Black Resistance in a Revolutionary Age* (Princeton, N.J.: Princeton University Press, 1991); Horton and Horton, *In Hope of Liberty*.

Sidebar, pages 22–23

Olaudah Equiano, *The Life of Olaudah Equiano or Gustavus Vassa, the African, Written by Himself,* reprinted in Arna Bontemps, *Great Slave Narratives* (Boston: Beacon Press, 1969), 30–31.

Chapter 2

1. George Washington Williams, *History of the Negro Race in America, 1619–1880* (New York: Putnam, 1883, reprint, New York: Arno Press, 1968), 332.

2. John Adams, quoted in Howard Zinn, *A People's History of the United States* (New York: Harper and Row, 1980), 67; Benjamin Thatcher, *Traits of the Tea Party Being a Memoir of George R.T. Hewes* (New York: Harpers, 1835), 103–104.

3. James Otis, *The Rights of British Colonies Asserted and Proved* (Boston: 1765), 37.

4. Richard S. Newman, *The Transformation of American Abolitionism: Fighting Slavery in the Early Republic* (Chapel Hill: University of North Carolina Press, 2002).

5. Arthur Zilversmit, *The First Emancipation: The Abolition of Slavery in the North* (Chicago: University of Chicago Press, 1967), 61–83.

6. David Brion Davis, *The Problem of Slavery in Western Culture* (Ithaca, N.Y.: Cornell University Press, 1966). Some historians argue that the role of the Quakers in the early antislavery campaigns has been overemphasized, and that they were far less effective than has been assumed. For this view, see Donald L. Robinson, *Slavery in the Structure of American Politics, 1765–1820* (New York: Harcourt Brace Jovanovich, 1970).

7. Petition of the Africans, living in Boston, 1773 (Boston: Boston Athenaeum).

8. Philip Foner, *History of Black Americans: From Africa to the Emergence of the Cotton Kingdom,* vol. 1 (Westport, Conn.: Greenwood Press, 1975), 297.

9. Petition of the Africans.

10. Circular letter Boston, April 20, 1773 (The New-York Historical Society).

11. Nathaniel Appleton, *Considerations on Slavery* (Boston: 1767), 19–20; Benjamin Rush, *An Address to the Inhabitants of the British Settlements in America, Upon Slave-Keeping* (Philadelphia: 1773), quoted in Philip S. Foner, *History of Black Americans,* I, 301; Gary B. Nash, *Race and Revolution* (Madison, Wis.: Madison House, 1990), 32. In 1775 the Pennsylvania Abolition Society was called The Society for the Relief of Free Negroes Unlawfully Held in Bondage. In 1787, when Benjamin Franklin was its president and Rush was its secretary, the organization changed its name to The Pennsylvania Society for Promoting the Abolition of Slavery, the Relief of Negroes Unlawfully Held in Bondage, and for Improving the Condition of the Colored Race.

12. Abigail Adams to John Adams, September 22, 1774, in Lyman H. Butterfield, ed., *Adams Family Correspondence*, vol. 1 (Cambridge, Mass.: Harvard University Press, 1963), 162, 13–14.

13. Quoted in Sidney Kaplan, *The Black Presence in the Era of the American Revolution, 1770–1800* (Greenwich, Conn.: New York Graphic Society, Ltd., 1973), 13.

14. Edmund and Helen Morgan, *The Stamp Act Crisis: Prologue to the Revolution*, 243, 249–251; Donald A. Grind, Jr., "Joseph Allicocker: African American Leader of the Sons of Liberty."

15. Ottley and Weatherby, eds., *Negro in New York*, 36–37.

16. *Samuel Howell v. Wade Netherland*, April, 1770.

17. *Virginia* Gazette, August 16, 1770.

18. Foner, *History of Black Americans*, 1: 318.

19. Gretchen Holbrook Gerzina, "Black Loyalists in London after the American Revolution," in John W. Pulis, ed., *Moving On: Black Loyalists in the Afro-Atlantic World* (New York: Garland, 1999), 85–102, 86.

20. Maryland report quoted in Howard Zinn, *People's History*, 81; Ellen Gibson Wilson, *Loyal Blacks* (New York: Capricorn Books, 1976). Many guerrilla soldiers continued to operate after the war ended.

21. Wilson, *Loyal Blacks*, 28. Leaders of the Southern Confederacy leveled a similar charge against President Lincoln in 1863 after he issued the Emancipation Proclamation.

22. Sylvia R. Frey, *Water from the Rock: Black Resistance in a Revolutionary Age* (Princeton, N.J.: Princeton University Press, 1991), 76.

23. Wilson, *Loyal Blacks*, 21; John Hope Franklin, *From Slavery to Freedom*, 6th edition (New York: McGraw-Hill, 1988), 70. See also Thomas Jefferson's Farm Book, cited in Peter Kolchin, *American Slavery, 1619–1877* (New York: Hill & Wang, 1993), 72–73.

24. Frey, *Water from the Rock*, 156.

25. Wilson, *Loyal Blacks*, 28–29; Foner, *History of Black Americans*, 364; Howard Zinn, *People's History*, 81.

26. Philip Foner, *History of Black Americans*, 1: 333.

27. Philip Foner, *History of Black Americans*, 1: 328.

28. Lorenzo Greene, "Some Observations on the Black Regiment of Rhode Island in the American Revolution," *Journal of Negro History* 37, 1 (January 1952): 142–172, 144.

29. Revolutionary War Pension Records of Cato Cuff, Samuel Coombs, Prince Whipple, Oliver Cromwell and Prince Bent, Records of the Veterans' Administration, Record Group #15, National Archives and Record Service, Washington, D.C.

30. John Mack Faragher et al., *Out of Many: A History of the American People*, 3rd edition (Upper Saddle River, N.J.: Prentice Hall, 2001), 115.

31. "Return of Negroes Employed as Artificers, Labourers and Servants in the Royal Artillery, " August 5, 1782, George Wray, Papers, 1770–1793, William L. Clements Library, University of Michigan, Ann Arbor, Michigan. Cited in Frey, *Water from the Rock*, 121–122.

32. Wilson, *Loyal Blacks*, 70–80.

33. Wilson, *Loyal Blacks*, 42.

34. George Washington to John Francis Mercer, September 9, 1786, George Washington Papers, Letterbook 13.

35. Foner, *History of Black Americans*, 1: 449; *Richmond Register*, June 6, 1802.

36. Horton and Horton, *Hard Road to Freedom*, 87–88.

37. Berlin, *Generations of Captivity: A History of African-American Slaves* (Cambridge, Mass.: Harvard University Press, 2003), 134.

38. By 1840 slave-produced cotton was more valuable than everything else the nation exported to the world combined.

39. Daniel L. Schafer, *Anna Kingsley*, revised and expanded edition (St. Augustine, Fla.: St. Augustine Historical Society, 1997).

40. Gary B. Nash, *Forging Freedom: The Formation of Philadelphia's Black Community, 1720–1840* (Cambridge, Mass.: Harvard University Press, 1988), 189–190.

41. Olive Gilbert, *Narrative of Sojourner Truth* (Battle Creek, Mich.:, 1878) quoted in Dorothy Sterling, ed., *Speak Out In Thunder Tones: Letters and Other Writings by Black Northerners, 1787–1865*, (Garden Grove, N.Y.: Doubleday, 1973), 128.

42. Nell Irvin Painter, *Sojourner Truth: A Life, A Symbol* (New York: W.W. Norton, 1996), 33.

43. For quotes, see Jacqueline Bernard, *Journey Toward Freedom: The Story of Sojourner Truth* (New York: The Feminist Press, 1990), 71. Also see Harriet Beecher Stowe, "Sojourner Truth, The Libyan Sibyl," *Atlantic Monthly* 2 (April, 1863): 473–481.

44. Charles Ball, *Fifty Years in Chains; or, The Life of an American Slave* (New York: H. Dayton, 1859), 24, 11.

45. Ball, *Fifty Years in Chains*, 12.

46. Ball, *Fifty Years in Chains*, 37, 96–97.

47. Charles H. Wesley, *In Freedom's Footsteps: From the African Background to the Civil War* (Cornwells Heights, Pa.: Publishers Company, 1979), 149–150.

48. James W. St. G.Walker, *Black Loyalists: The Search for a Promised Land in Nova Scotia and Sierra Leone* (Toronto: University of Toronto, 1992 [1976]), 389.

49. Kenneth Wiggins Porter, *Negro on the Frontier*: (New York: Arno Press, 1971), 223–262.

50. James Roberts, *The Narrative of James Roberts, A Soldier Under Gen. Washington in the Revolutionary War, and Under Gen. Jackson at the Battle of New Orleans, in the War of 1812: "A Battle Which Cost Me a Limb, Some Blood and Almost my Life."* (Chicago; Printed for the Author, 1858), 13.

51. *Ibid.*

52. Roberts, *The Narrative of James Roberts*, 17–18; James Oliver Horton and Lois E. Horton, *In Hope of Liberty: Culture, Community and Protest Among Northern Free Blacks, 1700–1860* (New York: Oxford University Press, 1997), 185–186.

Sidebar, p. 52

Massachusetts Historical Society *Collections*, 5th ser., 3: 432–33.

Sidebar, p. 73

Absalom Jones, *A Thanksgiving Sermon Preached January 1, 1808…on Account of the Abolition of the African Slave Trade…* (Philadelphia, 1808).

Chapter 3

1. Daniel L. Schafer, *Anna Kingsley*, revised and expanded edition (St. Augustine, Fla.: St. Augustine Historical Society, 1997), 19.

2. *Ibid.*, 23.

3. *Ibid.*, 28.

4. Peter M. Bergman and Mort N. Bergman, *The Chronological History of the Negro in America*, (New York: Mentor Books, 1969), 90–91; Thomas Jefferson, *Notes on the State of Virginia* (New York: Library of America, 1984), 266, 271.

5. Lamont Thomas, *Rise to Be a People* (Urbana: University of Illinois Press, 1986); Rosalind Cobb Wiggins, editor, *Captain Paul Cuffe's Logs and Letters, 1808–1817: A Black Quaker's "Voice from the Veil"* (Washington, D.C.: Howard University Press, 1996).

6. "Paul Cuffe to James Forten, Westport, January 8, 1817," quoted in Dorothy Sterling, ed., *Speak Out in Thunder Tones: Letters and Other Writings by Black Northerners, 1787–1865* (Garden City, N.Y.: Doubleday, 1973), 24–25; Thomas, *Rise to Be a People*.

7. William Wells Brown, *My Southern Home* (1880) included in William L. Andrews, ed., *From Fugitive Slave to Free Man* (New York: Mentor Book, 1993).

8. Alan Peskin, ed., *North into Freedom: The Autobiography of John Malvin* (Cleveland, Oh.: Press of Western Reserve University, 1966), 6-8; Philip S. Foner, *History of Black America: From the Emergence of the Cotton Kingdom to the Eve of the Compromise of 1850*, vol. 2 (Westport, Conn.: Greenwood Press, 1983), 584.

9. James Forten to Paul Cuffe, Philadelphia, January 25, 1817, in Shelton H. Harris, *Paul Cuffe: Black America and the African Return* (New York: Simon and Schuster, 1972), 243–245.

10. Harvey Wish, "American Slave Insurrections Before 1861," *The Journal of Negro History* 22, 3 (July 1937): 299–320.

11. David Robertson estimates that the Vesey conspirators recruited as many as 9,000 followers. David Robertson, *Denmark Vesey: The Buried History of America's Largest Slave Rebellion and the Man Who Led It* (New York: Alfred A. Knopf, 1999); Wish, "American Slave Insurrections Before 1861," 299.

12. Douglas R. Egerton, *He Shall Go Out Free: The Lives of Denmark Vesey* (Madison, Wis.: Madison House, 1999); Horton and Horton, *In Hope of Liberty*, 203.

13. Marie Tyler-McGraw, "Richmond Free Blacks and African Colonization, 1816–1832," *Journal of American Studies* 21, 2 (1987): 207–224.

14. Zephaniah Kingsley, *A Treatise on the Patriarchal, or Co-operative System of Society As It Exists in Some Governments, and Colonies in America, and in the Under the Name of Slavery, With Its Necessity and Advantages* (1829).

15. Schafer, *Anna Kingsley*, 40.

16. Martin E. Dann, ed., *The Black Press, 1827–1890: The Quest for National Identity* (New York: Capricorn, 1971); *Weekly Advocate*, 25 February 1837.

17. Peter Williams, *A Discourse Delivered in St. Philip's Church, for the Benefit of the Coloured Community of Wilberforce in Upper Canada, on Fourth of July, 1830* (New York: 1830), quoted in Leonard I. Sweet, *Black Images of America, 1784–1870* (New York: W.W. Norton, 1976), 55.

18. Theodore D. Weld, *Slavery and the Internal Slave Trade in the United States* (New York: Arno Press, 1969), 9.

19. Quoted in Steven F. Miller, "Plantation Labor Organization and Slave Life on the Cotton Frontier: The Alabama-Mississippi Black Belt, 1815–1840," in Ira Berlin and Philip D. Morgan, eds. *Cultivation and Culture: Labor and the Shaping of Slave Life in the Americas* (Charlottesville: University of Virginia Press: 1993), 157.

20. Foner, *History of Black America*, 2: 41; also see Michael Tadman, *Speculators and Slaves: Masters, Traders, and Slaves in the Old South* (Madison: University of Wisconsin, 1989).

21. Frederick Douglass, *Narrative of the Life of Frederick Douglass*, David Blight, ed. (Boston: Bedford Books, 1993), 73–74.

22. William Chambers, *Things as They Are in America* (Philadelphia: Lippincott, Grambo & Co., 1854), in Willie Lee Rose, editor, *A Documentary History of Slavery in North America* (New York: Oxford University Press, 1976), 143.

23. Foner, *History of Black Americans*, 2: 52.

24. Jack Hurst, *Nathan Bedford Forrest: A Biography* (New York: Alfred A. Knopf, 1993). Forrest became a general in the Confederate cavalry. In 1865 he helped found the Ku Klux Klan and became its first leader.

25. Ethan Allan Andrews, *Slavery and the Domestic Slave Trade in the United States* (Boston: Light & Stearns, 1836), 135–143, in Rose, *A Documentary History*, 138–139.

26. *Ibid.*, 139, 140.

27. Weld, *Slavery and the Internal Slave Trade*, 12–13.

28. George W. Featherstonhaugh, *Excursion through the Slave States, from Washington on the Potomac to the Frontier of Mexico: With Sketches of Popular Manners and Geological Notices* (New York: Harpers, 1844), 36–38, 46–47, 141–142, in Rose, *A Documentary History*, 157, 158.

29. Thomas Jefferson to John Holmes, April 22, 1820.

30. Joseph Holt Ingraham, *The South-West, by a Yankee*, vol. 2, (New York: Harpers, 1835), 192–197 in Rose, *A Documentary History*, 165.

31. Rose, *A Documentary History*,166.

32. Ann Patton Malone, *Sweet Chariot: Slave Family and Household Structure in Nineteenth-Century Louisiana* (Chapel Hill: University of North Carolina Press, 1992).

33. C. Peter Ripley, "The Black Family in Transition: Louisiana, 1860–1865," *Journal of Southern History* 41, 3 (August 1975): 369–380.

34. Frederic Bancroft, *Slave Trading in Old South* (New York: Frederick Ungar, 1931), 206–07.

35. Frederick Law Olmsted, *The Cotton Kingdom: A Traveler's Observation on Cotton and Slavery in the American Slave States*, vol. 1 (New York: Mason Brothers, 1861), 39–40, quoted in, Peter Kolchin, *American Slavery, 1619–1877* (New York: Hill and Wang, 1993), 117.

36. M[oncure] D. Conway, *Testimonies Concerning Slavery* (London: Chapman & Hall, 1864), 1–8, in Rose, *Documentary History*, 406–411, 410.

37. Thomas Jefferson, *Notes on the State of Virginia*, 289.

38. Solomon Northup, *Twelve Years a Slave. Narrative of Solomon Northup, a Citizen of New York, Kidnapped in Washington City in 1841, and Rescued in 1853, From a Cotton Plantation Near the Red River, in Louisiana* (Auburn, N.Y.: Derby and Miller, 1853).

39. Solomon Northup, *Twelve Years a Slave*.

40. *David Walker's Appeal*, 3rd edition. Edited with an introduction by Charles M. Wiltse (June 1830; N.Y.: Hill and Wang, 1965), 76.

41. Herbert Aptheker, *One Continual Cry: David Walker's Appeal to the Colored Citizens of the World, 1829–1830, Its Setting and Its Meaning* (New York: Humanities Press, 1965), 77, 137 137n.

42. John W. Cromwell, "The Aftermath of Nat Turner's Insurrection," *Journal of Negro History* 5, 2 (April 1920): 208–234, 209.

43. Harriet A. Jacobs, *Incidents in the Life of a Slave Girl*, Jean Fagan Yellin, ed. (Cambridge, Mass.: Harvard University Press, 1987), 63–64.

44. Cromwell, "The Aftermath," 215.

45. *Ibid.*, 220.

46. Marshall Rachleff, "An Abolitionist Letter to Governor Henry W. Collier of Alabama: The Emergence of A Crisis of Fear in Alabama," *Journal of Negro History* 66, 3 (Autumn 1981): 246–253, 247; William Courtland Johnson, "'A Delusive Clothing:' Christian Conversion in the Antebellum Slave Community," *Journal of Negro History* 82, 3 (Summer 1997): 295–311, 303.

47. James Oliver Horton and Lois E. Horton, *In Hope of Liberty: Culture, Community and Protest Among Northern Free Blacks, 1700–1860* (New York: Oxford University Press, 1997), 244–245.

48. *Colored American*, February 27, 1841.

Sidebar, p. 94

An Official Report of the Trials of Sundry Negroes, charged with an attempt to raise an insurrection in the State of South-Carolina… prepared and published at the request of the Court, by Lionel H. Kennedy and Thomas Parker, members of the Charleston bar and Presiding Magistrates of the Court (Charleston, 1822), 48–51, 66–67, in Herbert Aptheker, editor, *A Documentary History of the Negro People in the United States*, vol. 1 (N.Y.: Citadel Press, 1951), 76.

Chapter 4

1. *The North Star*, May 11, 1849; Edward D. Jervey and C. Harold Huber, "The Creole Affair," *Journal of Negro History* 65, 3 (Summer 1980): 196–211. In 1853 a joint U.S. and British commission awarded compensation to the slaveholders who had lost their slaves in the Creole affair.

2. C. Peter Ripley et al., eds., *Black Abolitionist Papers: The United States, 1830–1846*, vol. 3 (Chapel Hill: University of North Carolina Press, 1991), 409–410.

3. John Hope Franklin, *The Militant South, 1800–1860* (Cambridge, Mass.: Harvard University Press, 1956).

4. Robert E. May, "John A. Quitman and His Slaves: Reconciling Slave Resistance with the Proslavery Defense" *Journal of Southern History* 46, 4 (November 1980): 551–570, 561.

5. May, "John A. Quitman," 567.

6. William Wells Brown, *Narrative of William W. Brown, A Fugitive Slave* (1848) in William L. Andrews, ed., *From Fugitive Slave to Free Man* (New York: Mentor Books, 1993), 28.

7. Lewis Clark, *Narrative of the Sufferings of Lewis Clarke, During a Captivity of More than Twenty-five Years* (Boston: D. H. Ela, printer, 1845), 17; Harriet Jacobs, *Incidents in the Life of a Slave Girl: Written by Herself*, edited and introduction by Jean Fagan Yellin (Cambridge, Mass.: Harvard University Press, 1987), 28.

8. Elizabeth Fox-Genovese, *Within the Plantation Household: Black and White Women of the Old South* (Chapel Hill: University of North Carolina Press, 1988).

9. Solomon Northup, *Twelve Years A Slave*, Sue Eakin and Joseph Logsdon, eds. (Baton Rouge: Louisiana State University Press, 1968), 172.

10. William L. Van Deburg, *The Slave Driver* (Westport, Conn.: Greenwood Press, 1979).

11. Charshee Charlotte Lawrence-McIntyre, "The Double Meanings of the Spirituals," *Journal of Black Studies* 17, 4 (June 1987): 379–401, 386, 391.

12. The Fulbe people are also known as Fula or Fulani. Terry Alford, *Prince Among Slaves* (New York: Oxford University Press, 1977), 3, 42.

13. Alford, *Prince Among Slaves*, 47; See Bertram Wyatt-Brown, "The Mask of Obedience: Male Slave Psychology in the Old South," *American Historical Review* 93, 5 (December 1988): 1228–1252.

14. *The Raleigh Standard*, July 18, 1838.

15. "John J. Audubon Encounters a Runaway in Louisiana Swamps," from John James Audubon, *Ornithological Biography, or an Account of the Habits of the Birds of the United States of America*, vol. 2 (Edinburgh: Adam Black, 1834), 27–32, in Willie Lee Rose, ed. *A Documentary History of Slavery in North America* (New York: Oxford University Press, 1976), 262–266.

16. John Hope Franklin and Loren Schweninger, *Runaway Slaves: Rebels on the Plantation, 1790–1860* (New York: Oxford University Press, 1999).

17. Ripley et al., eds. *Black Abolitionist Papers*, vol. 4 (Chapel Hill: University of North Carolina Press, 1991), 56.

18. Steven Weisenburger, *Modern Medea: A Family Story of Slavery and Child-Murder from the Old South* (New York: Hill and Wang, 1998).

19. Charles Ball, *Fifty Years in Chains; or, The Life of An American Slave* (New York: H. Dayton Publisher, 1859), 251–260.

20. Pauli Murray, *Proud Shoes: The Story of an American Family* ([1956] N.Y.: Harper & Row, 1978), 99.

21. *Ibid.*, 99.

22. John Brown, *Slave Life in Georgia: A Narrative of the Life, Sufferings, and Escape of John Brown, a Fugitive Slave Now in England*, Electronic Edition, Louis Alexis Chamerovzow, ed. (1854), UNC-CH digitization project, *Documenting the American South* (1998), 14, 149.

23. *Ibid.*

24. In the 1880s, Parker dictated his memoirs, recounting the exciting and dramatic adventures of the Underground Railroad in southern Ohio. Stuart Seely Sprague, ed., *His Promised Land: The Autobiography of John P. Parker, Former Slave and Conductor on the Underground Railroad* (New York: W.W. Norton, 1996); quote from Nat Brandt, *The Town that Started the Civil War* (Syracuse, N.Y.: Syracuse University Press, 1990), 4.

25. Foner, *History of Black Americans*, 2: 194–195.

26. Ripley et al., eds., *Black Abolitionist Papers*, 4: 53–54, 56–57.

27. Earl Conrad, *General Harriet Tubman* (Washington, D.C.: Associated Publishers, [1943] 1990).

28. *Liberator*, April 19, 1834, cited in James Oliver Horton, *Free People of Color: Inside the African American Community* (Washington, D.C.: Smithsonian Institution Press, 1993), 59.

29. Alexander Crummell, *The Eulogy of Henry Highland Garnet, D.D. Presbyterian Minister, etc.* (Washington, D.C.: 1882), 25, n. 26.

30. "Report of the Condition of the People of Color in the State of Ohio" (April 1835), reprinted in Herbert Aptheker, ed., *A Documentary History of the Negro People in the United States* (New York: Citadel Press, 1965), 157–158.

31. Records of the Treasurer's Office, 1843, Oberlin College Archives, cited in Horton, *Free People of Color*, 69.

32. Union Baptist Church records, 1834, Union Baptist Church, Cincinnati, cited in Horton, *Free People of Color*, 69.

33. Paul Finkelman, *Defending Slavery: Proslavery Thought in the Old South* (Boston: Bedford/St. Martin's, 2003); Eugene D. Genovese, *The Slaveholders' Dilemma: Freedom and Progress in Southern Conservative Thought, 1820–1860* (Columbia: University of South Carolina Press, 1992).

34. James H. Hammond, *Selections from the Letters and Speeches of the Hon. James H. Hammond*

(Spartanburg, S.C.: The Reprint Co., 1978 [1866]), 43–44, quoted in Genovese, *Slaveholders' Dilemma*, 88.

35. Leonard L. Richards, *Gentlemen of Property and Standing: Anti-abolition Mobs in Jacksonian America* (New York: Oxford University Press, 1970).

36. James Brewer Stewart, *Holy Warriors: The Abolitionists and American Slavery* (New York: Hill and Wang, 1976), 69–72; Horton and Horton, *In Hope of Liberty*, 239.

37. Stewart, *Holy Warriors*, 81–82; Julie Roy Jeffrey, *The Great Silent Army of Abolitionism: Ordinary Women in the Antislavery Movement* (Chapel Hill: University of North Carolina Press, 1998), 87–88.

38. Frederick Douglass, "My Slave Experience in Maryland," an address delivered in New York City, May 6, 1845, in David W. Blight, ed., *Narrative of the Life of Frederick Douglass, An American Slave, Written by Himself* (Boston: Bedford Books/St. Martin's Press, 1993), 131; Frederick Douglass to Thomas Auld, September 3, 1848, in Blight, ed., *Narrative*, 139.

39. Frederick S. Voss, *Majestic in His Wrath: A Pictorial Life of Frederick Douglass* (Washington, D.C.: Smithsonian Institution Press, 1995), v.

40. Paul Finkelman, *An Imperfect Union: Slavery, Federalism, and Comity* (Chapel Hill: University of North Carolina Press, 1981), 17, 137.

41. Solomon Northup, *Twelve Years a Slave*, edited by Sue Eakin and Joseph Logsdon (Baton Rouge: Louisiana State University Press, [1853] 1968).

42. *Ibid.*

43. *Pennsylvania Freedman*, October 31, 1850, quoted in Ripley et al. eds., *Black Abolitionist Papers*, 4: 68.

44. *National Anti-Slavery Standard*, September 5, 1850, quoted in Robert C. Dick, *Black Protest: Issues and Tactics* (Westport, Conn.: Greenwood Press, 1974), 142.

45. *Liberator*, November 1, 1850.

46. Olivia Mahoney, "Black Abolitionist," *Chicago History* 20, 1&2 (1991): 22–37.

47. Finkelman, *An Imperfect Union*, 286, 296–310.

48. Finkelman, *An Imperfect Union*, 131.

49. James Oliver Horton and Lois E. Horton, *Black Bostonians: Family Life and Community Struggle in the Antebellum North* (New York: Holmes and Meier, 1979, 2nd edition, 1999).

50. Fred Landon, "The Negro Migration to Canada after the Passing of the Fugitive Slave Act," *Journal of Negro History* 5, 1 (January, 1920): 22–36, 23.

51. Wilbur H. Siebert, *The Underground Railroad from Slavery to Freedom* (New York: Macmillan, 1898), 249.

52. Landon, "The Negro Migration," 24.

53. James Oliver Horton and Lois E. Horton, *Hard Road to Freedom: The Story of African America* (New Brunswick, N.J.: Rutgers University Press, 2001), 153.

54. Horton and Horton, *Black Bostonians*.

55. Allan Nevins, *Ordeal of the Union: A Dividing House, 1852–1857* (New York: Scribners, 1947), 447.

56. Don Edward Fehrenbacher, *The Dred Scott Case: Its Significance in American Law and Politics* (New York: Oxford University Press, 2001).

57. "Address by Charles L. Remond," April 3, 1857, in Herbert Aptheker, *Documentary History of Negro People in the United States*, (New York: Citadel Press, 1951), 394.

58. *Douglass' Paper*, September 7, 1855; *Liberator*, November 27, 1857; Ripley et al., eds., *Black Abolitionist Papers*, 4: 319.

Sidebar, p. 150
Gilder Lehrman Collection.

Chapter 5

1. *Liberator*, May 28, 1858.

2. Benjamin Quarles, *Allies for Freedom: Black and John Brown* (New York: Oxford University Press, 1974), 86–87.

3. Allan Nevins, *The Emergence of Lincoln: Prologue to Civil War, 1859–1861* (New York: Scribners, 1950), 79, 81.

4. *Liberator*, December 9, 1859; Benjamin Quarles, ed., *Blacks on John Brown* (Urbana: Univ. of Illinois Press, 1972), 20–21.

5. *The Weekly Anglo-African*, December 1859.

6. *Liberator*, March 12, 1858.

7. James C. Humes, *The Wit and Wisdom of Abraham Lincoln* (New York: Gramercy Books, 1996), 55.

8. Maureen Harrison and Steve Gilbert, eds., *Abraham Lincoln: Word for Word* (San Diego, Calif.: Excellent Books, 1994), 129.

9. David Herbert Donald, *Lincoln* (New York: Simon and Schuster, 1995), 220.

10. Robert W. Johannsen, *The Lincoln-Douglas Debates* (New York: Oxford University Press, 1965), 216, 231.

11. *Liberator*, September 5, 1856.

12. "Equal Suffrage Defeated," *Douglass' Monthly*, December 1860, quoted in David W. Blight, *Frederick Douglass' Civil War: Keeping Faith in Jubilee* (Baton Rouge: Louisiana State University, Press, 1989), 61.

13. The 81.2 percent of eligible voters who cast ballots was the highest percentage of voters at that time

and the second highest in American history, surpassed only by the election of 1876 with an 81.8 percent turnout.

14. Quoted in James M. McPherson, *The Negro's Civil War: How American Negroes Felt and Acted During the War for the Union* (New York: Vintage Books, 1967), 11. See also James O. Horton, "'Making Free': African Americans and the Civil War," in Frances H. Kennedy, ed., *The Civil War Battlefield Guide* (Boston: Houghton Mifflin, 1990), 261–263.

15. *Chicago Daily Times and Herald*, November 20, 1860.

16. *New Orleans Bee*, December 5, 1860.

17. "Joseph E. Brown's Secessionist Public Letter, December 7, from Milledgeville," William W. Freehling and Craig M. Simpson, eds., *Secession Debated: Georgia's Showdown in 1860*, (New York: Oxford University Press, 1992), 147. Reprinted from (*The Milledgeville Weekly*) *Federal Union*, December 11, 1860.

18. Quoted in Drew Gilpin Faust, *The Creation of Confederate Nationalism: Ideology and Identity in the Civil War South* (Baton Rouge: Louisiana State University Press, 1988), 60.

19. "South Carolina Ordinances of Secession," *The War of the Rebellion: Official Records*, (Washington: War Department, 1891), Series 4, 1: 1.

20. Quoted in Allen C. Guelzo, *Abraham Lincoln: Redeemer President* (Grand Rapids, Mich.: William B. Eerdmans Publishing Company, 1999), 250.

21. The Constitution of the Confederate States of America, adopted unanimously March 11, 1861, Montgomery, Alabama.

22. Daniel L. Schafer, *Anna Kingsley*, revised and expanded edition (St. Augustine, Fla.: St. Augustine Historical Society, 1997), 43–47.

23. Abraham Lincoln, "Presidential Inaugural Address, on March 4, 1861" in *Inaugural Addresses of the Presidents of the United States: From George Washington to George W. Bush*, Senate document (Washington, D.C.: U.S. Government Printing Office, 1989), 101–110.

24. Hondon B. Hargrove, *Black Union Soldiers in the Civil War* (Jefferson, N.C.: McFarland & Co., 1988).

25. McPherson, *Negro's Civil War*, 19.

26. Peter H. Clark, *The Black Brigade of Cincinnati: Being a Report of Its Labors and a Muster-Roll of Its Members; Together with Various Orders, Speeches, Etc. Relating to It* (Cincinnati: Joseph B. Boyd, 1864; reprint New York: Arno Press, 1969), 4–5.

27. *New York Tribune*, February 12, 1862; *Douglass' Monthly*, September 1861.

28. *Montgomery Advertiser*, November 6, 1861.

29. *Douglass' Monthly* August 1861, quoted in McPherson, *Negro's Civil War*, 38.

30. James M. McPherson, *The Struggle for Equality: Abolitionists and the Negro in the Civil War and Reconstruction* (Princeton, N.J.: Princeton University Press, 1964).

31. Report of the Joint Committee on the Conduct of the War, Report 108, Part III, 37th Congress, Third Session, 632–645, quoted in William Loren Katz, *Eyewitness: The Negro in American History*, 3rd edition (Belmont, Calif.: Fearon Pitman Publishers), 219.

32. McPherson, *Struggle for Equality*, 73–74.

33. Willie Lee Rose, *Rehearsal for Reconstruction: The Port Royal Experiment* (New York: Vintage Books, 1964).

34. *The Principia*, December 21, 1861.

35. Constance McLaughlin Green, *Washington: A History of the Capital, 1800–1950* (Princeton, N.J.: Princeton University Press, 1962).

36. McPherson, *Negro's Civil War*, 44–45

37. *Harper's Weekly*, February 7, 1863.

38. Janice Sumler-Edmond, "Charlotte L. Forten Grimké," in Darlene Clark Hine, ed. *Black Women in America: An Historical Encyclopedia* (Brooklyn, N.Y.: Carlson Publishing, 1993), 505–507; Charlotte L. Forten, *The Journal of Charlotte L. Forten*, ed. and introduction by Ray Allen Billington (New York: Collier Books, 1953), 144–145.

39. Earl Conrad, *General Harriet Tubman* (Washington, D.C.: Associated Publishers, [1943] 1990), 153; Catherine Clinton, *Harriet Tubman: The Road to Freedom* (New York: Little, Brown, 2004), 148–149.

40. *Liberator*, September 12, 1862.

41. Quoted in Katz, *Eyewitness*, 210.

42. Herbert Aptheker, "The Negro in the Union Navy," *The Journal of Negro History* 32, 2 (April 1947): 169–200, 175.

43. *The War of the Rebellion: A Compilation of Official Records of the Union and Confederate Armies*, 128 vols. (Washington, D.C., 1880–1901), 3 ser., 2: 43.

44. Dudley Taylor Cornish, *The Sable Arm: Negro Troops in the Union Army, 1861–1865* (New York: W. W. Norton, 1966).

45. McPherson, *Struggle for Equality*, 196.

46. Thomas Wentworth Higginson, *Army Life in a Black Regiment*, biographical introduction by John Hope Franklin (Boston: Beacon Press, 1962), xii–xiii.

47. Quoted in McPherson, *Negro's Civil War*, 163.

48. Higginson, *Army Life in a Black Regiment*, xiii.

49. *Ibid.*

50. Quoted in McPherson, *Negro's Civil War,* 166–167.

51. Quoted in McPherson, *Negro's Civil War,* 50.

52. Noah Andre Trudeau, *Like Men of War: Black Troops in the Civil War, 1862–1865* (Boston: Little, Brown, 1998), 19–20.

53. Higginson, *Army Life in a Black Regiment,* 40–41.

Chapter 6

1. *The Commonwealth* (Boston), Friday, July 10, 1863, in Earl Conrad, *General Harriet Tubman* (Washington, D.C.: Associated Publishers, 1990), 169–175, quote 175. *The Commonwealth* reported 300 soldiers went on this mission, Clinton in *Harriet Tubman* puts the number at 150, and Rose in *Rehearsal for Reconstruction* reports there were 250.

2. In 1864 Congress authorized equal pay for blacks who had been free before the war, but did not include those who had been slaves at the time of enlistment until March 1865. At that time, equal pay was made retroactive to the date of enlistment. Ira Berlin, Joseph P. Reidy, and Leslie S. Rowland, *Freedom: A Documentary History of Emancipation, 1861–1867* (Cambridge: Cambridge University Press, 1982), Series 2, 363, 367–368.

3. Frederick Douglass, *The Life and Times of Frederick Douglass* (London: Collier-Macmillan Ltd., [1892], 1962), 348.

4. Noah Andre Trudeau, *Like Men of War: Black Troops in the Civil War, 1862–1865* (Boston: Little, Brown, 1998), 254.

5. George Washington Williams, *History of the Negro Race in America, 1619 to 1880,* vol 2 (New York: Putnam, 1883), 331.

6. Albert Bushnell Hart, *Slavery and Abolition* (New York: Harpers, 1906), 209.

7. Philip Foner, *History of Black Americans,* vol. 3 (Westport, Conn.: Greenwood Press, 1983), 376.

8. *New Orleans Daily True Delta,* April 23, 1861.

9. James G. Hollandsworth, Jr., *The Louisiana Native Guards: The Military Experience During the Civil War* (Baton Rouge: Louisiana State University Press, 1995), 2–6.

10. Hollandsworth, *Louisiana Native Guards,* 16–17.

11. Frances H. Kennedy, ed., *The Civil War Battlefield Guide* (Boston: Houghton Mifflin, 1998), 181–184.

12. Howard C. Wright, *Port Hudson: Its History from an Interior Point of View* (St. Francisville, La., 1937), reprint ed., (Baton Rouge, La.: The Eagle Press, 1978), 51.

13. Edward Bacon, *Among the Cotton Thieves* (Bossier City, La., [1897] 1989), 288–289.

14. Hollandsworth, *Louisiana Native Guards,* 65.

15. *New York Times,* June 11, 1863.

16. Henry T. Johns, *Life with the Forty-ninth Massachusetts Volunteers* (Pittsfield, Mass.: For the author, 1864), 254–255.

17. Jack Hurst, *Nathan Bedford Forrest: A Biography* (New York: Alfred A. Knopf, 1993), 172–178, 186; James M. McPherson, *The Negro's Civil War: How American Negroes Felt and Acted During the War for the Union* (N.Y.: Vintage Books, 1965), 217.

18. R. J. M. Blackett, *Thomas Morris Chester: Black Civil War Correspondent* (Baton Rouge: Louisiana State University Press, 1989), 125; Hurst, *Nathan Bedford Forrest,* 178; McPherson, *Negro's Civil War,* 222.

19. Mark A. Weitz, *A Higher Duty : Desertion Among Georgia Troops During the Civil War* (Lincoln: University of Nebraska Press, 2000).

20. Blackett, *Thomas Morris Chester,* 247.

21. James Ford Rhodes, *History of the Civil War, 1861–1865* (New York: Macmillan, 1917), 417.

22. Blackett, *Thomas Morris Chester,* 248.

23. James M. McPherson, *For Cause and Comrades: Why Men Fought in the Civil War* (New York: Oxford University Press, 1997), 172.

24. Blackett, *Thomas Morris Chester,* 248.

25. *New Orleans Tribune,* February 25, 1865, quoted in Du Bois, *Black Reconstruction,* 119; Blackett, *Thomas Morris Chester,* 248.

26. Leon Litwack, *Been in the Storm So Long: The Aftermath of Slavery* (New York: Alfred A. Knopf, 1979), 168.

27. Virginia M. Adams, ed., *On the Altar of Freedom: A Black Soldier's Civil War Letters from the Front* (Amherst: Univ. of Massachusetts Press, 1991), 18–19.

28. Litwack, *Been in the Storm So Long,* 169.

29. Litwack, *Been in the Storm So Long,* 168; Mark E. Neely, Jr., *The Last Best Hope on Earth: Abraham Lincoln and the Promise of America* (Springfield: Illinois State Historical Library, 1993); *Liberator,* April 7, 1865.

30. Gavin Wright, *The Royal Economy of the Cotton South* (New York: W.W. Norton, 1978); James L. Roark, *Masters Without Slaves: Southern Planters in the Civil War and Reconstruction* (New York: W. W. Norton, 1977), 77, 120. Both cotton and sugar recovered relatively quickly. The planters' greatest loss was the value of human capital that the end of slavery took from them and redistributed to the former slaves themselves.

31. James Mc Pherson, *Battle Cry of Freedom: The Civil War Era* (New York: Oxford University Press, 1988), 852.

32. Donald Yacovone, ed. *Freedom's Journey: African American Voices of the Civil War* (Chicago: Lawrence Hill Books, 2004), 303–304.

33. Abraham Lincoln, "Second Inaugural Address," Washington, D.C., March 4, 1865, in Maureeen Harrison and Steve Gilbert, eds., *Abraham Lincoln: Word for Word* (San Diego, Calif.: Excellent Books, 1994), 375–377, 377.

34. Trudeau, *Like Men of War*, 433.

35. Moses Grandy, *Narrative of the Life of Moses Grandy, Late a Slave in the United States of America* (London: Gilpin, 1843), 53–54.

36. Litwack, *Been in the Storm So Long: The Aftermath of Slavery* (New York: Alfred A. Knopf, 1979), 229.

37. *Colored Tennesseean,* Aug. 12, 1865, in Litwack, *Been in the Storm So Long,* 232.

38. Joel Williamson, *After Slavery: The Negro in South Carolina During Reconstruction, 1861–1877* (New York: W.W. Norton, [1965] 1975), 59–60.

39. Litwack, *Been in the Storm So Long,* 252.

40. Litwack, *Been in the Storm So Long,* 448.

41. Steven Mintz, ed., *African American Voices: The Life Cycle of Slavery* (St. James, N.Y.: Brandywine Books, 1993), 166, 170.

42. Mintz, ed., *African American Voices,* 166.

43. Eric Foner, *Reconstruction: America's Unfinished Revolution, 1863–1877* (New York: Harper and Row, 1988); *New York Tribune,* June 30, 1869.

44. Leslie A. Schwalm, *A Hard Fight for We: Women's Transition from Slavery to Freedom in South Carolina* (Urbana: University of Illinois Press, 1997), 232.

45. Thomas Holt, *Black Over White: Negro Political Leadership in South Carolina during Reconstruction* (Urbana: University of Illinois Press, 1977), 34–35; Sharon Harley, *The Timetables of African American History* (New York: Simon and Schuster, 1996), 174.

46. Litwack, *Been in the Storm So Long,* 281.

47. Hollandsworth, *Louisiana Native Guards,* 106–107.

48. W. E. B. Du Bois, *Black Reconstruction in America, 1860–1880* (New York: Atheneum, 1973), 465.

49. Du Bois, *Black Reconstruction,* 465.

50. James G. Hollandsworth. *An Absolute Massacre: The New Orleans Riot of July 30, 1866* (Baton Rouge: Louisiana State University Press, 2001).

51. Hurst, *Nathan Bedford Forrest*; Foner, *Reconstruction.*

52. Lerone Bennett, Jr., *Black Power U.S.A.: The Human Side of Reconstruction, 1867–1877* (Chicago: Johnson, 1967).

53. Daniel L. Schafer, *Anna Kingsley* (St. Augustine, Fla.: St. Augustine Historical Society, 1997), 49.

54. *Ibid.,* 48–49.

55. Joe M. Richardson, "Francis L. Cardozo: Black Educator During Reconstruction," *Journal of Negro Education* 48, 1 (Winter, 1979): 73–83; William C. Hine, "Black Politicians in Reconstruction Charleston, South Carolina: A Collective Study," *Journal of Southern History* 49, 4 (Nov. 1983): 555–584.

56. Bennett, *Black Power U.S.A.* As lieutenant governor, Pinchback ascended to the governorship when the white Republican governor was impeached.

57. Du Bois, *Black Reconstruction,* 389–399, 638.

58. Edward A. Miller, *Gullah Statesman: Robert Smalls from Slavery to Congress, 1839–1915* (Columbia: University of South Carolina Press, 1995).

59. Du Bois, *Black Reconstruction,* 686.

60. George C. Wright, *Racial Violence in Kentucky, 1865–1940* (Baton Rouge: Louisiana State University Press, 1990).

61. Litwack, *Been in the Storm So Long,* 269.

62. Howard Zinn, *A People's History of the United States,* revised edition (New York: Harper Perennial, 1995), 199.

63. Foner, *Reconstruction,* 550.

64. Joel Williamson, *After Slavery: The Negro in South Carolina During Reconstruction, 1861–1877* (New York: W.W. Norton, 1965), 410–411; Thomas Holt, *Black Over White: Negro Political Leadership in South Carolina During Reconstruction* (Urbana: University of Illinois Press, 1977), 212.

65. Foner, *Reconstruction,* 571.

66. Litwack, *Been in the Storm So Long,* 168–169; Mark E. Neely, Jr., *The Last Best Hope on Earth: Abraham Lincoln and the Promise of America* (Springfield: Illinois State Historical Library, 1993); *Liberator,* April 7, 1865.

67. Nell Irvin Painter, *Exodusters: Black Migration to Kansas after Reconstruction* (New York: W.W. Norton, 1976).

68. Compiled from the U.S. Census, 1860 and 1880.

Sidebar, p. 208

Black Republican, New Orleans, Louisiana, April 29, 1865. Library of Congress.

Sidebar, p. 228

Schomburg Center, New York Public Library.

Chronology

1619

Twenty Africans brought to Jamestown, Virginia, by a Dutch ship and sold as involuntary laborers to British colonists. They are the first Africans sold in British North America.

1635

Angolan-born Antonio (Anthony) Johnson gains his freedom in Virginia.

1641

Massachusetts Bay prohibits the enslavement of people not taken in just wars, thereby becoming the first colony to give legal status to slavery.

1662

Virginia law declares a child's slave or free status to follow the status of the mother.

1664

Maryland becomes the first British colony to prohibit interracial marriage.

1672

Royal African Company chartered in England and granted a monopoly in British slave trading.

1676

Slaves and white indentured servants participate in Bacon's Rebellion in Virginia.

1688

Quakers in Germantown, Pennsylvania, register the first formal protest against slavery and the slave trade by a white organization.

1700

African American population of 27,817 is 11 percent of the estimated total population of British North America excluding Canada.

1712

Nine whites killed in New York City slave rebellion. Twenty-one slaves executed.

1739

Slaves rebel in Stono, South Carolina. Twenty whites and more than forty blacks are killed.

1741

Suspicious fires in New York City result in the execution of 31 blacks and 5 whites convicted of slave conspiracy.

1750

African American population of 236,420 is 20 percent of the estimated total population of British North America excluding Canada.

1751

Slavery becomes legal in Georgia, formerly a free colony.

1765

Blacks participate in protests against the Stamp Act passed by the British Parliament.

1770

African American population of 459,822 is more than 21 percent of the total population of British North America excluding Canada.

Crispus Attucks, a sailor and fugitive slave, is the first person killed at the Boston Massacre.

1775

Lord Dunmore, Royal Governor of Virginia, issues a proclamation offering freedom to all slaves and servants who fight for the British.

1776

Declaration of Independence adopted by the Continental Congress on July 4. Signers remove a section denouncing the slave trade.

1777

Vermont state constitution abolishes slavery.

1778

After prohibiting slaves in the Continental Army in 1775, the Continental Congress authorizes George Washington to recruit free blacks. Five thousand African Americans served in the American military.

1787

United States Constitution adopted. The words "slavery" and "slave" do not appear in the document.

1789

George Washington inaugurated as first President of United States.

Olaudah Equiano publishes his autobiography.

1790

The first United States Census records nearly 4 million residents, more than 750,000 (19 percent) of whom are black.

1793

First federal Fugitive Slave Law passed.

Eli Whitney invents the cotton gin, greatly increasing cotton production. By 1840 the American South is producing 75 percent of the world's cotton.

1800

U.S. population is 5,308,483, of whom 1,002,037 (19%) are black.

Gabriel's slave revolt in Richmond, Virginia, involving 100 slaves, is betrayed. Sixteen slaves including Gabriel are hanged.

1803

U.S. purchases territory of Louisiana from France for 15 million dollars, more than doubling land area of nation.

1808

Congress prohibits U.S. involvement in the international slave trade.

1815

Andrew Jackson commands U.S. troops, including at least 600 African Americans, defeating the British at the Battle of New Orleans.

1816

American Colonization Society established.

1819

Florida purchased by the U.S. from Spain for 5 million dollars.

1820

Missouri Compromise maintains balance of slave and free states (twelve each). Missouri admitted as slave state and Maine as free.

1821

West African colony of Liberia founded by the American Colonization Society for settlement of former slaves.

1822

Denmark Vesey's plans for a slave revolt discovered in Charleston, South Carolina. Thirty-five blacks executed.

1827

Freedom's Journal, first black newspaper, published in New York City.

1829

David Walker's *Appeal to the Coloured Citizens of the World* published.

1831

Nat Turner leads a slave rebellion in Southampton County, Virginia.

1833

Slavery abolished in the British empire.

American Anti-slavery Society founded.

1838

Frederick Douglass escapes slavery in Maryland.

1839

Slaves led by Cinque rebel aboard the ship *Amistad*; they are captured and charged with murder and piracy.

1841

Slaves revolt aboard the slave ship *Creole* and gain freedom in the Bahamas.

1845

Narrative of the Life of Frederick Douglass published.

1849

Harriet Tubman escapes from slavery in Maryland.

1850

New federal Fugitive Slave Law makes recovering fugitives easier for slaveholders.

1852

Harriet Beecher Stowe's *Uncle Tom's Cabin* published.

1854

Armed conflict between antislavery and proslavery forces in Kansas after passage of the Kansas-Nebraska Act.

Fugitive slave Anthony Burns returned to Virginia from Boston.

1859

John Brown, thirteen whites, and five blacks attack the federal arsenal at Harpers Ferry, Virginia.

1860

Abraham Lincoln elected president.

African American population of 4,441,830 is 14 percent of the total U.S. population of 31,443,790.

1861

Civil War begins with firing on federal Fort Sumter, South Carolina. African Americans volunteer for military service but are rejected.

1862

Slavery abolished in the District of Columbia, and slave owners are compensated for the emancipation of their slaves.

1863

Abraham Lincoln issues Emancipation Proclamation.

Black troops enlisted in the U.S. army.; African American troops of the Fifty-fourth Massachusetts Volunteers engage in battle at Fort Wagner.

1864

Fort Pillow massacre under command of Confederate General Nathan Bedford Forrest.

General William T. Sherman issues Field Order No. 15 distributing 40 acres of land per black family in the Sea Islands and surrounding countryside. The order is later rescinded.

1865

Congress passes Thirteenth Amendment to the Constitution abolishing slavery; ratified the same year.

Bureau of Refugees, Freedmen, and Abandoned Lands established (Freedmen's Bureau).

Surrender of Confederate General Robert E. Lee to General Ulysses S. Grant at Appomatox Courthouse on April 9.

Abraham Lincoln shot on April 14; he dies the following day.

Andrew Johnson becomes president. Mississippi Black Codes enacted.

1866

Congress passes Fourteenth Amendment to the Constitution giving blacks equal citizenship rights.

1868

Fourteenth Amendment ratified.

President Andrew Johnson impeached but not convicted.

Ulysses S. Grant elected president.

1869

Congress passes Fifteenth Amendment to the Constitution, guaranteeing the right to vote.

1870

Hiram R. Revels elected to U.S. Senate to fill seat formerly occupied by Jefferson Davis.

Fifteenth Amendment ratified.

1874

Blanche Kelso Bruce elected to the U.S. Senate from Mississippi.

1875

Congress passes Civil Rights Act prohibiting discrimination in public accommodations, conveyances, theaters, and other places of public amusement.

1877

Wormley Hotel Agreement settles contested election, giving Rutherford B. Hayes the presidency and providing for withdrawal of the last federal troops from the South.

Black town of Nicodemus, Kansas, founded.

1883

U.S. Supreme Court declares Civil Rights Act of 1875 unconstitutional.

1884

Robert Smalls elected to U.S. House of Representatives from South Carolina.

1895

Booker T. Washington delivers Atlanta Compromise Speech at Cotton States Exposition.

Frederick Douglass dies.

1896

U.S. Supreme Court establishes doctrine of separate but equal in *Plessy v. Ferguson*.

Further Reading and Web Sites

Aptheker, Herbert, ed. *A Documentary History of the Negro People in the United States.* New York: Citadel Press, 1965.

Ball, Charles. *Fifty Years in Chains.* Mineola, N.Y.: Dover, 2003.

Berlin, Ira. *Generations of Captivity: A History of African American Slaves.* Cambridge, Mass.: Harvard University Press, 2003.

Berlin, Ira. *Many Thousands Gone: The First Two Centuries of Slavery in North America.* Cambridge, Mass.: Harvard University Press, 1998.

Berlin, Ira, and Philip D. Morgan, eds. *Cultivation and Culture: Labor and the Shaping of Slave Life in the Americas.* Charlottesville: University Press of Virginia , 1993.

Bernard, Jacqueline. *Journey Toward Freedom: The Story of Sojourner Truth.* New York Feminist Press, 1990.

Blassingame, John W. *The Slave Community: Plantation Life in the Antebellum South.* New York: Oxford University Press, 1972.

Blight, David W. *Race and Reunion: The Civil War in American Memory.* Cambridge, Mass.: Harvard University Press, 2001.

Bontemps, Arna, ed. *Great Slave Narratives.* Boston: Beacon Press, 1969.

Davidson, Basil. *The Search for Africa: History, Culture, Politics.* New York: Random House, 1994.

Davis, David Brion. *The Problem of Slavery in Western Culture.* Ithaca, N.Y.: Cornell University Press, 1966.

Douglass, Frederick. *Narrative of the Life of Frederick Douglass.* David Blight, ed. Boston: Bedford Books, 1993.

Eltis, David. *The Rise of African Slavery in the Americas.* New York/UK: Cambridge University Press, 2000

Engerman, Stanley, Seymour Drescher, and Robert Paquette. *Slavery.* New York: Oxford University Press, 2001.

Engerman, Stanley, and Eugene Genovese, eds. *Race and Slavery in the Western Hemisphere.* Princeton, N.J.: Princeton University Press, 1975.

Finkelman, Paul. *Defending Slavery: Proslavery Thought in the Old South.* Boston: Bedford/St. Martin's, 2003.

Finkelman, Paul. *An Imperfect Union: Slavery, Federalism, and Comity.* Chapel Hill: University of North Carolina Press, 1981.

Fogel, Robert William, and Stanley L. Engerman. *Time on the Cross: The Economics of American Negro Slavery.* Boston: Little, Brown, 1974.

Fox-Genovese, Elizabeth. *Within the Plantation Household: Black and White Women of the Old South.* Chapel Hill: University of North Carolina Press, 1988.

Franklin, John Hope, and Loren Schweninger. *Runaway Slaves: Rebels on the Plantation, 1790–1860.* New York: Oxford University Press, 1999.

Frey, Sylvia R. *Water from the Rock: Black Resistance in a Revolutionary Age.* Princeton, N.J.: Princeton University Press, 1991.

Genovese, Eugene D. *Roll, Jordan, Roll: The World the Slaves Made.* New York: Pantheon, 1974.

Genovese, Eugene D. *The Slaveholders' Dilemma: Freedom and Progress in Southern Conservative Thought, 1820–1860.* Columbia: University of South Carolina Press, 1992.

Gomez, Michael A. *Exchanging Our Country Marks: The Transformation of African Identities in the Colonial and Antebellum South.* Chapel Hill: University of North Carolina Press, 1998.

Gutman, Herbert G. *The Black Family in Slavery and Freedom, 1750–1925.* New York: Pantheon, 1976.

Haley, Alex. *Roots: The Saga of an American Family.* Garden City, N.Y.: Doubleday, 1976.

Higginbotham, A. Leon, Jr. *In the Matter of Color: Race and the American Legal Process.* New York: Oxford University Press, 1978.

Hinks, Peter P. *To Awaken My Afflicted Brethren: David Walker and the Problem of Antebellum Slave Resistance.* University Park: Pennsylvania State University Press, 1997.

Hodes, Martha. *White Women, Black Men: Illicit Sex in the Nineteenth Century South.* New Haven, Conn.: Yale University Press, 1997.

Holt, Thomas. *Black Over White: Negro Political Leadership in South Carolina During Reconstruction.* Urbana: University of Illinois Press, 1977.

Horton, James Oliver, and Lois E. Horton. *Black Bostonians: Family Life and Community Struggle in the Antebellum North.* 2nd edition. New York: Holmes and Meier Publishers, 1999.

Horton, James Oliver, and Lois E. Horton. *Hard Road to Freedom: The Story of African America.* New Brunswick, N.J.: Rutgers University Press, 2001.

Horton, James Oliver, and Lois E. Horton. *In Hope of Liberty: Culture, Community and Protest Among Northern Free Blacks, 1700–1860.* New York: Oxford University Press, 1997.

Jacobs, Harriet A. *Incidents in the Life of a Slave Girl.* Jean Fagan Yellin, ed. Cambridge, Mass.: Harvard University Press, 1987.

Jeffrey, Julie Roy. *The Great Silent Army of Abolitionism: Ordinary Women in the Antislavery Movement.* Chapel Hill: University of North Carolina Press, 1998.

Johnson, Walter. *Soul by Soul: Life Inside the Antebellum Slave Market.* Cambridge, Mass.: Harvard University Press, 1999.

Jones, Jacqueline. *Labor of Love, Labor of Sorrow: Black Women, Work, and the Family from Slavery to the Present.* New York: Basic Books, 1985.

Joyner, Charles W. *Down by the Riverside: A South Carolina Slave Community.* Urbana: University of Illinois Press, 1984.

Kaplan, Sidney. *The Black Presence in the Era of the American Revolution, 1770–1800.* Greenwich, Conn.: New York Graphic Society, 1973.

Katz, William Loren. *Eyewitness: The Negro in American History.* Belmont, Calif.: Pitman, 1974.

King, Wilma. *Stolen Childhood: Slave Youth in 19th Century America.* Bloomington: Indiana University Press, 1998.

Kolchin, Peter. *American Slavery, 1619–1877.* New York: Hill and Wang, 1993.

Kolchin, Peter. *Unfree Labor: American Slavery and Russian Serfdom.* Cambridge, Mass.: Harvard University Press, 1987.

Levine, Lawrence W. *Black Culture and Black Consciousness: Afro-American Folk Thought from Slavery to Freedom.* New York: Oxford University Press, 1977.

Malone, Ann Patton. *Sweet Chariot: Slave Family and Household Structure in Nineteenth-Century Louisiana.* Chapel Hill: University of North Carolina Press, 1992.

Morgan, Edmund. *American Slavery, American Freedom: The Ordeal of Colonial Virginia.* New York: W.W. Norton, 1975.

Morgan, Phillip D. *Slave Counterpoint: Black Culture in the Eighteenth-Century Chesapeake and Lowcountry.* Chapel Hill: University of North Carolina Press, 1998.

Nash, Gary. *Forging Freedom: The Formation of Philadelphia's Black Community, 1720–1840.* Cambridge, Mass.: Harvard University Press, 1988.

Nash, Gary. *The Urban Crucible: Social Change, Political Consciousness, and the Origins of the American Revolution.* Cambridge, Mass.: Harvard University Press, 1979.

Newman, Richard S. *The Transformation of American Abolitionism: Fighting Slavery in the Early Republic.* Chapel Hill: University of North Carolina Press, 2002.

Northup, Solomon. *Twelve Years a Slave.* Sue Eakin and Joseph Logsdon, eds. Baton Rouge: Louisiana State University Press, 1968.

Olwell, Robert. *Masters, Slaves and Subjects: The Culture of Power in the South Carolina Low Country, 1740–1790.* Ithaca, N.Y.: Cornell University Press, 1998.

Painter, Nell Irvin. *Exodusters: Black Migration to Kansas after Reconstruction.* New York: W.W. Norton, 1976.

Painter, Nell Irvin. *Sojourner Truth: A Life, A Symbol.* New York: W.W. Norton, 1996.

Phillips, Ulrich Bonnell. *American Negro Slavery.* New York: D. Appleton, 1918.

Rose, Willie Lee, editor. *A Documentary History of Slavery in North America.* New York: Oxford University Press, 1976.

Stampp, Kenneth M. *The Peculiar Institution: Slavery in the Antebellum South.* New York: Vintage Books, 1956.

Stevenson, Brenda E. *Life in Black and White: Family and Community in the Slave South.* New York: Oxford University Press, 1996.

Stewart, James Brewer. *Holy Warriors: The Abolitionists and American Slavery.* New York: Hill and Wang, 1976.

Stuckey, Sterling. *Slave Culture: Nationalist Theory and the Foundations of Black America.* New York: Oxford University Press, 1987.

Tadman, Michael. *Speculators and Slaves: Masters, Traders, and Slaves in the Old South.* Madison: University of Wisconsin Press, 1989.

Thornton, John. *Africa and Africans in the Making of the Atlantic World, 1400–1680.* New York: Cambridge University Press, 1992.

Uya, Okon Edet. *From Slavery to Public Service: Robert Smalls, 1839–1915.* New York: Oxford University Press, 1971.

Vlach, John Michael. *By the Work of Their Hands: Studies in Afro-American Folklife.* Ann Arbor, Mich.: UMI Research Press, 1991.

White, Debra Gray. *Ar'n't I a Woman?: Female Slaves in the Plantation South.* New York: W.W. Norton, 1987.

White, Shane. *Somewhat More Independent: The End of Slavery in New York City, 1770–1810.* Athens: University of Georgia Press, 1991.

White, Shane. *Stories of Freedom in Black New York.* Cambridge, Mass.: Harvard University Press, 2002.

Wood, Peter. *Strange New Land: Africans in Colonial America.* New York: Oxford University Press, 2003.

Wright, George C. *Racial Violence in Kentucky, 1865–1940: Lynchings, Mob Rule, and "Legal Lynchings."* Baton Rouge: Louisiana State University Press, 1990.

Zinn, Howard. *A People's History of the United States, 1492–Present.* New York: Harper Collins, 1995.

Web Sites

The African-American Mosaic
A Library of Congress Resource Guide for the Study of Black History and Culture
http://www.loc.gov/exhibits/african/afam001.html

Chicago Historical Society
Just the Arti-facts: Slavery
http://www.chicagohs.org/AOTM/nov97artifact.html

Cornell University Library
"I will be heard!": Abolitionism in America
http://rmc.library.cornell.edu/abolitionism/

Digital History
http://www.digitalhistory.uh.edu/

Library of Congress
The African American Odyssey: A Quest for Full Citizenship
http://memory.loc.gov/ammem/aaohtml/exhibit/aointro.html

Library of Congress
American Memory: Historical Collections for the National Digital Library
http://lcweb2.loc.gov/ammem/ammemhome.html

Mystic Seaport, Connecticut
Exploring *Amistad*
http://amistad.mysticseaport.org/main/welcome.html

National Park Service
Aboard the Underground Railroad: A National Register Travel Itinerary
http://www.cr.nps.gov/nr/travel/underground/ugrrhome.htm

Public Broadcasting Service
Africans in America
http://www.pbs.org/wgbh/aia/home.html

University of North Carolina at Chapel Hill Libraries
Documenting the American South: North American Slave Narratives
http://docsouth.unc.edu/neh/neh.html

Index

Page numbers in italics represent Illustrations.

A

Abdy, Edward S., 98
abolitionism/abolitionists, 49–50,
   66–67, 139–159, 175
   American Anti-Slavery Almanac, *107*
   Amistad (ship), 117
   John Brown, 162
   communications between slaves and
      free people, 140–141
   Frederick Douglass's involvement
      with, 144–146 (*See also* Douglass,
      Frederick)
   Fugitive Slave Act (1850), 136,
      148–156
   fugitive slaves, regulations for,
      146–156 (*See also* fugitive slaves)
   Kansas territory, 156–157
   Lincoln and, 177, 186
   popularity of during Civil War,
      178–179
   Southern Homestead Act (1866)
      influenced by, 216
   Southern reaction against, 143–144
   Harriet Beecher Stowe, 153–154
   David Walker, 111–112
Adams, Abigail, 53
Adams, Dock, 224
Adams, John Quincy, 117, 127
Africa, 13–21, 24
   diversity of, 18–19
   map of *12, 21*
   resettlement of African Americans
      in, 65
   slavery in, 20–21, 24
   trade with Europe, 13–18
Alabama, 98
Alexandria, Virginia, 160
Allicocke, Joseph, 54
American Anti-Slavery Almanac, *107*
American Anti-slavery Society,
   139–140, 144
American Colonization Society, 86–87,
   90–91
   Paul Cuffe working with, 88
   Liberia resettlement, 95
American Indians, 28, 32
   See also Native Americans
American Revolution, 47–66, 57–58,
   61–64
   African Americans serving in military,
      57–58

antislavery sentiment rising during,
   49–50
Boston Massacre, 47–48
Thomas Jefferson's ambivalence
   towards slavery, 54–56
petition of slaves for freedom in
   Massachusetts, 50–54
James Roberts fighting in, 82
slaves siding with British for free-
   dom, 58–61
Somerset Case, 56–57
Amistad (ship), 116–117, 233n22
Anderson, Osborn Perry, 163, 164
Andrew, John, 181, 194, 195
Andrews, Ethan Allen, 100
Ansdell, Richard, 102
Appleton, Nathaniel, 49
Ashley, John, 66
Atlanta Compromise, 229
Atlantic Creoles, 15–16
Attucks, Crispus, *46*, 47–48
Audubon, John James, 128–129

B

Bacon, Nathaniel, 31–32
Bailey, Frederick, 144–145
   See also Douglass, Frederick
Ball, Charles, 77–80, *81*, 101–103,
   130–131
Banks, Nathaniel P., 200
Bass, Samuel, 148
Baumfree, Isabella (Sojourner Truth),
   74–77
Beecher, Henry Ward, 156
Bell, John, 167, 169
Benezet, Anthony, 50
Benin Empire, 14, 16, 19
Bennett, Rolla, 94
Berlin, Ira, 10, 15–16, 101
Bethel Church, Philadelphia,
   Pennsylvania, 90–91
Birch and Company, *160*
Birth of a Nation (film), 8, 230
black codes, 213–214
Blacke, Henry, 215
Black Republican (newspaper), 208
Blake: The Cabins of American
   (Delany), 115
Blassingame, John, 9
"Bleeding" Kansas, 156–157
   See also Kansas
Booth, John Wilkes, 206–207

Boston, Massachusetts, 155–156
   See also Massachusetts
Boston Gazette (newspaper), 49
Boston Massacre, *46*, 47–48
Boyer, Jean Pierre, 96
Brazil, 27
Breckinridge, John C., 167, 169
breeding slaves, 98–99
British Abolitionist Society, 25
Brooks, Preston, 157
Brown, Henry "Box," *139*
Brown, John, 156–157, 161–166
Brown, John (Fed), 134–135
Brown, Joseph E., 170
Brown, William Wells, 122–123, 139
*Brown v. the Board of Education of
   Topeka, Kansas*, 231
Bruce, Blanche K., 220
Buchanan, James, 159, 164
Bucks of America, 62, 63
Burke, Edmund, 59–60
Burns, Anthony, 155
Butler, Andrew P., 157
Butler, Benjamin, 175, 181, 199, 202
Butler, Eleanor, 30

C

Caesar (fugitive slave), 134
Caldwell, Charles, 223
Calhoun, John C., 87, 143, *145*
Canada, 64, 154–155
cannibalism, 20
Cardozo, Francis Louis, 220
cargo ships for slaves, *25, 26*
Carney, William H., *197*
carpetbaggers, 217
Cary, Lott, 95
Chambers, Frederick Law, 99
Chester, Thomas Morris, 203–204, 205
Chidgigine, Sophie, 72
Christophe, Henri, 63
churches, 90–91
Cinque, Joseph, 116, 117, 233n22
Civil Rights Act (1866), 215
Civil Rights Act (1964), 231
civil rights groups, 230–231
Civil War, 173–207
   Confederacy debate on enlisting
      slaves, 203–205
   District of Columbia, emancipation
      of slaves in, 179

Emancipation Proclamation (1863), 186–189, *192*
First South Carolina Volunteers, 191, 193
fugitive slaves as contraband, 175–177
Louisiana Native Guard, 198–200
military service, African Americans recruited for, 184–186
military service, African Americans turned away from, 174–175, 183–184
military service, inequalities for African Americans, 194–196, 201–202, 271n2
Richmond, Virginia, captured, 205–206
sailors, African Americans enlisting as, 183
Sea Islands, South Carolina and Georgia, captured, 177–178 (*See also* Sea Islands, South Carolina and Georgia)
Harriet Tubman volunteering during, 181–182 (*See also* Tubman, Harriet)
The Clansman (Dixon), 8
Clarke, Lewis, 123
class system, 38
Clay, E. W., 121
Clay, Henry, 86, 127
Cobb, Howell, 203
Coburn, Titus, 57
Coker, Daniel, 95
Collins, Robert, 152–153
Colonial America, 27–45
culture of Africans in America, 41–43
Jamestown settlement, 27–28
slave codes instituted, 32–33
slavery in northern colonies, 43–44
Spanish Florida, 36–37
Stono River Rebellion, 37–38
Colored American (newspaper), 97
community institutions of free blacks, 89
Confederacy, 171
black soldiers captured by, 195–196
enlisting slaves, debate on, 203–205
pardons given to members of, 212–213
Port Hudson, siege at, 200–201
Congress, United States
Preston Brooks's attack on Charles Sumner, 157
gag rule to abolitionists, 144
Andrew Johnson antagonizing, 215–216
land grants to freed slaves, 212
Congressional Medal of Honor, 197
Connecticut, 66
Constitution of the United States *See* U.S. Constitution
Continental Congress, 61

contrabands, fugitive slaves as, 175–177
Coombs, Samuel, 63
Cooper, Grant, 57
Copeland, John Anthony, Jr., 163, 164, 165
Cornish, Samuel, 96
cotton, 69, 71, 83, 97, 109–110, 235n38, 241n30
Cotton Kingdom, 71
Covey, Edward, 98–99
Cowan, Jacob, 116
Craft, Samuel, 57
Craft, William and Ellen, 152–153
crafts, *14, 16*, 42
Crawford, David, 116
Creole (ship), 119, 237n1
Cromwell, Oliver, 63
crops maintained by slavery, 10
cotton, 71 (*See also* cotton)
rice, 33, 42
sugar, 27 (*See also* sugar crop)
tobacco, 28, 33
Crummel, Boston, 88–89
Cuff, Cato, 63–64
Cuffe, Paul, 87–88, 91
culture of Africans in Colonial America, 41–43

D

Davis, Jefferson, 172, 203, 219
debts, 214–215
Declaration of Independence, 55, *56*
Deep South, slave conditions in, 110–111
See also Southern states
Delany, Martin R., 115
Democratic Party
blocking African Americans' voting rights, 226–227
presidential election of 1876, 225–226
during Reconstruction, 222, 223
southern states walking out on, 167
Deslondes, Charles, 91
Dew, Thomas R., 143
Dickinson, John, 7
diseases, 17, 33
District of Columbia, 179
Dixon, Charles, 64
Dixon, Thomas, 8
Dodson, Ben and Betty, 210
Dodson, Caroline, 211
Dodson, Jacob, 174
Douglas, Stephen A., 167–168, 169
Douglass, Frederick, 139, 144–146, 169, 170, 177, 179
John Brown's raid, refusing to participate with, 163
Lincoln, interview with, 195
on U.S. refusal to enlist African Americans for Civil War, 175
Douglass, H. Ford, 170
Dred Scot v. Sandford (1857), 157–158

drivers, 123–124
Du Bois, W. E. B., 230
Dunmore, Lord, 59–60, 61
Dunn, Oscar J., 219
Dutch system of slavery, 34

E

Edo people, 14
education
of black political office holders, 219–220
Freedmen's Bureau running schools, 221
teachers sent to Sea Islands of South Carolina and Georgia, 180–181
election for president in 1860, 167–170
election for president in 1876, 225–226
Elkins, Stanley, 9
Emancipation League, 177
Emancipation Proclamation (1863), 186–189, *192*
Emanuel, 29–30
Engerman, Stanley, 10
Equiano, Olaudah, 18, 19–20, 24, 233n9
autobiography of, 67
experiences as a slave, 35–36
Middle Passage, account of, 22–23
supervision of Sierra Leone colony, 65
Estabrook, Prince, 57
Europe, trade with Africa, 13–18
Evans, Joshua, 50
exodusters, 225, 228

F

family ties, 106–108
fugitive slaves, 128–129
searching for after Civil War, 208, 209–211
Featherstonhaugh, George W., 103
Fed (fugitive slave), 133–135
festivals, 44–45, 89
Fifteenth Amendment to the U.S. Constitution, 216, 229
Fifty-fourth Massachusetts Volunteers, 194, 196–197
Finley, Robert, 86
First Bryan African Baptist Church, Savannah Georgia, *90*
First Corps d'Afrique, 199
First Great Awakening, 45
First Kansas Colored Volunteer Infantry, 188–189
First South Carolina Volunteers, 185–186, 191, 193
Fitzgerald, Thomas, 133
Florida, 171–172
See also Spanish Florida
Fogel, Robert, 10
Foote, Kate, *181*

Forrest, Nathan Bedford, 100
  as Confederate general, 202–203
  in the Ku Klux Klan, 217–218,
    237n24
Forten, Charlotte, 180, 182, 185
Forten, James, 91
Fort Pillow, Tennessee, 202–203
Fort Sumter, South Carolina, 173
"Forty acres and a mule" plan, 211–212
Foster, Thomas, 126
Fourteenth Amendment to the U.S.
  Constitution, 215, 229
Fourteenth Colored Rhode Island
  Heavy Artillery, 195
Fourth U.S. Colored Infantry in Civil
  War, *198*
Franklin, Benjamin, 48, 50
Franklin and Armfield, 100, 160
Fraunces, "Black Sam," 54
free blacks, 91–92
  Bethel Church, Philadelphia meeting,
    90–91
  communications to slaves, 140–141
  Anthony Johnson, 29
  Republican Party, skepticism of, 169
  restrictions against in North, 89–90
  Denmark Vesey, 92–95
  vulnerability to kidnapping, 136–137
Freedman, Peter, 137
Freedmen's Bureau, 209
  finding family members, 211
  running schools during
    Reconstruction, 221
  on white attitudes towards African
    Americans, 215
freedom of speech, 144
Freedom's Journal (newspaper), 96, 97
Freeman, Elizabeth (Mum Betts), 66,
  66
Free Soil Party, 145, 156
Fremont, John C., 176
Fugitive Slave Act (1850), 136,
  148–156
  Canada, black exodus to, 154–155
  Ellen and William Craft case,
    152–153
  Northern states' response to, 149, 151
fugitive slaves, *106*, 127–129, 131–138
  Robert Brown, *84*
  decision to escape, 105–106
  Frederick Douglass as, 144–145 (*See
    also* Douglass, Frederick)
  Fed, 133–135
  regulations concerning, 69, 146–156
  Underground Railroad, 132–133
    (*See also* Underground Railroad)
  See also Ball, Charles

G

Garner, Margaret, 130
Garnet, Henry Highland, 119
Garrett, Thomas, 138

Garrison, William Lloyd, 139, 144, *145*
Geneva Club, 39–40
Genovese, Eugene, 9
Georgia, 177–178, 211
  See also Sea Islands, South Carolina
    and Georgia
Gerzina, Gretchen Holbrook, 57
Gibbons, Joseph, 134
Gibbons, William, 134
Gibbs, Jonathan, 220
Gone with the Wind (Mitchell), 9
Goodell, William, 179
Grant, Ulysses S., 197, 219
Great Britain, 7
  Dutch ousted from Hudson Valley
    by, 33–34
  slaves gaining freedom by siding
    with, 65
  slaves siding with during American
    Revolution, 58–61
  Somerset Case, 56–57
  taxing American colonies, 48–49
  War of 1812, 80–83
Greeley, Horace, 145, 178
Green, Shields, 163, 164
Greene, Lorenzo, 63
Grenville, George, 49
Griffith, D. W., 8, 230
guns, 16
Gutman, Herbert, 9

H

Haiti, 62–63
  African Americans settling in, 96
  slave rebellion in, 68
  Denmark Vesey appealing to, 93
Haley, Alex, 10
half freedom, 34
Hamlet, James, 152
Hammond, James Henry, 143
Hampton, Wade, 222
Hancock, John, 63
Hanks, Dennis, 167
Hannahan, Abraham, 72, 96
Harper's Ferry, Virginia, 161–162,
  163–164
Hayes, Rutherford B., 226
Heathcock, Edwin, 136
Hemmings, Sally, 56
Higginson, Thomas Wentworth,
  185–186, 189, 191
holidays, 44–45, 89
Holland, 34
Horton, Reverend, 218, 219
house slaves, 122–123
Houston, Charles, 230
Howell, Samuel, 54–55
Hughson, John, 40
Hunt, John, 50
The Hunted Slaves (Ansdell), *102*
Hunter, David, 181
Hunter, General, 184

I

impressment, 40–41, 57
indentured servants, 28, 38
Ingraham, Joseph Holt, 105
inheritance rights, 171–172
interracial heritage, 15, 198–199
interracial marriages, 30–31, 34, 39
  See also race relations

J

Jackson, Andrew, 81–82, 83, 144
Jacobs, Harriet, 106, 113–114, 123
Jamestown, Virginia, 27–28
Jefferson, Thomas, 54–56, 71, 104,
  109
  Louisiana Purchase, 70
  on outlawing slavery in territories,
    67
  resettlement of African Americans,
    endorsement of, 114
  on separation of races, 87
  on slaves joining the British, 60
  David Walker criticizing, 112
Jennison, Nathaniel, 66
Jim Crow laws, 11, 227, 229
Johnson, Andrew, 212, 215–216
Johnson, Anthony, 29
Johnson, Eastman, 128
Johnson, Lyndon, 231
Jones, Absalom, 73
Jones, Jacqueline, 10
Juba dance, *41*
Jupiter (Thomas Jefferson's slave), 54

K

Kajor kingdom, 16
Kansas, 156–157
  African Americans migrating to, 225,
    228
  First Kansas Colored Volunteer
    Infantry, 188–189
  Thomas Wentworth Higginson in,
    185
Kentucky, 136
Key, Francis Scott, 86
King, Wilma, 10
Kingsley, Anna Madgigine Jai, 85–86
  after Confederate states seceded,
    171–172
  grandson elected to Florida State
    Senate, 220
  Haiti, moving to, 96
  See also Njaay, Anta Majigeen
Kingsley, Zephaniah, 71, 72
  Florida's purchase from Spain affect-
    ing, 95–96
  leaving property to his wife, 171
  during War of 1812, 85–86
Knights of the White Camilla, 217
Kolchin, Peter, 10
Kongo empire, 24
Ku Klux Klan, 217, *218*, 230

Nathan Forrest as leader of, 237n24
measures against, 219
Kumba, Amari Ngoone Ndella, 13

L

LaBaron, Lazarus, 43–44
Land ownership, 211–212
Leary, Lewis, Sheridan, 163, 164
Lee, Robert E., 164, 203, 206, 212
Lemmon, Jonathan, 149, 151
The Liberator (newspaper), 139
Liberia settlement, 95, 97, 225
Lincoln, Abraham, 167–168, 169–170,
    179, 195, 205–206
    death of, 206–207
    Emancipation Proclamation (1863),
        186–187, *192*
    encouraging African American
        enlistments, 197
    inauguration as president, 172–173
    reluctance to enlist African
        Americans in military, 183–184
    revoking Fremont's order to free
        slaves in Missouri, 176
Little George (ship), 26
Locke, John, 49
Louisiana, 198–200, 200–201
    See also New Orleans, Louisiana
Louisiana Purchase, 70–71
Louuverture, Toussaint, 63, 69
Lovejoy, Elijah P., 144
Lowery, Lucinda, 211

M

Madison, James, 85
maroons, 92
Marshall, Thurgood, 230
Maryland
    enlistment of African Americans in
        the army (American Revolution), 62
    as escape route to North, 131
    regulations for slavery, 30
    restrictions on free black population
        in, 91
Massachusetts
    abolition of slavery in, 66
    black militia in, 158
    Boston Massacre, *46*, 47–48
    Anthony Burns captured in Boston,
        155–156
    Fifty-fourth Massachusetts
        Volunteers in the Civil War, 194
    interracial relationships prohibited
        in, 30
    Lazarus LaBaron's slaves, 43–44
    petition of slaves for freedom, 50–54
Massasoit Guard, 158
McClellan, George, 184
Mercer, Charles Fenton, 86
Michigan, 132
Middle Passage, 22–23, 25–27, 101
military service, African Americans in
    black militia units, independent,

158–159, 166
black militia units after the Civil
    War, 222–223
Civil War, African Americans accepted
    in during, 184–186
Civil War, African Americans turned
    down for enlisting during,
    174–175, 183–184
Civil War, inequalities for African
    Americans during, 194–196,
    201–202, 271n2
Fifty-fourth Massachusetts
    Volunteers in the Civil War, 194,
    196–197
First Kansas Colored Volunteer
    Infantry in Civil War, 188–189
First South Carolina Volunteers,
    191, 193
Fourth U.S. Colored Infantry in
    Civil War, *198*
Seventy-third United States Colored
    Troops, 199
Tennessee Colored Battery camp, *190*
Third Louisiana Native Guards,
    199–200
War of 1812, 80–81
War for Independence. *See* American
    Revolution.
Missouri, 176
Missouri Compromise, 103–104
Mitchell, Margaret, 9
mixed race heritage, 15, 198–199
Monroe, James, 70, 85, 86
Montgomery, James, 193
Morgan, Phillip D., 10
mothers, slave status passed through,
    30
mulattoes, 198–199
Murray, Anna, 145
Musa, Mansa Kango, 24
music, 125

N

names of slaves, 36, 44, 209
*Narrative of the Life of Frederick
    Douglass* (Douglass), 145–146
National Association for the
    Advancement of Colored People
    (NAACP), 230
National Era (newspaper), 154
Native Americans, 28, 32
Native Guard military unit of
    Louisiana, 198–200
Negro Charles, 30
Negro Seaman Act, 95
New Amsterdam, 34
Newby, Dangerfield, 163, 164, 165
Newby, Harriet, 163, 165
New Jersey, 35, 51, 66
New Netherlands, 34
New Orleans, Louisiana, 82, 91–92
    massacre at state constitutional con-
        vention, 218–219

Native Guard military unit, 198–200
    as slave depot, 98
New Orleans Tribune (newspaper), 204
New York City, 34, 97, 149, 151
    abolishing slavery in, 75
    Isabella Baumfree born in, 74–75
    criminal activity in, 39–40
    James Hamlet arrested as fugitive, 152
    Stamp Act riots, 54
New York Times (newspaper), 201
Niagara Movement, 230, *230*
Njaay, Anta Majigeen, 13, 72
    See also Kingsley, Anna Madgigine Jai
Norcom, James, 106
North, Lord, 64
northern states
    abolitionism rising in after American
        Revolution, 66–67
    granting freedom to fugitives, 149,
        151
    presidential election of 1860, 169
    racial discrimination in, 89–90
    slavery declining in, 74
    slavery in Colonial America, 43–44
    See also individual states
Northrup, Henry B., 148
Northrup, Solomon, 109, *110*
    kidnapping and enslavement of,
        147–148
    as slave driver, 124
Nott, Josiah C., 143

O

Oberlin College, Ohio, 163
Ogden, Mahlon, 137
Ohio, 135
Olmsted, Frederick Law, 99, 108
Otis, James, 49
overseers, 124
Owens, Leslie Howard, 9

P

The Pale Face Brotherhood, 217
Parker, John, 135–136
Penn, William, 35
Pennsylvania, 35, 78, 147, 155
Pennsylvania Abolition Society, 48, 50,
    234n11
Pentecost holiday, 44–45
Pereira, Pacheco, 21
personal liberty laws, 146
Phillips, U. B., 8–9
Pinchback, Pinckney Benton Stewart,
    220, 242n56
plantation culture, 122–125
Planter (ship), 182
Plessy v. Ferguson (1896), 229, 231
political office, African Americans
    holding during Reconstruction,
    219–221
political structure for slaves, 44
Poor, Salem, 57
Port Hudson, Louisiana, 200–201

presidential election of 1860, 167–170, 239n13
presidential election of 1876, 225–226
press gangs, 40–41, 57
Prigg v. Pennsylvania (1842), 147
Punch, John, 29
Purvis, Robert, 117

Q

Quakers, 35, 50, 234n6
Quando, Quasho, 43–44
Queen's Head tavern, 54
Quitman, John and Eliza, 120–121

R

race relations
  after Civil War, 213
  in antebellum South, 108–109
  in Colonial America, 29–31
  interracial marriages, 30–31, 34, 39
racial discrimination, 201–202
  after Civil War, 215, 223–224
  black codes, 213–214
  in Midwest in 1800s, 89–90
  in north after Civil War, 225
  segregation, 8, 11, 227, 229
Rahman Ibrahima, Abd al-, 126–127
Randolph, John, 68
Rankin, John, 135
rationalizations for slavery, 121, 141–143
rebellions by slaves, 68–70, 119–120
  Creole (ship), 119
  Stono River, 37–38
  Nat Turner, 112–114
  Vesey's Rebellion, 92–95
Reconstruction, 209–231
  African Americans' voting rights restricted after, 226–227, 229
  Freedmen's Bureau running schools during, 221–222
  Andrew Johnson's presidency, 215–216
  land given to freed slaves, 211–212
  pardons given to plantation owners, 212–213
  political office, African Americans holding during, 219–221
  sharecroppers, African Americans as, 214–215
  violence during, 217–219, 222–225
Red Shirts, 223
regulations on race relations, 29–31
See also race relations
religion
  African American preachers, 115
  Bethel Church, Philadelphia Pennsylvania, 90–91
  First Bryan African Baptist Church, 90
  First Great Awakening, 45
  holidays, 44–45, 89
  sermon of Absalom Jones, 73
Remond, Charles Lenox, 158

Republican Party, 167
  African Americans during Reconstruction, 217
  opposing slavery, 169
  presidential election of 1876, 225–226
  during Reconstruction, 215–216, 223
resettlement of African Americans in Africa, 65, 86–88
  during the Civil War, 179
  controversy amongst African Americans about, 90–91, 96–97
  Liberia settlement, 95, 97, 225
  during Reconstruction, 225
  See also American Colonization Society.
resistance to slavery by slaves, 119–122, 126–138
  escapes to freedom, 127–129, 131–138 (*See also* fugitive slaves)
  Abd al-Rahman Ibrahima, 126–127
  rebellions, 68–70 (*See also* rebellions by slaves)
  suicide, 130–131
Revels, Hiram Rhodes, 219–220
Revere, Paul, engraving of Boston Massacre, 46
Revolutionary War, *see* American Revolution.
Rhode Island, 33
  abolition of slavery in, 66
  enlistment of African Americans in the army (American Revolution), 61
  law against entertaining slaves, 39
rice, 33, 42
Rice, Thomas "Daddy," 227
Richmond, Virginia, 205–206
Rifle Clubs, 223
Roberts, James, 81, 99
Rock, John, 166
Rodrigues, Jan (Juan), 34
Rolfe, John, 27
Romme, John, 39
Ruggles, David, 145
runaway slaves
  See fugitive slaves
Rush, Benjamin, 53
Russwurm, John, 96

S

sailors, African American, 95, 140–141, 183
St. Dominique, 68
  See also Haiti
Salem, Peter, 57, 63
Sammis, Egbert, 220
Sammis, John, 172
Savannah River Baptist Association, 107
Saxton, Rufus, 184–185
scalawags, 217
Scott, Dred, 157–158

Sea Islands, South Carolina and Georgia, 177–178
  Emancipation Proclamation, reaction to, 189
  First South Carolina Volunteers, 191, 193
  teachers sent to, 180–181
  secession from the United States, 170–171, 173
Second Middle Passage, 101
Second South Carolina Volunteers, 193–194, 241n1
Sedgwick, Theodore, 66
segregation, 8, 11, 227, 229
  "separate but equal" doctrine, 229
Seventy-third United States Colored Troops, 199
Seward, William H., 207
sexual harassment of female slaves, 123
sharecropping, 214–215
Sharp, Granville, 56
Shaw, Robert Gould, 196–197
Shepherd, Hayward, 162
Sheridan, Philip H., 219
Sherman, Thomas W., 184
Sherman, William T., 211
Sierra Leone, 65, 87
Simmons, J. J., 159
slave codes, 32–33
slave drivers, 123–124
slave factories, 17
slave status, 30
slave trade, 67, 70
  holding pens, 75
  Joseph Holt Ingraham describing sale, 105
  from Upper South to Deep South, 74, 98–100, 103
smallpox, 33
Smalls, Robert, 182–183, 221–222
Smith, Calvin, 81, 82
Smith, Venture, 18
Somerset, James, 56–57
songs of slaves, 125, 138
Sorubiero, Margaret (Peggy), 40
South Carolina
  American Revolution, enlistment of African Americans in the army during, 61–62
  American Revolution, guerrilla bands during, 58
  Charles Ball as slave in, 79
  constitutional convention during Reconstruction, 221
  Fort Sumter, 173
  Fort Wagner battle, 196–197
  Sea Islands captured in Civil War, 177–178 (*See also* Sea Islands, South Carolina and Georgia)
  seceding from the United States, 170
  slave code, 32–33

Stono River Rebellion, 37–38
tags required of free blacks in
   Charleston, 95
Harriet Tubman's raid, 193–194,
   241n1
Vesey's rebellion, 92–95
Southern Democratic Party, 167, 169
Southern Homestead Act (1866), 216
southern states
   conditions in Deep South, 110–111
   economy destroyed by Civil War,
      206, 241–30
   enforced migration of slaves to,
      97–98
   fugitive slaves, 131–132 (See also
      fugitive slaves)
   interracial relationships in, 108–109
   reactions against abolitionism,
      143–144
   reaction to Nat Turner's rebellion,
      115–116
   seceding from the United States,
      170–171, 173
   secessionist movement, 159
   slave trading in, 98–100
   walking out on the Democratic
      Party, 167
   See also under individual states
Spanish Florida, 36–37, 72
   sold to United States, 95–96
   in War of 1812, 85–86
   See also Florida
Stamp Act Crisis, 7, 54
Stampp, Kenneth, 9
Stanton, Edwin M., 211
Stanton, Elizabeth Cady, 146
stealing, 122
Steel, Sidney, 129
Stevenson, Brenda E., 10
Stewart, Charles, 56
Still, William, 118, 137
Stono River Rebellion, 37–38
Stowe, Harriet Beecher, 153–154
Stuart, J. E. B., 164
sugar crop, 27, 98, 110, 111, 241n30
suicides of slaves, 130–131
Sumner, Charles, 157, 179
Supreme Court, United States, 226
   Brown v. the Board of Education of
      Topeka, Kansas, 231
   Dred Scot v. Sandford (1857), 157–158
   "separate but equal" doctrine, 229

T

Taney, Roger B., 158
taxes, British of American colonies, 49
Tennessee, 202–203
Tennessee Colored Battery camp, 190
Tenure of Office Act, 216

Third Louisiana Native Guards,
   199–200
Thirteenth Amendment to the U.S.
   Constitution, 209, 210, 229
Thornton, John, 24
Tilden, Samuel J., 225
Timbuktu, 15
tobacco, 28, 33
Towne, Laura, 180
trade
   between Africa and Europe, 13–18
   of slaves to U.S., 67, 70, 74 (See also
      slave trade)
Truman, Harry, 230
Truth, Sojourner (Isabella Baumfree),
   74–77, 139
Tubman, Harriet, 118, 137–138
   John Brown, support for, 162
   Civil War, volunteering during,
      181–182
   at Fort Wagner battle, 197
   Second South Carolina Volunteers,
      as part of, 193–194, 241n1
Turner, Henry M., 187
Turner, Nat, 112–115
Tuskegee Institute, 227, 229
Twelve Years a Slave (Northrup), 110
Twenty-second U.S. Colored
   Regiment, 207
Tye, Captain, 58, 59
Tyler, John, 87

U

Uncle Tom's Cabin (Stowe), 154
Underground Railroad, 132–133,
   134–139
   John Brown helped by, 134–135
   Harriet Tubman, 137–138 (See also
      Tubman, Harriet)
U.S. Constitution, 67–68
   changes to during Reconstruction,
      229
   Fifteenth Amendment, 216
   Fourteenth Amendment, 215
   Thirteenth Amendment, 209, 210
upper classes, 38

V

Vassa, Gustavus, 36
   See also Equiano, Olaudah
Vermont, abolishing slavery, 66
Vesey, Denmark, 92–95, 122, 236n11
Virginia
   American Revolution, enlistment of
      African Americans during, 62
   Anthony Johnson as freedman in, 29
   Harper's Ferry raid, 161–162,
      163–164
   Jamestown settlement, 27–28

"luxuries" in, 31
regulations for slavery, 30
restrictions on free black population
   in, 91
Richmond captured during Civil
   War, 205–206
slave rebellions in, 68, 69–70
Nat Turner's rebellion, 112–115
voting rights, 89, 224
   Fifteenth Amendment to the U.S.
      Constitution, 216–217
   New York African Americans, 169
   southern states move to block
      African Americans', 226–227
   Voting Rights Act (1965), 231

W

Walker, David, 111–112
Walker, Quock, 66
Walker, William, 195
War of 1812, 80–83
War for Independence, see American
   Revolution.
Washington, Booker T., 227, 229
Washington, Bushrod, 86
Washington, George
   on abolishing slavery, 67
   enlistment of African Americans in
      the army, 57, 61, 63
   fugitive slave law in 1793, 69
Washington, Madison, 119
weapons, 16
Webster, Daniel, 86
western migration of blacks after Civil
   War, 225, 228
Whipple, Prince, 63
White, Debra Gray, 10
White, Garland, 205
White League, 218, 223
white supremacy beliefs, 213
Whitney, Eli, 69
Whittemore, Cuff, 57
Williams, Henry, 141
Williams, Peter, 97
Wilmot, David, 145
Wilson, Woodrow, 8
winnowing basket for rice, 42
women
   role during elections in
      Reconstruction, 216–217
   sexual harassment of female slaves,
      123
   slave status passed through mothers,
      30
Wood, Cato, 57
Woolman, John, 50

Z

Zong (ship), 65

Acknowledgments

We would like to thank Lauren E. Borchard, Laurel A. Clark, Kevin Strait, and Betsy O. Wiley for providing valuable research assistance for this book. Stanley Engerman, in his characteristically thorough and supportive way, did a complete reading of the manuscript and provided us with invaluable comments. We owe him yet another debt of gratitude. We are grateful to Christine Berry, who read and commented on early drafts of the chapters, and to colleagues on two continents—at the University of Amsterdam, the University of Leiden, George Washington University, and George Mason University—who indulged our excited conversation as we sought to reconstruct the lives of the many actors in this book. The Woodrow Wilson International Center for Scholars generously provided partial support for this project. We greatly benefited from the comments of Lindsay Collins and Kent Hughes and the assistance of Erin Carrier.

We thank Michael and Kelly Horton-Geer for their patience, and we thank Dana Jeffrey Horton-Geer and Alex James Horton-Geer, both of whom are descendants of this story. Their infectious smiles and encouraging hugs kept us going when few other things could have.

Picture Credits

Producer's Acknowledgments

The public television series
Slavery and the Making of America
is a production of THIRTEEN/WNET

VICE PRESIDENT AND DIRECTOR OF PROGRAMMING
Tamara E. Robinson

EXECUTIVE PRODUCER
William R. Grant

SERIES PRODUCER
Dante J. James

NARRATED BY
Morgan Freeman

Program 1: The Downward Spiral
Written, produced, and directed by Dante J. James

Program 2: Freedom in the Air
Written, produced, and directed by Gail Pellett

Program 3: Seeds of Destruction
Written, produced, and directed by Chana Gazit

Program 4: The Challenge of Freedom
Written, produced, and directed by Leslie D. Farrell

The sole funder of the PBS series
Slavery and the Making of America is